FRINGE SHIFTS

**Transforming planning
for new sub>urban habitats**

0 NETWORK OF CITIES

**0.1 The Role of URBACT in the Development of
a New Culture of Urban Planning in Southern Italy**
Salvatore Napolitano p.6

0.2 Reinventing the Fringe
Anna Attademo and Enrico Formato p.10

0.3 Five reasons why Casoria is a model for other cities
Simone d'Antonio p.26

1 IN EUROPE

1.1 Sub>urban network: challenges in the urban fringe
Maarten van Tuijl p.34

1.2 Antwerp. Transforming planning
Mieke Belmans p.46

1.3 Oslo. Transforming for intensified use
Peter Austin p.56

1.4 AMB (Barcelona). Transforming for social inclusion
AMB URBACT Team p.66

1.5 Five Cities
Baia Mare - Brno - Düsseldorf - Solin - Vienna p.80

Dossiers

1.6.1 Private Europe. What's up in the fringe
Antwerp - Baia Mare - AMB (BARCELONA) - Brno - Casoria -
Düsseldorf - Oslo - Solin - Vienna p.90

1.6.2 Ownership, Commons and the Right to the City
Carmine Piscopo p.104

Interviews

1.7.1 Antwerp 2003-2018: 15 Years of Work on the City
Interview with Paola Viganò, *by Bruna Vendemmia and Anna Livia Friel* p.108

1.7.2 The Time Scaling
Interview with Michel Desvigne, *by Francesca Garzilli* p.120

2 CASORIA, ITALY

2.1 Initial situation p.132

2.2 The Integrated Action Plan p.136

2.3 Principles, methods, new perspectives p.148

Dossiers

2.4.1 Casoria: the new Municipal City Plan
Enrico Formato and Salvatore Napolitano p.154

**2.4.2 NO.WALL:S
New Openness. Wide Accessible Local Life: Scenarios**
Anna Attademo and Enrico Formato p.160

**2.4.3 Motion, Energy, Nature for rethinking Wastescapes
CAR: MEN: Casoria Remix**
Libera Amenta, Anna Attademo and Enrico Formato p.164

**2.4.4 Participation and Empowering.
The GOPP Method for the Co-management of Common Property**
Francesca Scafuto p.168

**2.4.5 Asse Mediano Stories.
Living in an infrastructured wasteland**
Fabrizia Ippolito p.176

2.4.6 The Metropolitan Dimension
Michelangelo Russo p.182

**2.4.7 SbS_Lab after URBACT. Starting points for innovation
in facing the new challenges of the fringe**
Francesca Avitabile, Ermelinda Clarino, Pietro Salomone,
Bianca Senese, Pasquale Volpe p.186

Interviews

2.5.1 From here to diversity
Interview with Pablo and Miguel Georgieff, *by Danilo Capasso* p.194

2.5.2 Eco-Regional perspective
Interview with Michael Neuman,
By Libera Amenta, Anna Attademo, Enrico Formato, Federica Vingelli p.206

References p.212

0. NETWORK OF CITIES

- Oslo
- Antwerp
- Düsseldorf
- Brno
- Vienna
- Solin
- AMB (Barcelona)
- Casoria

0.1 Preface

The Role of URBACT in the Development of a New Culture of Urban Planning in Southern Italy

Salvatore Napolitano
Supervisor of Planning for the City of Casoria

In May 2015 the Planning Committee for the city of Casoria made a proposal to town council administration to apply for the URBACT III Programme.

The decision to participate in the programme was based on the desire to "learn" from cities that had gained important experience in the redevelopment and regeneration of urban fringe areas, and the awareness that sharing these reflections could offer beneficial and enriching effects on our world, through experimenting with inclusion practice with the citizens.

The lab that worked on the proposal for participation in the URBACT programme was named "Casoria SbS _ Lab" and consisted of young motivated professionals who had collaborated on the drafting of the Municipal Urban Plan (PUC2013)[1]. The team, hosted in Municipal spaces, distinguished themselves for their content and innovative work strategies: working on the crest of theoretical and technical innovation, pushing for the involvement of local communities, producing a decidedly unusual plan compared to the standard. The plan wasn't directed towards growth, nor was it dictated or organised by functional areas or building regulations, with clear divisions between the structural and operational components, adaptive and process-oriented.[2]

With this new urban plan a well-defined choice was made, aimed at safeguarding and renewing all the areas which had remained unused during the intense construction of the past fifty years,[3] knowing that only by facing this tangle, and well aware of its complexity, could a real process of urban redevelopment begin.

---

1. The Planning Office, coordinated by the Supervisor of Planning for the City of Casoria, was composed of a group of architects (who had graduated no more than five years previously), a scientific consultant, Enrico Formato from the Department of Architecture of Federico II University of Naples, and Michele Moffa and Paolo Sacco from *Suburbia Mode* architecture firm.

2. The work was packaged by "pressing" on the innovative elements outlined in the most recent urban planning reform of Regione Campania for the Regulation to implement the *Governo del Territorio* n. 5/2011 (B.U.R.C. n. 53 of 8 August 2011) acting on Regione Campania Law n. 16/2004.

3. Most construction after the 1960s and during the last century in the territory of the City of Casoria is in contrast with current regulations, and is currently under examination for approval for building sanction.

In brief, the strategies illustrated in the PUC2013 were employed, right from the proposal stage, as the basis for the participation in the URBACT programme, thereby being accepted into the group of cities successively financed as part of the *Sub>urban – Reinventing the Fringe* network which included the cities of Antwerp, Baia Mare, the Metropolitan Area of Barcelona, Brno, Casoria, Düsseldorf, Oslo, Solin and Vienna.

A fundamental difference between the city of Casoria and the other cities of the network – among which are some of the most important European cities, even capital cities, cities that have at their disposal large and efficient planning offices – is to have counted on a team of professionals whose daily work is to manage the technical departments of the Municipality. This overlapping of roles, caused by the lack of technical personnel in the administration of Southern Italy, on the one hand indisputably demonstrates organizational difficulties, with serious consequences also on the management of European funds (including ERDF funds, for which Casoria is the intermediate Organism for management). On the other hand, it offered, thanks to its considerable commitment on the part of the *SbS_Lab* members, a clear advantage because it provided the opportunity to act directly on the skills of those who now are implementing the transformation outlined in the programme.

During the URBACT experience in Casoria, the convergence of different levels of responsibility- from the management of technical offices to the finalised works, to the drafting of the Local Action Plan- all became the opportunity to transform, in real time, knowledge into action. This occurred in particular by:

a. identifying two areas, already present in the operational component of the Municipal Urban Plan (acquired free of cost according to the regulations regarding "public concession federalism") as target areas on which to put into action the strategies in general,

b. the implementation of minimal urban renewal intervention within the plan for local action, allocating a limited part of the Economic Management Plan from Public Works to carry out interventions needed to open an area of the park to the public (Via Michelangelo Park). The URBACT programme actually led to a process which brought about the construction of the largest park in the town of Casoria,

c. the inclusion in the target area of construction on the part of a private investor, thus defining a new public-private relationship and interfacing with continually evolving Italian regulations,

d. the pursuit of different forms of collaboration with those involved in the town – from the planning of park equipment being shared with school pupils to the actualisation of these by local private individuals – thereby fostering trust in the institutions and the effectiveness of inclusion programmes.

The Local Action Plan, for these reasons, provided the opportunity to enhance the work on the general setting, while simultaneously carrying out actions on different levels: the municipal territory, and its connections with the metropolitan area of Naples, the planning of the park and its equipment, can all be seen as the trigger for an expansion strategy in other urban settings of the city.[4]

---

4. In December 2018 Casoria presented a project for "green infrastructure" to the Metropolitan City of Naples. The Via Michelangelo Park became a starting point for regeneration guided by sustainable mobility, extended to adjacent roads. The project was financed with €390,000 and will be put into effect in the first six months of 2020.

The URBACT III experience, in its duration (2015-2018) had to face a succession of four different political administrations, two elected and two government-appointed.[5] This situation didn't allow the politicians to fully follow through with the implementation of the programme, although none of the administrations withdrew their support. However, due to the transitory situation, the most senior administrators could not satisfactorily fulfil their role of launching the inclusion of the community that the existing models required. Furthermore, as often happens in regional administrations in Southern Italy, and particularly in the metropolitan city of Naples, the uncertainty of political guidance produced a gap between drafting and implementation times (medium to long) for urban planning. Paradoxically, URBACT III programme's Local Action Plan included an urban plan which has not yet been put into action.

This minor example underlines the importance and usefulness of community programmes like URBACT, capable of placing Italian public administration in a position of positive tension: between the undeniable organisational difficulties and exposed to discontinuity of administrative action, to the lack of social recognition and distrust on the part of the population – and an awareness of the many resources that the culture – social, technical and administrative- of the nation, if given the right conditions, is still today capable of providing, at the service of sustainable and democratic development.

---

5. During the period in which the municipal administration had undergone a vote of no confidence, Italian law requires that commissioners nominated by the Prefect lead the local community until the next elections. The alternating of political administrations before completing their natural terms of office is frequent in most cities in southern Italy.

Transnational Meeting of Sub>urban.
Reinventing the fringe, Antwerp,
june – july 2016.

Copyright: Jochen by Lucid Lucid

0.2 Introduction

Reinventing the Fringe

Anna Attademo and Enrico Formato*

URBACT NETWORK SUB>URBAN. REINVENTING THE FRINGE
URBACT is a programme financed by the European Commission to incentivize the exchange of knowledge between cities in order to help them develop innovative solutions capable of combining urban, economic, social and environmental themes. The final product of the URBACT programme is the Local Action Plan, drafted by each partner through the participation in local communities and exchange of skills, with the support of accredited leading experts.

Sub>Urban. Reinventing the Fringe is a network that was born in 2015 as a part of the URBACT III programme which witnessed the drafting of Local Action Plans in nine European cities differing greatly in size and role: Antwerp, Belgium was the leading proponent: Baia Mare (Romania), Metropolitan Area of Barcelona (AMB) (Spain), Brno (Czech Republic), Casoria (Italy), Düsseldorf (Germany) Oslo (Norway), Solin (Croatia) and Vienna (Austria). The Local Action Plans, the outcome of the network, were derived from participating in local networks and the integration of skills between the network partners which occurred during conferences, exhibitions, workshops and field trips.

Sub>urban is involved with the fringe: the area of transition, often coinciding with post-war expansion, which was born and consolidated around the historical centres of European cities. This belt, sandwiched between the compact centre and the more external suburbs, presents different functions and densities; it acts as an area of transition whose landscape is characterised by transportation infrastructures, slabs of residential buildings, planned and unplanned low density settlements, old rural nuclei interspersed with commercial and production platforms, unutilised and in decline. The presence of public property generally centres around infrastructures and the *grand ensemble* of social buildings, while private areas appear to be fragmented as far as topology and ownership is

* This introduction was written collectively by the authors following extensive discussions, however paragraphs 2, 4, 5 and 7 were written by Anna Attademo; and paragraphs 1, 3, 6 and 8 by Enrico Formato.

concerned. Territorial amenities and services appear to be insufficient. Although various functions are fulfilled, even though they are contiguous, they present a high degree of sectorisation. Density is also variable, due to the recurrence of alternation between compact urban pockets and low density areas, *terrain vague* and other underutilised open spaces. In several cases -especially in Italy, Croatia and Spain – part of the construction originates from unauthorised unplanned settlements established between the sixties and the eighties.

Even though the fringe may present itself as in critical conditions, it can be considered a fundamental area for the regeneration of European cities, as long as work is based on a growth model differing from that from which it originated. For this reason, it is clear that, through a *shared project*, a *different* growth must be based on new models for planning and the inevitably complex management of the regeneration process which will be put into play (Russo, 2014; Bergevoet and van Tuijl, 2016). The inherent qualities must be considered without losing sight of the long term prospective.

Particularly, three strategic prospects seem to be emerging as opportunities for direct action:

1. the opportunities offered by *recycling*, through the exploitation of existing materials and their possibly even radical potential for transformation,

2. the need for integration, to be pursued via densification and connections between existing and newly introduced urban functions,

3. the expansion of accessibility, both internal and outward-bound towards the urban areas of the fringe, achieved by the creation of previously inexistent permeability (visual, functional and ecological) through barriers; thereby recovering the centrality of open public spaces, and developing a multi-pronged network of sustainable mobility.

It is also useful to recognise, among the characteristic elements of the fringe belt, several values from which to begin: its structural closeness to the city centre, for instance, defines an advantageous condition both for providing functions *par excellence* and for developing sustainable modes of transport. The great presence of undeveloped, underutilised or neglected land offers the opportunity for developing new compact and sustainable urban development. Residential delocalization can trigger policies for overcoming the mono-functional aspect, and simultaneously provide a solution to demographic transition and migration, along with their associated pressing issues. Lastly, the presence of an infrastructure network can be seen as an opportunity to reconnect with nature, providing cycling and footpaths through nature, with positive consequences on the regeneration of the local landscape and on health and comfort for those who will live in the fringe and those passing through, commuting from or between the suburbs and the compact centre.

IN THE URBAN FRINGE

Following the Second World War, the historical compact city had to face demographic changes caused by the economic boom. Almost all European cities expanded drastically with new areas located contiguous to the centre, leaning on the centre's infrastructure and identity. In ex-Socialist countries this growth occurred as mono-functional blocks of residential buildings, now mostly privatised and in transformation. This type of urban growth, developing in concentric circles, has determined a harsh interruption of pre-existing networks of residential settlements, landscape and environmental continuity that connected the city with its non-urbanised territory. (Donadieu, 1998). Connection lines (railway lines, highways and freeways, electric lines etc.) became entry corridors into this expanding city, with a consequential increase in traffic congestion between the city and the inland area. The latter then subsequently absorbed, over the last three decades in a multipolar and fragmentary manner, further expansion, generating what has been defined as "post-metropolis" (Forman, 2008; Soja, 2000). These are the belts of post-war expansion which became transition belts, the stronghold of an overflowing city, and preceded the industrial and tertiary industry's dislocation, and the progress of residential sprawl in today's world. Thus, starting some decades ago, while the edge of the conurbation was bustling (Gallent et al., 2006), the internal areas, the urban fringe, were in crisis, in need of an identity, new functions, physical and environmental regeneration (Beauregard, 2006).

Many European cities display signs of this crisis in the internal geography of their contemporary landscape. As a result of the post-metropolitan expansion process and the structural inadequacy for new requirements of the modern world, post-war urban fringes started to meet at their own fringes. This phenomenon produced:

-the abandonment of early industrial areas, having become obsolete following production developments and post-industrialisation;

-neglect and underutilisation of electricity, communication and transportation infrastructure due to the reorganisation of the economic sectors in the modern city;

-residual territories, in-between spaces open to multiple opportunities, at times non-authorised use;

-the progressive closing in of the barriers of the "active" platforms, such as residences, services, and production (especially tertiary and quaternary). A closing off that today reveals the dramatic laceration inside the peri-urban areas, often true jumbles of mono-functional blocks, socially homogeneous inside, accumulated and unplanned in a space which is devoid of any landscape elements.

Nowadays these fringe areas are all involved in transformation and re-appropriation. They offer an extraordinary opportunity for supplying solutions to the main challenges that cities await, both those related to the expansion of growing urban systems and those experienced in urban areas in crisis, over the course of shrinkage (Oswalt et al., 2006). The main issue then becomes finding alternative solutions to improve the liveability of the cities, while taking into consideration the size of demographic transition, as well as patterns connected to population aging and migration, spatial isolation and segregation.

All these challenges converge in a paradigm of growth which passes through a reconversion of what exists, working on marginal areas, stimulating the development of a sustainable and compact city, offering a viable alternative to sprawl and land consumption. Urban fringes are becoming the next places to re-think about the city, following the successful regeneration of the historical centres of many European cities. But in order to build an alternative for the future, fringe areas need to be redesigned and rebuilt meaningfully.

"Re-inventing the fringe", in this sense, with the above-mentioned elements, means reinventing fringe areas critically and focussing on the URBACT project's founding themes: sustainability (environmental and other) of urban transformation, social cohesion, democratic participation, sustainable mobility, attention to everyday living, well-being and health (Houk et al., 2015).

The nine cities in the URBACT network, notwithstanding their differences in size, history and current conditions, have faced this challenge of reconversion by grouping potential interventions around five common themes (later explained in further detail) (Van Tuijl and Verhaert, 2018). Each of these five themes - - *transforming planning, transforming for intensified use, transforming for social inclusion, transforming the relationship with the region, transforming private space* – emphasise the need to deeply transform the way of viewing, planning and living in the urban fringe.

TRANSFORMING PLANNING
FOR A FLEXIBLE, ADAPTIVE AND PROCESS-ORIENTED PROJECT

The reconversion of the urban fringe seems to require a radical change compared to the traditional urban model, both as far as expansion is concerned, and for the recovery of its historical composition. One of the emerging problems is linked to the contrast, apparent in current conditions, between the expectations of the transformation and the availability of resources. The starting point presents complex conditions offset by difficulties in the sustainability of modification, not only in economic terms, but also in social and political sustainability. One of the recurring problems is further related to the need for awakening interest towards urban areas which are seen as neglected and deteriorating by the general public.

The contradiction between what is imagined for the future and the current condition can be dealt with by innovating the urban plan on a processual level: shifting from a linear, traditional and comprehensive planning model, in which the plans are defined by small teams of experts, to a more flexible model, in which the institutions give up their more traditional regulatory roles in favour of a more active one, facilitating the launch and experimenting with participatory processes. The planners give up part of their ownership and deconstruct their expectations in favour of the opportunity of letting reality interact, over time, on the definition of the transformative scene in the urban space (Formato, 2015).

This model has been trialled for some years in the urban policies of the City of Antwerp which developed, using the Structure Plan drafted by Bernardo Secchi and Paola Viganò as a starting point, the skills to work on transformative implementation based on the "research-by-design" approach centring around *visioning* and multi-scenario work (Secchi and Viganò, 2009). This model has formed, more in general, the fundamental philosophy of *Sub>urban*, calling upon Antwerp to guide the selection of network partners.

Within the programme each partner city has worked on their fringe on the basis of two areas of reflection: one strategic and one tactical, all based on trials during pilot schemes. The tangible transformative action of the pilots serves to refine skills, strength and progressively to earn the trust of the citizens and other stakeholders in the opportunity for transformation. Following this model, for example, the city of Casoria set up a public park in the ex-military area of Via Michelangelo, demonstrating what this means in real terms, thanks to a collective action of re-appropriation and a strategy of "social forestation" proposed by the Structure Plan for the city, now pending approval.

In the same way, the City of Oslo has identified pilot sites, all within the Hovin City quarter, in which to activate the transformation, in accordance with the general Strategic Plan approved for this area. By encouraging the active participation of private investors and new forms of collaboration between public agencies, municipal departments and local stakeholders, the city has set up a process of social construction of the urban plan, handing over the responsibility to the participants who have been invited to personally deal with the issues at hand. Through open and transparent procedures, the stakeholders were presented with the need to collaborate to resolve controversial issues, notwithstanding any prejudicial or ideological positions held.

TRANSFORMING FOR INTENSIFIED USE
INTENSIFYING FUNCTIONAL DIVERSITY, FAVOURING INTEGRATION AND FLEXIBILITY OF USE

One of the critical characteristics of the fringe, as mentioned above, is the extreme sectorisation of the single parts that compose it. This condition is accompanied by a fragmentary topology made up of adjacent barriers, each of which presents a strong sectorised function. Taken as a whole, therefore, the post-war fringe fulfils many functions. However, they cohabitate in close physical contact but they have very little reciprocal connection.

Another theme related to uses involves the neglect and underutilisation of both many open spaces offering potential connections between the barriers, and of some of the building amalgamations. For example, there are many neglected factories – brownfields – or large tertiary commercial or office complexes in critical or abandoned conditions. This phenomenon is due to the progressive decentralisation of production to areas outside the fringe which are better connected and offer more available land. As far as residential dwellings are concerned, it is not rare to see building and urban areas in decline, where the residential issue presents a paradoxical lack of balance between supply and demand. This is often due to family models, and allocation and lifestyle prospects which are no longer feasible. This presents another, even more complex theme when faced in areas which were built without authorisation or regulation, and that now are in remarkably critical conditions as far as risk factors, functional suitability and appearance are concerned (Attademo 2017; Curci, Formato, Zanfi, 2017).

In regards to open space, lastly, the list of neglected and underutilised spaces is lengthy. These are located near the major infrastructures, buffer areas or subject to restrictions, ex agricultural fields, spaces "serving" as parking lots for shopping or business centres, ex-military or ex-public facility areas dating back to the early modern period (abattoirs, military hospitals etc.). How can these areas in crisis be reactivated and connected to current urban uses?

In this case too it is beneficial to collocate the actual spatial strategy within its expected timeline. First of all, overcoming the fragmentary nature means offering attractive alternatives to the sprawl of the fringe by intensifying its uses. This implies a better use of public spaces and of underutilised buildings, creating a mixture not excluding a volumetric densification. In actual fact, it appears to be useful to promote the introduction of new uses and buildings without affecting the fringes' remaining natural land, but by focussing on the densification of existing construction. This also means *working towards complexity*, a typical characteristic of central urban areas, and multiplying the range of potentially connected uses, weakening the regulatory statutes that are typical of zoning plans and pushing the hybridisation and mixture of uses even within the same building.

Moreover, this form of densification mustn't be seen as a toughening of conditions, but rather, it must be introduced within a process of growth, so as to allow reutilisation as soon as possible, as well as the promotion of more radical transformation interventions in the future, to be introduced when conditions permit.

In this sense, "temporary uses" are one of the most successful paths followed in many European cities to trigger the reactivation of use in fringe areas, especially, but not only, with an eye towards public spaces (Inti, 2011).[1]

---

1. See also URBACT III network study "Refill": https://urbact.eu/Refill

Several cities in the network have worked on the reutilisation of publically owned spaces, as well as privately owned buildings, with temporary reutilisation and bottom-up practices, particularly in abandoned areas and buildings. However, it is important to recognise that the path towards more consolidated and less temporary future practices must inevitably pass through the stimulation of a debate between private owners, public agents and persons involved, for obvious reasons, in order to reach the expected outcomes (entrepreneurs, citizens, associations and local committees).

In order to carry this out, several years ago the City of Antwerp set up *Lab XX* with the aim of intervening on the densification of its industrial districts. In the areas of Lageweg and Hoboken, for instance, they preserved the existing activities alongside those which were being promoted for new mixed uses, like residential dwellings and light industry.

In Oslo the revitalisation of a large peri-urban industrial area began with the conservation and reutilisation of the Oxer Tower, a sort of relic of early industrialisation, whose peak offers a view of the whole quarter. On the top floor of the tower a space for meetings and events has been built. This hosts public discussions involving citizens and entrepreneurs as participants, and serves to set up, as needed, the actions required for the functional regeneration and densification of the quarter. The area includes several infrastructural elements that are traditionally excluded from the urban fabric, like an incinerator plant and other activities connected to waste disposal. This pre-existing aspect, nonetheless, is not considered to be a limitation to the densification prospects which will potentially involve tertiary and quaternary sectors.

TRANSFORMING FOR SOCIAL INCLUSION
TACKLING SOCIAL SEGREGATION IN FAVOUR OF INTEGRATION

Internal fringe areas often experience the *paradox of timing*, meaning that they can't manage to offer adequate solutions to the residential and productive demands made by contemporary society. These demands are better met in the compact centre (density, integration, accessibility) and external suburbia (nature, quiet, availability of large spaces).

In any case, the fringe shouldn't be seen as a unidirectional gradient with diversified urban uses that gradually fades into agricultural use: the presence of tertiary commercial and productive functions is possibly the same as that in the centre but it's the settlement model that is different.

The lack of buildings in low density areas, together with a lack of public spaces, networks and sustainable transportation lines provides a completely different prospect on life than that in more central areas. Spatial segregation often coincides with socio-economic segregation: fringe areas generally present high levels of unemployment, lack of public facilities and a concentration of the disadvantaged segments of the population. They cannot afford the economic standards of more central areas, while seeing their condition further worsened by a landscape that includes all the functions which the city centre has expelled and a desolate and neglected environmental system. The presence of the disadvantaged contrasts with the persistence of several middle-class enclaves that settled in post-war years, and are now affected by issues related to the aging population. Then again, second or third generations often prefer to live elsewhere and inherited apartments often lay unrented and unutilised for years, due to the lack of a meeting point between the owners' demands and the economic disposal of those who are interested in living in those areas.

Within the *Sub>urban* network much has been done on the theme of social segregation. In Düsseldorf, for instance, events and public debates were held in order to gradually strengthen the identity of the community by reconstructing its collective image with a project called "Neighbourhood Branding". Much debate was held regarding the intensification of uses and the types of businesses that would reactivate several central areas of the quarter, in relation to the various ethnic communities who had settled there and in view of reciprocal integration.

In the Metropolitan Area of Barcelona (AMB) in the municipality of Bahia del Valles, the vision for a more inclusive city coincides with a diversification of the supply and the quality of accommodation, promoting the cultural scene and relaunching local economic activities. In this way there has been an attempt to introduce new inhabitants and smaller, more transitory types of residences into a quarter which had been born for a determined social class and inhabited by an aged population.

In Vienna the transformation is taking place through the reinvention of large residential complexes from the seventies in the north of the city, and relocating part of the residences to other areas which thus become densified, in a strategy of reactivation and reconstruction of the community in areas that are not necessarily neighbouring. This operation is tightly coordinated by the public administration, a tradition which dates back to the times of the Red Vienna of the early 20th century.

In Casoria, in a setting which has long been associated with high rates of unemployment, this theme has been developed in relation to the social economy, attempting to create matches between the availability and the reutilisation of abandoned public spaces and buildings, the opportunity of creating new jobs capable of generating wealth and, at the same time, promoting the environmental renewal of the fringe.

TRANSFORMING RELATIONS WITH THE REGION
OVERCOMING INFRASTRUCTURAL AND IMMATERIAL BARRIERS

To contain monocentric urban growth, modern urban planning has developed multipolar and extensive regional models. Dating back to the theories of Howard and Geddes and the conferences held by the International Federation for Town and Country Planning and Garden Cities, regional planning has been put into practice, starting in the Thirties, in several cities. Some examples, like the Greater London Plan (1944) or the Five Fingers Copenhagen Plan (1951), define the figure of a metropolis which aspires to build a gemmation of nuclei in equilibrium with a system of parks and interspersed rural areas, in different geometrical patterns, out to the edges of the 20th century fringe. However, over the century, only a few European cities managed to successfully pursue this regionalist development, avoiding the influence that real estate income was having on determining the progressive expansion of pre-existing urban centres. Generally speaking, this only occurred in the countries where public control over peri-urban land was exercised in a more coherent manner and urban development policies were coordinated with social and economic policies (in Great Britain, The Netherlands, Germany and Scandinavian countries).

More frequently the post-metropolitan boom of the last decades occurred outside a ring of already existing fringe settlements; in this context, the tension present between the compact centre and suburban nuclei transformed the fringe into a transition belt, chopped up by infrastructural barriers - highways, pipelines, power lines, railway tracks etc. – connecting the historical centre to the external areas. Depending on the situation, the barriers might have been the result of: sectorisation policies overlapping over time; the lack or surplus of planning regulations, plans that were "born" old, plans approved decades after their elaboration and indifferent to the changes in the meantime profit from real estate speculation. What can be seen today, especially, is a scene of obsolescence and excess, exhausted life cycles of the territory, especially on the edges and in no man's land areas, and running along the barriers of the major infrastructure and logistics platforms.

The metabolism of the peri-urban areas is ringed by these waste areas in an actual assembly of *drosscape* (Berger, 2006) and operational spaces (for the interpretation of these spaces as *wastescapes* see: Geldermans et al., 2018), whose sectorisation produces marginality and separation. The diversified sum of the uses therefore ends up only being a container for the uses and services that cannot be materially located in the centre. The space running along the infrastructure remains abandoned, the network corridors cut up by public or private transport are not planned to be "intermediate stops" and so the aspects of the frailty of this territory are not easily visible to the casual flâneur of the urban region.

These passages deeply mark the landscape and condemn today's fringe to a subordinate role as a "servant" to the city. An even more dramatic situation is where the post-war urban boom took place in a total lack of any form of general territorial plan, like in Southern Italy or other coastal areas of the Mediterranean.

In all of this, it seems clear that to operate successfully on the fringe it is worthwhile to consider two different scales: on the one hand, reinforcing the coordination between policies and plans at a Regional level in order to overcome rigid administrative division and to tackle solutions to problems at the appropriate level: on the other hand, clustering neighbouring urban nuclei which still feel separate as far as identity is concerned, and working, in the short term, on mending the systems of continuity of the environment as well as of public spaces.

The lowest common denominator, as far as levels and themes are concerned, is that related to accessibility. By strengthening public transport and the development of an effective network of sustainable mobility, supported by existing networks and infrastructures, the area would be capable of offering an alternative connection between the fringe and the city centre. This challenge involves both the Regional administration (this is the only way that inter-municipality connection will assume any significance), and material manufacturing, which can be carried out immediately where conditions permit.

Within *Sub>urban*, several cities, especially those covering a suitably-sized area- AMB, Antwerp, Düsseldorf, Oslo, Vienna –have drawn up policies of sustainability on a regional level, acting on a strong reduction of automobile use and, simultaneously on the improvement of public transport and a network of cycling paths. Through the size of the urban plan, they are also encouraging those who pass through the fringe, on their way from one municipality to another, to take a longer look. Other cities like Casoria and Solin directed their attention to existing infrastructure for which they planned improvements for public passages and the environmental and landscape recovery of surrounding areas, with green paths and new public spaces. Solin, in particular, during the URBACT experience achieved a remarkable improvement in the connection with the coastal belt which is separated by a substantial infrastructural barrier. The impossibility of acting on the structure or size or position of the existing barrier – a condition which had previously also paralysed any initiative – was tackled by improving the quality of pedestrian tunnels and promoting the "rediscovery" of the city beach which is now being used and looked after by the citizens.

TRANSFORMING PRIVATE SPACE
OVERCOMING THE IMPASSE OF FRAGMENTED OWNERSHIP

Fringe areas are characterised by fragmentation of ownership, mostly privately-owned property. This condition makes the activation and coordination of urban regeneration operations extremely difficult.

Besides, there is a clear relationship between ownership fragmentation, spatial and functional fragmentation and urban fringe landscape.

As far as this is concerned, this book contains a collection of photographs displayed at the "*What's up in the fringe*" exhibition, organised at the Casoria Contemporary Art Museum in 2016, along with the materials that document the fragmentation of the private space in the fringe of the nine cities involved in the *Sub>urban* network. The exhibition provides a view of the private space which intentionally focuses on the spaces of the fringe as a landscape of daily life, the result of a thousand small collective and individual gestures. At the same time, insisting on the private and inevitably fragmented character of the fringe, it offers an image of a complex mosaic of distrustful acts, individualistic choices often in juxtaposition with each other. It shows fences and barriers, small-scale ones rather than infrastructural barriers – placed to obstruct and close off the public realm from sight; pathways and connections with denied access, in the attempt of negating the public space and an extreme fight for survival and self-affirmation.

The existence of this conflict, like the evidence that although the fringe is decayed it is also lived in by the citizens, presents the need to stimulate a process of collaboration capable of reconstructing common values and a group identity of the social groups, before even planning new public and publicly-used spaces

Transforming private space means starting off from collective spaces (like the entrance to a condominium, informal spaces and private gardens) as a place for mediation which can connect the individuals' interests; interpreting the need for seclusion, but without denying the need for cooperation (Mattei, 2012; Formato, 2012). In this way, the collective space offers a guarantee of success and its own existence in the reasoning and care of the community that cultivates it daily, animating it, managing it and assuming the responsibility for its maintenance. Informing/training the community in the autonomy of use of the space allows for a sort of communal management, overcoming on the one hand selfish impulses and on the other the patterns of passive delegation to the institutions (Arena, 2006; Magnaghi, 2012). Results can be patchy (depending on the historical context, differences in governing legislation etc.) and can conflict with the different transformations of private spaces, in several cities of the project the intervention focused on an extension of uses and of caretaking:

In Baia Mare, in a quarter composed of mono-residential blocks, extensions were added to existing buildings, in exchange for a renovation and general improvement of environmental sustainability and the recovery of several public services.

In Brno interventions were performed on large public building settlements, revitalising them through the introduction of new models of private buildings. In both cases, the ownership fragmentation – which had occurred after the fall of the socialist regimes – was fought but the transformations were stimulated "utilising" several of its typical aspects.

In Vienna, on the other hand, the operations used to manage the fragmentation follow the model of centralised coordination, based on the intervention of very efficient urban transformation companies, in the well-established urban tradition of the Austrian capital city.

In Antwerp, a public agency is now assisting in matching up demand and supply for accommodation by offering guarantees and insurance to private citizens to facilitate low-income renters in accessing residences that the owners have committed to offering at rent-controlled prices.

Casoria has planned a complex system of incentives (urban, fiscal and procedural) to trigger regeneration operations, in exchange for temporary public use and the assignment of spaces for public use beyond the minimum standards dictated by the law. In the large abandoned industrial areas, it is now possible to rebuild as long as this is connected to the decompression of a densely-populated part of the city. Meanwhile, the municipality, in exchange for fiscal incentives, is aiming at acquiring the public use of some of the large decades-long abandoned barriers to allow for the installation of public use facilities in these areas between the compact city and the fringe.

CONCLUSION

Reinventing the urban fringe presents several issues, but also provides solutions: for the territory and its uses, on what to plan and how to do it, on the idea that in a plan for a modern city no space should be left "behind". In a disordered landscape the fringe counts an indefinite number of landfills, warehouses, shopping centres and industrial plants – alongside heterogeneous elements of the environmental system, in some case natural habitats with significant levels of biodiversity: resilient native elements of nature, which run through the incoherent continuum of the fringe, offering a previously unknown and often chaotic alternative to fallow or neglected land and desertification areas. Nature, in the urban fringe, is capable of penetrating, if conditions are favourable, the fabric of the compact city: growing along the waterways, in the intersections between environmental networks, in the in-between areas in non-authorised use, in anticipation of transformation, open to many opportunities. These are spaces of "subtraction" that urban transformation will be able to generate, in the future, even within the heart of the city and its fringe.

Furthermore, the characteristics of fragmentation and compartmentalisation in the urban fringe do not exclude the possibility of becoming a space for a different kind of growth which takes into consideration recovery and densification, but without stripping the identifying elements of a composite and hybrid landscape, interpreting the evolution of these areas into soft configurations of mixed uses and models of interposed settings, in opposition to planning policies which have focussed on the clear separation between countryside and city, functions and social classes.

In this sense the urban fringe seems to combine the best of both worlds (Van Tuijl and Verhaert, 2018) –the urban and the suburban worlds – in unusual assemblies and life cycles in continual change. The main element of the plan therefore becomes time: the life cycles of the landscape and open spaces, of buildings and infrastructures, all create a correspondence between time and form in the space; between the aspirations of the planners and an evolving society, between the long-term visions and the tangible transformations that will be made, day by day, in a space of uncertainty that the new projects for the territory will put into play (Sassen, 2008).

The uncertain aspect of the project also involves the role and the nature of uses and services, in flexible proposals for the definition of use which are not fixed in time; services that are appropriate but not predetermined and that are set up as far as procedures are concerned –temporary and ever-evolving – to also be capable of overcoming the limits related to planning and policies. Nevertheless, this process needs public action to avoid any potential spatial inequalities in the access to property and services.

The project for the fringe rebuilds a role for all the areas waiting to re-enter into the metabolism of the city as a whole through integrative collaborative processes which activate a dialogue between public, private and social institutions, associations and local groups, as a lever to develop awareness and skills. This work model determines an overriding of the traditional planning model which is purely prescriptive and conceived by public players, going from providers to enablers of transformation. It also considers the redefinition of welfare (and welfare spaces) as an effect of the global crisis. The search for transparency in decisional processes and the opening up of democratic conditions for the management, access and use of urban spaces all constitute the conditions under which the above-mentioned concept of flexibility can fully come about. In addition, several principles – like that of maximum environmental sustainability, in terms of land use, best practices in water resource management, more in general than in contrast to climate changes – now seem to be non-negotiable values. So much so as to be defined as the cornerstone that directs uncertainty towards predefined political directions (Secchi, 2011 e 2013; Latour, 2018).

In actual fact, innovating the role of the fringe means bringing to the table decisions made solely by local stakeholders, because human capital and property are key factors in urban regeneration. This process requires a willingness to reinvent administrative procedures by strengthening the public structures for management and planning, while also focusing on new flexible and adaptive instruments capable of opening up the project to social interaction which focuses on the specific features of the location and the participation of the residents, in order to reach a collaborative definition of the uses of these new territorial instruments and of the system of open space.

The processes of co-creation, combined with actions of urban regeneration and inclusion policies, reflect the fairness of a demand which is constantly changing. In this way, fringe areas pose a fundamental question for the construction of the city, as well as for a need for integrated and collaborative welfare beyond existing public welfare.

Examples like the URBACT network clarify that there is a great desire, on the part of European cities, for innovation, experimentation, hybridising practices and for following wider and transdisciplinary process.

Best practices resulting from each experiment cannot be simply reproduced in other contexts, but must be re-defined through customised strategies and by building new decisional models which are appropriate to each local context. On a larger scale the involvement becomes increasingly complex, and experiences like those gained by URBACT demonstrate that expert knowledge must inevitably be measured and merged with knowledge of the context in question.

Transforming planning
For a flexible, adaptive and process-oriented project

Transforming for intensified use
Rafforzare la mixité funzionale, favorendo l'integrazione e la flessibilità degli usi

Transforming for social inclusion
Contrastare la segregazione sociale e favorire l'integrazione

Transforming the relationship with the region
Superare le barriere infrastrutturali e immateriali

Transforming private space
Superare l'impasse della frammentazione proprietaria

0.3 Introduction

Five reasons why Casoria is a model for other cities

Simone d'Antonio
ANCI, National URBACT Point

In the URBACT jargon the so-called "unusual suspects" are those actors able to change the rules of the game in an unexpected way, to subvert the existing order, enthusiastically bringing innovative elements able to permeate the whole process.

What if an entire city is an "unusual suspect"? In the vibrant Italian community of URBACT cities Casoria held perfectly that role.

As often happens in similar cases, the recognition was not formally assigned but was gained by Casoria in a spontaneous and maybe uncommon way for this 80.000 inhabitants-city in the Northern outskirt of Naples bringing on itself all the signs of its industrial past, such as brownfields and abandoned buildings.

Casoria is the ideal ground for testing the impact of innovative ideas and visions on how to reinvent the Sub>urban landscape and to set up concrete and visible actions for its future growth.

The participation to Sub>urban network contributed to activate solutions able to improve the urban governance towards a more sustainable and integrated urban development promoted thanks to the participation to the URBACT programme. This action model may be valid also for many other Cities in the North as well as in the South of Europe.

What are the main reasons characterizing the experience of Casoria, especially if compared to other Italian cities?

The capacity to work on equal terms with big cities is a key factor in the framework of a network as Sub>urban which was one of the few to embed cities very different in terms of territorial size. Giving a look at the list of the partners, Casoria would seem quite out of place among cities such as Vienna, Barcelona, Antwerp and Oslo, but the topics and the approaches promoted along the network activities contributed to make Casoria a valuable partner, representing the whole metropolitan area of Naples.

The regeneration of the metropolitan fringe is a central theme in the national debate, considered in relation to the National Plan for Suburbs and the introduction administrative entity of Metropolitan Cities. A comparison with the strategies adopted by other European countries, where strategic planning is a consolidated element, is able to enrich the regional and local debate, offering useful sparks for the regeneration of Sub>urban areas, highlighting the role of the commons and the active participation of the residents.

In an area such as the Casoria's area with a rate of urbanization of 90%, the regeneration of abandoned spaces offers a great opportunity to initiate new forms of urban development. The first step is updating the Urban Masterplan and fostering the reuse of the former military area located in Via Michelangelo and in Via Boccaccio, both turned into public parks. The green surface of 60000 square meters has been given back to the residents, following similar models of regeneration of unused areas in other cities, also in the framework of URBACT Networks such as Naples, Genoa and Piacenza involved respectively in 2nd Chance and MAPS Networks.

The connection with the metropolitan dimension of urban regeneration is another element characterizing the strong networking action carried out by Casoria in the framework of Sub>urban.

The Metropolitan City of Naples is defining the key elements of its Metropolitan strategic plan, focusing on areas of intervention on which the metropolitan government can intervene on medium and long term.

Following the framework defined by the national law instituting the Metropolitan cities, Casoria is acting in a very concrete and effective way in order to reverse the industrial decline, one of the main issue in the entire metropolitan area.

Areas as the former Rhodiatoce factory and the abandoned shopping mall Euromercato are symbols of the industrial expansion that brought the population to grow from 19000 residents in 1951 to 68000 in 1981 and up to 81000 in 2001.

Counteracting to the urban sprawl , or urban shrinkage, as the only possible reaction to the economic crisis strongly hitting this fraction of the metropolitan area of Naples, is the main challenge faced by Casoria in line with its former Provincial General Planning, adopted in 1999 and updated in 2004 but never entered in force.

A coherent strategy of integrated regeneration enriched by participatory approach is the start of the debate on the future of the Sub>urban fringe at the core of the project.

Starting an unprecedented participatory process constituted a unique element, even more relevant in a comparison with the action of neighbouring municipalities.

In an area where the participation of the residents has rarely been put in place, the massive involvement of a wide range of local actors since the beginning of the Sub>urban activities is a valuable point for Casoria, with the power of defining a model for the local government to be spread also in other fields of action. The variety of the actors involved in co-designing the future of the city is having concrete impacts on the every day life of the residents.

Local NGOs such as Legambiente, youth volley teams, scouts and the NGO on sustainable mobility l'Mobility are among the subjects involved in the pilot actions launched to revive a sense of ownership of the places regained through the participation to the Sub>urban network. Cycling through the brownfields or gardening in Michelangelo Park are just some of the actions which involved

unusual local actors, elementary school students and the asylum seekers involved in the local project of inclusion.
Furthermore, the Transnational Meeting with the other partner cities hosted in Casoria contributed to give visibility to another excellent reference point, the Casoria Contemporary Art Museum that is one of the most interesting and eclectic collection of contemporary art in Southern Italy. The participation of Casoria to Sub>urban contributed in an unexpected way to highlight the social capital of a city left in the shadow by the storytelling on urban revival in recent years.

The strong connection with the local University is another distinctive element of the Casoria's experience in the framework of Sub>urban. The Department of Architecture of Naples University "Federico II" offered more than just a technical and scientific support. In fact professors and students of the department contributed to frame the issues emerging from the dialogue between citizens and stakeholder in the broader framework of the development of the Metropolitan Area. Issues as the seismic and hydrogeological risk, the density of population, the contrast to illegal practices and the creation of a green urban belt are affecting many municipalities of the metropolitan area of Naples. All of them were the research focus of interdisciplinary groups, involving young academics and city officials, with the aim of making the results of the research useful to face and solve the most urgent challenges of the area. This partnership with the University is making Casoria a living lab to test practices and innovative actions also in the framework of other EU co-funded programs, such as Horizon2020.

A team composed by young and motivated city officials, united in the Step by Step Lab, is a powerful example of innovation in terms of governance, able to permeate the entire action of the local government of Casoria.
The city would not have reached the same results without a team composed by eight young professionals, with an average age of 30 and a strong academic background gained with experiences abroad. Since this group was hired by the City Hall in 2015, many interesting results were gained such as the definition of the Urban Masterplan and the regeneration of streets of the city, also through a more efficient use of EU and national financial resources.
The participation to the actions of the Sub>urban Network and to the rest of the activities organized by the URBACT Programme at national and European level contributed to the professional growth of the members of the team.

Logo of Sub>urban Reinventing the fringe.
Corporate Identity designed by Antwerp URBACT team.

Group picture from the Transnational Meeting of Sub>urban. Reinventing the fringe, Antwerp, July 2016.

Copyright: Jochen by Lucid Lucid

1. IN EUROPE

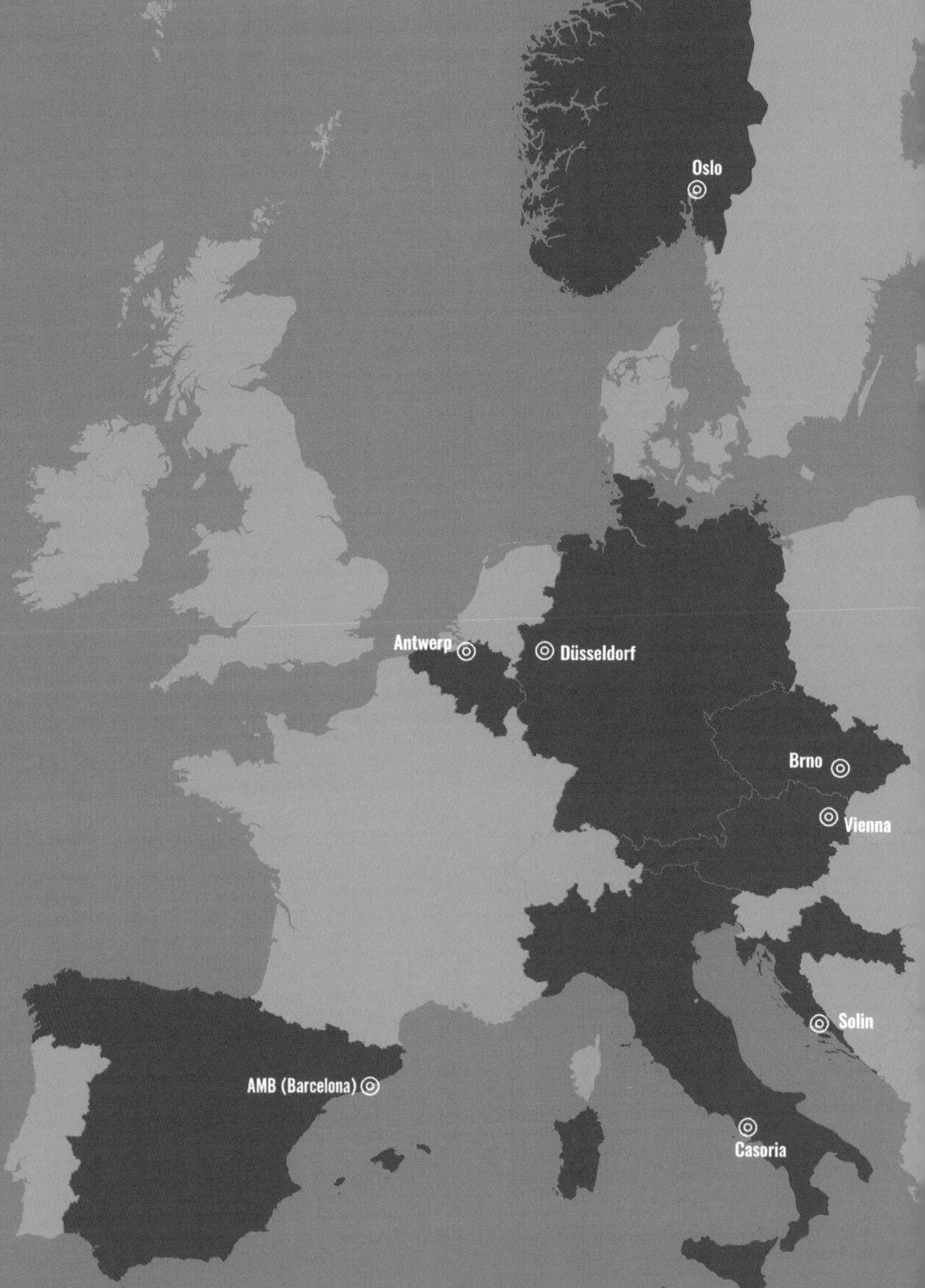

- Oslo
- Antwerp
- Düsseldorf
- Brno
- Vienna
- Solin
- AMB (Barcelona)
- Casoria

1.1
Sub>urban network: challenges in the urban fringe

Maarten van Tuijl
Lead expert of "Sub>urban. Reinventing the fringe"

ARE YOU WORKING ON YOUR FRINGE?

The urban fringe area is the zone between high density urban and low density Sub>urban areas, where development pressure is or has been often intense. It appears as a fragmented car based collage landscape, made up of modernistic urban areas, old village nuclei, industrial zones and recreational areas, cut by heavy infrastructure. Most of the property is privately owned – and therefore often lacks a collective layer for achieving improvements. For many cities the fringe is a fragmented unsustainable belt of often sub-optimal land usage close to their inner cities. Inefficient landuse and urban highways create high car-dependency and underused space. In some cities that are already further in their development process, like the polycentric conurbation of Barcelona or the Naples metropolitan area for instance, the fringe area is already very dense but is lacking quality and is facing social issues. Socioeconomic segregation in the urban fringe with pockets of social deprivation, often coexist with low-waged jobs. Sub>urban is aimed at developing physical planning approaches and tools, that should guide and stimulate transformation processes in the urban fringe. Transformation that aims to achieve more attractive and efficiently organised areas that can both include and improve the lives of existing communities, while also creating sustainable new homes and jobs when necessary. The cities in our network want to revive these areas and create a newer, high-quality urban environment. Overall, the objective is to intensify the use of underused and poorly used space, increase the quality and availability of housing and amenities, find effective and transparent ways to deal with private and fragmented ownership, improve the connectivity of these areas and rethink the identity of the urban fringe. Since these fringe areas and their restrictions are very different from the inner city and the suburbs, an entirely new approach toward urban planning as a whole will be required.

THE CITY OF THE FUTURE IS ALREADY HERE

In the wake of the Second World War, many historical cities found themselves unable to cope with the demographic changes and growth occasioned by the post-war economic boom. Nearly every European city expanded rapidly and drastically, with the result that there are now many large post-war districts close to the city centre (fringe areas) in urgent need of renewal. By the same token, such areas offer a tremendous opportunity for tackling many of the major challenges facing our cities today, such as rapid growth or, conversely, depopulation. As well as tackling these quantitative demographic changes, cities will also have to find ways of dealing with qualitative demographic changes, such as ageing and migration, and their possible negative effects like social isolation and segregation. Existing buildings, infrastructure and mobility will have to become more sustainable. Cities will increasingly have to offer compact living and working environments that are attractive and affordable. All these challenges converge and, at the same time, can be solved, in the fringe. A successful transformation of these fringe areas can help stimulate the development of compact sustainable cities by offering an attractive alternative to sprawl. Following the successful renewal of the historical centres of many European cities, the fringe is the next logical place in which to locate a city of the future based on an existing one. To become future-proof, the fringe needs an update. If it is to fulfil its promise, it needs to be improved and in some instances redesigned. "Reinventing the fringe" is a critical reconsideration of post-war urban areas on the fringe of nine European cities, viewed from the perspectives of sustainability, social cohesiveness, mobility and land use.

THE DILEMMA OF THE FRINGE

The urban fringe area, also known as the transitional belt, is the post-war zone around the city centre, which has diverse urban functions and often a relatively low density. It appears as a fragmented car-based collage landscape made up of modernist urban areas, old village nuclei, industrial zones and recreational areas, intersected by heavy infrastructure.

Viewed at the city region level through the eyes of the planner, the often underused fringe appears to offer opportunities for densification. Its fragmented, individualized and frequently monofunctional characteristics need to be addressed. Its proximity to the centre also offers excellent opportunities for the extension of public transport and the stimulation of sustainable mobility. Dealt with in this way, fringe areas could contribute to the aim of sustainable and compact city development.

When you zoom in, however, things are more nuanced. There are already people there, the buildings and land are already owned, used and serving purposes such as logistics, production, recreation or housing. Furthermore the physical fringe sometimes also coincides with a social fringe where people experience exclusion. Zooming in on the existing situation will reveal its own needs and desires.

So how can we intervene here? Planning for the fringe is a complex process that involves making difficult choices that take account of the interests of the people who are already there as well as sustainable ambitions and goals at the scale of the entire city region. Offering housing for new residents in the fringe is more sustainable than sprawl, but might lead to gentrification or push production and jobs further out of the city. Decisions made here by the city need to be well informed. Therefore, reinventing the fringe means simultaneously thinking about the consequences of new plans and ambitions on two levels: the level of the city region and the local level of the intervention site and its [immediate] vicinity. Challenges, opportunities and consequences need to be transparently discussed, weighed and considered in relation to one another.

FRINGE CHALLENGES

The fringe presents many specific challenges. The five challenges below are not all-encompassing, but are the ones that the nine cities have worked on, because they considered them to be the most relevant.

How can we manage complex urban transformation projects with fewer resources?

Maybe the biggest challenge of all is changing the way we plan itself. Urban transformation requires a different approach than urban expansion owing to its complexity and the number and diversity of people involved. Instead of determining the outcome by design early on, focusing on the process and its dynamics is much more productive. Good communication is the key, but is also very time-consuming.

How can we reverse sprawl and stimulate compact and mixed neighbourhoods in the fringe instead?

For many cities the fringe is currently an unsustainable belt of often suboptimal and monofunctional land usage close to their inner cities. Vacant and underused buildings and land, such as large, one-storey supermarkets with vast outdoor parking lots, make for inefficient land use. Part of the challenge is to offer attractive alternatives to sprawl.

How can we counter social segregation?

Socio-economic segregation in the urban fringe, with pockets of social deprivation, often coexists with high levels of unemployment and suboptimal accessibility of public facilities and care, which might cause escalations, as we saw with the Banlieue riots in Paris and other French cities in 2005, but also in the fringes of other cities in Europe. Authorities often react by demolishing entire buildings and neighbourhoods and replacing them, while leaving the root causes untouched.

How can we overcome barriers?

Fringe areas are often divided by barriers, like highways, pipelines, cables and rail tracks, mostly servicing the historical centre. Infrastructure is one example of the subordinate role of the fringe and it highlights the need to rethink its identity and relation to the centre. It also shows that the fringe and its implications do not stop at the administrative boundary of a municipality, making regional coordination between often competing municipalities a crucial challenge.

How can we transform fragmented and privately-owned places?

The fringe appears as a fragmented area and, for the most part, has fragmented ownership, in which each individual plot is self-centred. Most of the property is privately owned and often lacks the collective layer necessary for achieving improvements. This is also due to its monofunctional and spatially segregated layout. Cross-plot development and collaboration needs to be stimulated, but this implies a very intensive and complex process.

FRINGE OPPORTUNITIES

The fringe has the potential to become the city of the future due to its size, its location close to the city centre, the specific qualities of a mixed urban-green zone, and its age.

Scale (size)

Owing to the size of the fringe, its future use will have a real impact for better or for worse. There are large areas in the fringe with room for improvement and the potential to absorb more programmes.

Proximity

As part of the existing morphological urban area, most fringe areas are close to existing city centres. This provides opportunities for both existing and future residents and for sustainable mobility concepts.

Best of both worlds

The fringe holds the promise of combining the best of both worlds, having more amenities and being closer to the city centre than the low-density suburbs, but also offering more space and greenery than the city centre.

Momentum for change

The fringe areas in the nine partner cities were built after the Second World War. The buildings are often in need of renovation or repurposing. This provides an opportunity to use this momentum of change to regenerate and rethink entire areas. Private parties are often not yet interested. The time for cities to make up their minds about these areas and act, is now!

TOWARDS A MORE SUSTAINABLE AND INCLUSIVE FRINGE IN FIVE STEPS

For the last two years, nine European cities have both re-thought their fringes on a city and regional scale and worked on the implementation of local action plans on pilot sites. What did we learn?

Step 1
Embrace existing qualities

Step 2
Adapt parts with lesser quality

Step 3
Encourage interaction

Step 4
Increase sustainable mobility

Step 5
Transforming planning

Embrace existing qualities

◯ Step 1

*Start with a careful analysis of what is already there.
Know your fringe: the buildings and the people.*

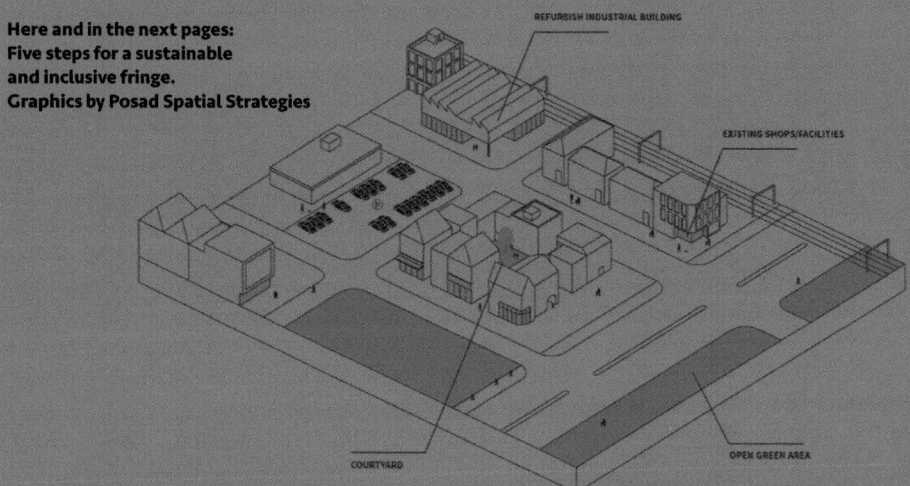

Here and in the next pages:
Five steps for a sustainable
and inclusive fringe.
Graphics by Posad Spatial Strategies

What are the characteristics of the present fringe? How does it function at the moment? What are the assets? Who are living and working there? Who are the owners of the land and buildings? Who should be involved (participation)? What exactly should be done for whom? These are questions that all cities have to reflect on when planning for the fringe. It is not only about analysis, it is about recognising and reinforcing these qualities.

How can one renovate post war flats to improve their quality, in situations where ownership is fragmented? The opportunities for renovating collective buildings are closely linked to the way the housing is organised. For example in Bulgaria and Romania, there are no associations of home owners by law. Collective renovations are therefore exceptions. In Hungary on the other hand, the percentage of private ownership is similar, but the residents of apartment buildings are grouped in associations and subsidies are linked to these associations. This is a powerful incentive to organise, in order to achieve more qualitative renovations. But even without a strict law and conditional subsidies, stakeholders can initiate collective renovation. In Baia Mare this process is made possible by a private developer. He organises the residents of an apartment building and renovates the building. In return he can add and sell one extra floor.

The City of Antwerp coerces the property management of collective buildings to carry out renovations for more energy efficiency. The city finances a masterplan and technical expertise. This way the property managers are better able to facilitate the entire renovation process. The management of collective buildings will be a challenge that we will increasingly have to deal with in compact cities.

Besides the issues of management, there is also the problem of the impact of the renovation works. Examples in France and the Netherlands however show us that major renovations are possible without having to move the residents for the duration of the works. One of the best known examples is the renovation of Lacaton Vassal in Bordeaux, where residents were able to stay in their apartments while balconies were renovated.

Adapt partswith lesser quality

○ Step 2

Find new typologies for housing.
Create mixed urban areas.
Integrate social infrastructure, jobs and production.
Use vacant buildings.
Open up fenced areas.

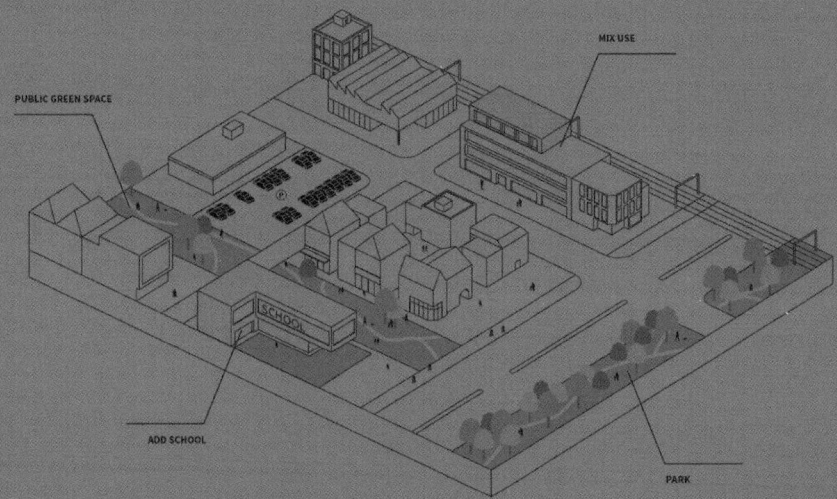

What are new typologies for housing? To attract more people and families into our cities, one has to find ways to combine the benefits of a single family home with compact housing in the fringe. Somehow, we have to find ways of managing everything in an apartment building that you could manage in a villa. When we think of housing typologies we can look at the Havenhuizen of Amsterdam. Here the designers literally took the single family house typology and transformed them in high density buildings in Amsterdam.

Other examples illustrate new ways to transfer the typical activities and uses of a single family house into other housing typologies. There are more and more examples of collective spaces in apartment buildings, where you can paint your furniture, clean your bikes, or rent spaces for visiting guests. In Malmö for example, there is a bicycle building. This is a collective building with rental apartments and a hotel. The residents can bring their cargo bikes into the kitchen. The elevators and doors are adapted so you can get your groceries easier from your bike into the kitchen fridge. This is comparable with having the garage next to the kitchen of a single family house.

In Oslo, we visited the office building of the project developer NCC. It is located in a monofunctional business neighbourhood that is slowly starting to transform. The building is constructed as a collective building which houses different firms. It is the home of the project developer himself who rents out some offices. But at the same time this building can easily be converted to a small office building with flats. The internal patio can be transformed into a collective garden.

How to create mixed urban areas? For many years, mixing functions has been an explicit goal for urban development policies and projects. But when we see the results, it is often not been put into practice at the end of the journey. In practice there are more barriers to mixed use than we often assume at the start and a lot of these plans get somehow stuck in the implementation, sale and management phase. But we have also seen some good practices:

Split 3 was built during the communist period in Croatia and is designed and constructed as a mixed-use neighbourhood. The central boulevard is flanked by large apartment buildings. The original plans were to run the boulevard through to the sea but the development stopped after the first stage. The ground-floors are shops and the first and second floors are office buildings. Above there are flats. The neighbourhood was built in the 70s and is still succesful today. There are almost no vacancies in the shops and office buildings and the homes are still in demand.

We witnessed a similar success in the Alt Erlaa estate in Vienna. As in Split, high density housing was successfully combined with a large number of amenities. There are swimming pools on top of each block and recreational facilities, such as bowling alleys, integrated in the towers. A sociological study pointed out that the Alt Erlaa residents go on holidays or short vacations less frequently than residents in other areas. The residents indicate that the quality of the amenities and flats in their neighbourhood give them less need to travel elsewhere in their free time.

In Oslo we visited the Vulkan area, a new development with different shops and restaurants, a marketplace, offices and two hotels. The project developer explained that, apart from the housing, most of the space was rented out. This gave the developer the opportunity to look for the right partners. If for example the shops were causing noise polution in one area, he could move them to another place and install a quieter meeting room underneath. This flexibility in management also gave the opportunity to organise car and bike sharing systems, since most of the parking space was still held by them.

Another interesting development is that of Sundstadt in Tübingen, Germany. This development not only created 6000 houses, but also yielded 2000 jobs. Here the primary actors were the residents who worked together with designers and the municipality. To encourage the construction of affordable houses, the municipality organised a competition to make plots available for private building cooperatives. By excluding the intermediate developer, the construction price was 15 to 20% less than the regular price.

These last two examples show that if the builder of a project stays in the area, there can be more opportunities to build more for mixed and flexible use.

Encourage interaction

○ **Step 3**

Create a collective layer.
Create new communities through temporary use and placemaking.
Encourage multifunctional use of spaces.

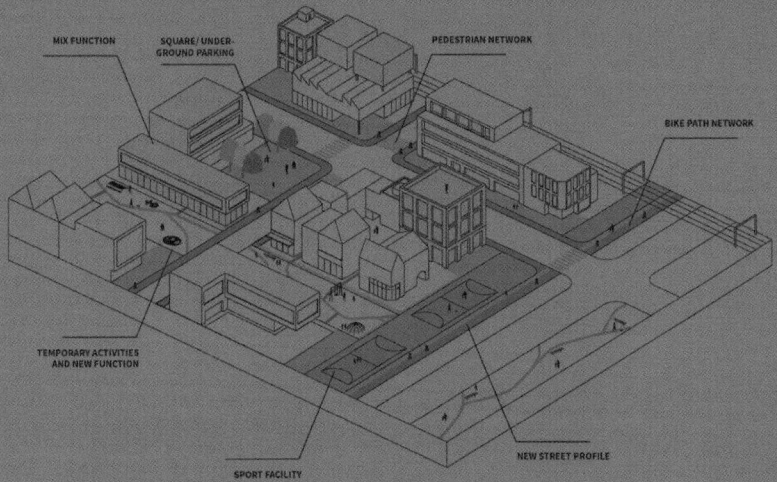

Collective spaces and venues - also called a collective layer - are missing in most of the fringe areas in our network. These are the places where neighbours can meet. The collective development and management of part of the public domain, for example of a tree or a communal allotment garden, stimulates social interaction between neighbours and workers, as well as relieving the city's management services! To encourage social interaction in a neighbourhood, these meeting places should be attractive and accessible, so people stay longer and make better use of them. This can be as easy as improving the doorway of an apartment building.

We saw a beautiful example of a building in Kabelwerk that is used for housing students and for short term renting, where the collective spaces (the doorway and hall, the collective laundry room, swimming pool and fitness area) were all constructed with such care that people chose to spend more time in them.

Other collective spaces are the little paths next to the private gardens where all the children of the neighbourhood play.

One can facilitate space for social interaction in the public domain. However in Solin for examples the URBACT team worked together with the University of Split and placed installations on a pedestrian road that was under-used. The effect is that these installations are now used as a playground by the residents and schools and it has become a place where residents can meet informally with their children.

Increase sustainable mobility

○ Step 4

From roads to streets.
Deal with barriers.
Promote sustainable transport.

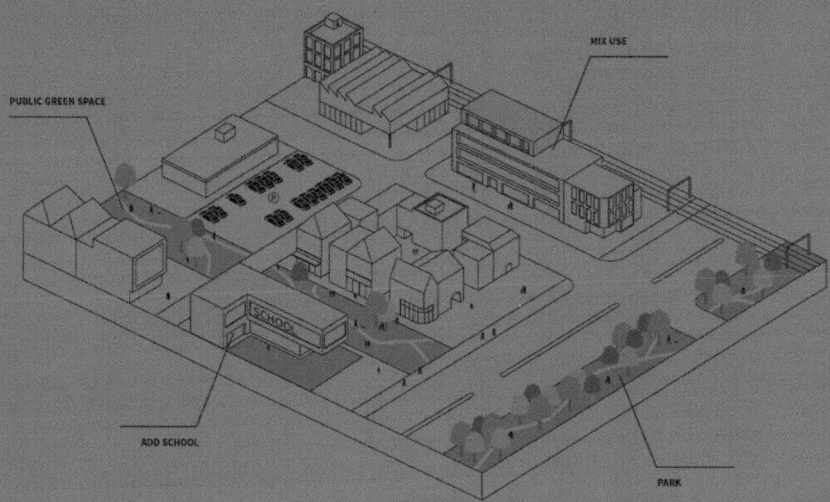

By changing the scale and mode of transport infrastructure, we can reduce barriers and encourage denser and mixed land-use. Downgrading roads, eg. from motorways to streets or from roads to cycleways, are important tools for enhancing the life quality of an area.

In Stockholm, the main 4-lane highway of "Enskedevägen" links the transformation area in the southern part of Stockholm to the outer ringroad. Options such as reducing the speed of traffic and road capacity, encouraging more cycling and planting a boulevard were under consideration. This could help to open up one of the main roads for more access for pedestrian and cyclists and to reduce its barrier effect.

The strategic role of infrastructure as a barrier for development was also shown clearly in Brno. Here, the City was faced with a big dilemma, linked to uncertainty and local controversy about the relocation of their main railway station, to be financed under the TEN-T programme. The new station will be the key to open up a large section of the cityfringe for transformation. In the meantime stakeholders are developing creative ideas for temporary use of the sites around and behind the station, which will generate interest in the development potential before the final railway investment is approved.

Many cities are seeking ways to plan for less road space, when car traffic appears to be a constant pressure. Recent studies in Oslo have monitored the effects of closing some of the urban highways due to tunnel maintenance. The researchers have looked at a number of independent road sections, and concluded that many cars actually seemed to "disappear". So by carefully reducing road capacity, in combination with advanced warning and reliable transport alternatives, people seem to find alternatives that work.

Transforming planning

○ **Step 5**

Create a living lab.
Plan in 1-5-15 years.
Use a flexible process, learn and adapt.
Plan, implement and organise management simultaneously.
Modify rules to govern.
Stimulate cooperation.

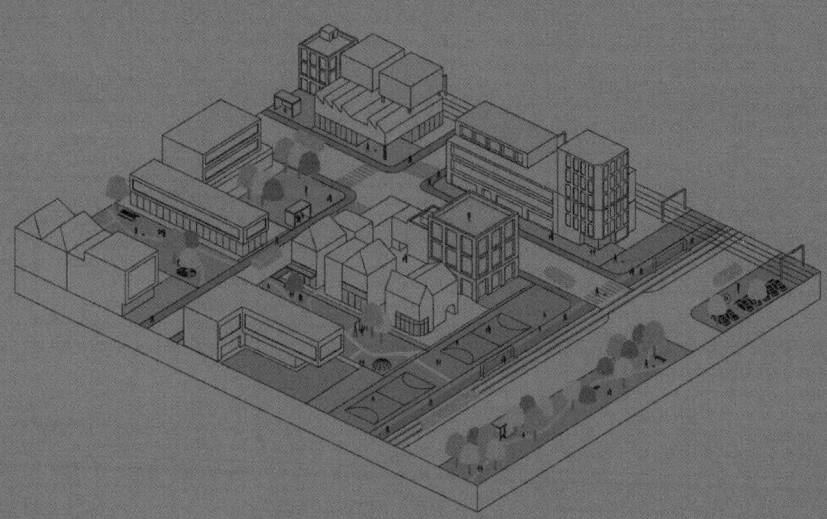

How to create a living lab? It is important to create a space where cities can develop new methods and planning approaches, through testing and learning. Being part of a knowledge-exchange network has created this "testing space" in all our partner cities. A living lab like this must be well-facilitated and carefully documented so that we can learn in a systematic way. It can create uncertainty for the stakeholders at the start, but it enables taking advantage of new possibilities and can lead to a mental shift.

Work on the level of the cities' urban strategy.
Test this strategy in one or more pilot cases simultaneously.
Integrate interaction and reflection on both levels.

All of the partners in the URBACT network are working on two levels. They work on the level of the cities' urban strategy, and they test this strategy in one or more pilot cases. The idea is that the vision influences the cases, and the experience of the cases influences the overall city strategy. Antwerp created a testing site with the project Lageweg. After discussions with politicians, this was communicated to all stakeholders, while working on the level of a big area through research by design in Lab XX. In Olso the Integrated action plan works on 5 pilot sites in Hovinbyen, an area where there is already a proces of planning on the level of the entire area.

Work with the current context, learn from it and anticipate the new operational phase by already organizing management.

Planning, implementation and management are all crucial for developing neighbourhoods with long term, qualitative improvements. Understanding the impact of interventions is also important, as well as the wider effects that the organisation of communities can have, especially in compact urban areas. Developers who take on new roles in the same areas as their investment projects, for example as landowners, housing cooperative or with other responsibilities, are likely to have stronger committments and contribute to sustainable and high quality results in the longer term.

Planning, implemention and management are not always clearly defined, sequential phases in developing a neighbourhood. These activities will invariably overlap in the fringe areas, where people already live and work. Two of our partner cities already started to take action during this planning network. It is significant that these are the two smallest municipalities of the network. In larger cities, the administration is often strictly divided, which makes implementation together with planning very difficult. But the municipality of Casoria already started to plant trees in a park and Solin has collected private funding from the larger companies to restore a former beach area. We should all seek ways to plan, implement and organise the management at the same time. To work with a flexible plan and integrate learning moments. Work today on short, intermediate and long term plans. Plan for the fringe based on the full life cycle of an area.

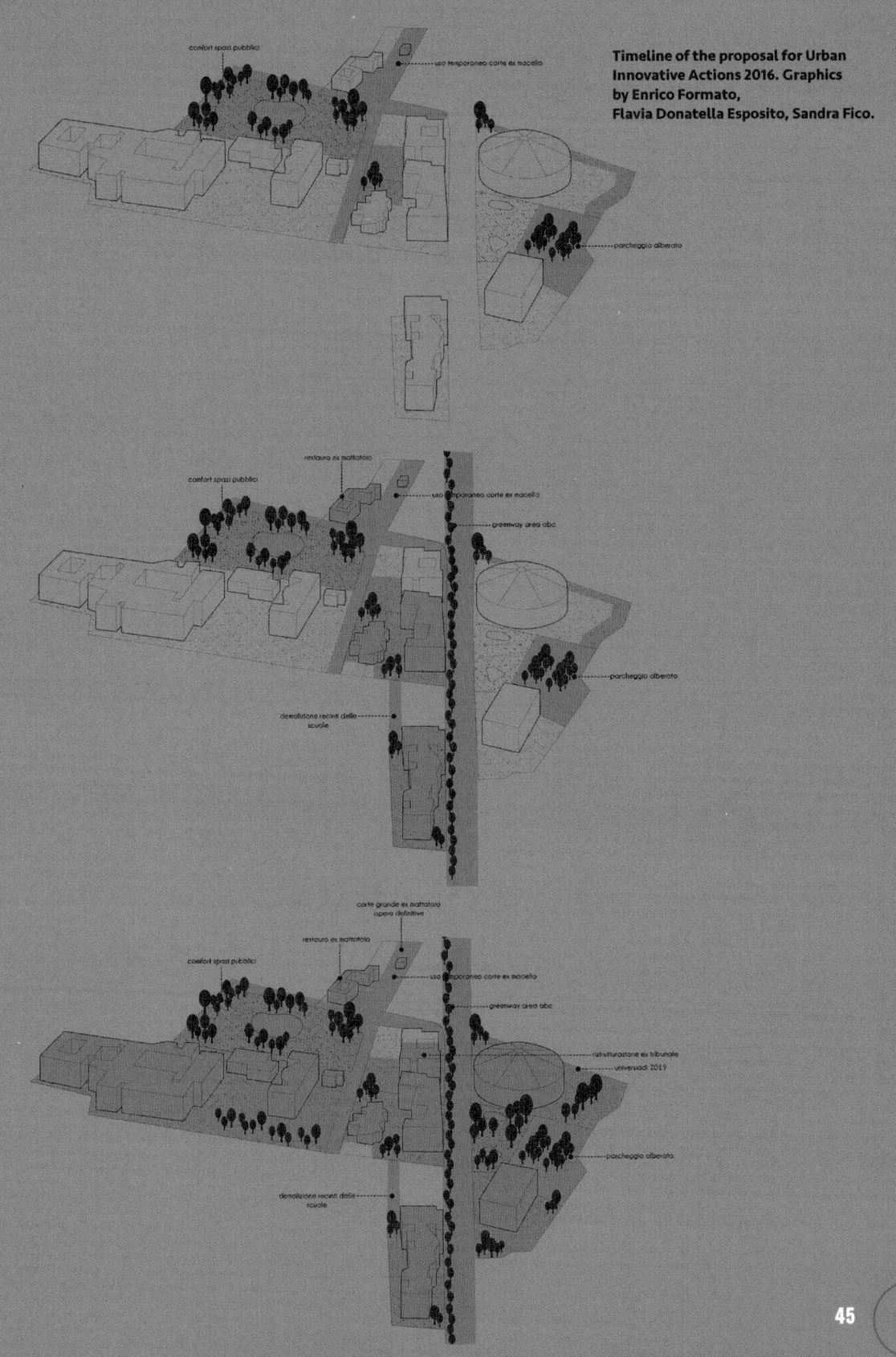

Timeline of the proposal for Urban Innovative Actions 2016. Graphics by Enrico Formato, Flavia Donatella Esposito, Sandra Fico.

1.2

Antwerp.
Transforming planning

Mieke Belmans
*Urban planner for the city of Antwerp
and project coordinator of Sub>urban*

European fringe areas are in need of transformation. Large parts are built after the Second World War and wait for renovation and repurposing. This provides an opportunity to use this momentum of change to rethink entire areas. However, the fringe appears as a different landscape than the inner city and 19th century belt. Modernist urban areas, old village nuclei, industrial zones and recreational areas forms a fragmented tissue, intersected by heavy infrastructure. The set of instruments which are used in the inner city and 19th century belt are not suitable for the fringe area.

The aim of the Sub>urban network is to develop useful strategies for reinventing and transforming the urban fringe by uncovering new planning practices, processes, instruments and partnerships. Instead of making a fixed blueprint plan, this involves flexible planning and working with strategic pilots. In this way a parallel development of an experimental setting as well as an action plan for tangible ideas can be achieved. The ambition is to plan, learn and implement at the same time. Feeding discoveries on the concrete scale of the site with the ambitions of the strategic plan and viceversa.

Flexible Planning

Linear blueprint planning, where plans are fixed by a small group of experts, has proven not to be able to deal very well with the complexity, unpredictability and limited funds usually associated with urban regeneration. Instead of determining the outcome by design, focusing on the process and its dynamics is much more productive. This does not mean letting go of quality related goals but rather adding a broader definition instead of looking at these as the only possible outcome. It also means clearly excluding and setting the scope of ambition. The possibilities for developments or redevelopments are determined by these ambitions, often described in a strategic plan, together with process-related, legal, financial and spatial boundaries. If a development is seen as a stepwise incremental process rather than a single undertaking, it can gradually take shape based on existing qualities, allowing users and other stakeholders to gain more influence, thereby making it easier to respond to and take advantage of unforeseen and unforeseeable social dynamics. In the field of flexible area development, each individual development explicitly part forms of a conti-

Aerial view of Lageweg pilot site.

nuous process. Each step can feed the learning and can help the masterplan grow.

In this quest for planning practices that enable transformation, the Sub>urban partners are not only interested in strategies as such. They are eager to discover the roles of local and regional governments in the ongoing development of their cities. The local governments' roles in the renewal of their inner cities have mostly been to initiate, coordinate and/or direct projects that are generally well-defined.

Should we prepare for a substantial shift towards enabling and facilitating roles in mostly organic and informal processes? What are the tools needed to take on these new roles and are these instruments within reach of local and regional governments today?

Strategic Pilots

In addition to thinking on a strategic level on the scale of the city and the region, the Sub>urban project is also about the implementation of local action plans as strategic pilots and on a more zoomed-in scale, it serves as a testing ground with an urban acupuncture approach. Sub>urban aims at renewing the city by rethinking our concept of the city. By doing research through concrete pilot projects, the partners aim to improve current concepts of urban development and find and test new strategies, partnerships, financial models, procedures and regulations and new building typologies for housing, amenities, school buildings and offices. As it is impossible to finance and initiate everything at the same time, it is important to choose these strategic sites well, so they can influence and contribute the planning on a larger scale. Modest steps, even temporary ones, that are well chosen can ultimately have big consequences.

Transforming flexible planning in Antwerp:

Lab XX[1]

«The development of a new urban renewal culture takes time», says Michiel Dehaene, associate professor of urban design at Ghent University. Which was why he proposed setting up a permanent living lab in Antwerp for knowledge gathering and experimenting in the fringe. Lab XX started operating in 2013.

1. Verhaert, 2018

Regeneration of housing development, Zanderroth Architekten.
Source: Integrated Action Plan of the City of Antwerp, 2018.

Transforming design of public facilities in a micro-node.
Source: Integrated Action Plan of the City of Antwerp, 2018.

Dehaene explains: According to general prognoses, the city was expecting a large increase in population (+ 20% in 15 years). We observed the first effects of an unmonitored population increase on children, who were unable to find a place in schools. At the same time, the departments of planning and building permits were confronted with more and more building applications for developments in the 20th-century fabric. The city's urban strategies and regulations were tailored to brownfield redevelopment and to the rigid 19th-century building blocks and older areas of central Antwerp. However, our standard solutions did not seem to be suited to the 20th-century fabric in the fringe. We didn't know how to intervene effectively in this hybrid context.

The planning department of Antwerp got inspired by Bordeaux's "50.000 logements" process directed by La CUB (Communité Urbaine de Bordeaux/Bordeaux Métropole). In particular, the parallel research by different design teams, each with their own specific perspective, caught our attention.

That's why Lab XX selected four design teams. It is important to note that the teams did not have to provide a solution for the entire challenge or the entire area. The assignment procedure made it possible to select four complementary approaches. Together the teams produced a vision for the 20th-century belt made up of four different scenarios. This is what is called "research by design": different scenarios that reveal the potential of an area are used to guide the discussion and to communicate with a wider audience.

The design based research that was conducted within Lab XX is primarily a study of the area's potential. The outcome of Lab XX is not a final plan for how and where to compact the city. In fact, it mainly helps us to understand what is feasible and how densification can be linked to qualitative urban renewal. Gradually the assignment changed. Instead of being treated as a bad thing, population growth was to be welcomed in the 20th-century belt as a necessary condition for qualitative and sustainable transformation. The living lab experience enabled us to reformulate our question.

Lageweg as test case[2]

The scenarios of the four design teams were explored in test cases. Lageweg was one of them. The Lageweg project site is situated in a semi-industrial part of the Antwerp fringe. The city has no ownership of the site's 30 hectare of land, which are characterized by a hybrid environment of small and large industry, schools, houses, big apartment buildings and privately-owned green space. There is no real social connection between inhabitants and users of the place. The Lageweg is called the "Ugly Duckling" at the entrance of the district Hoboken. The area is in need of transformation as it continues to deteriorate.

This area is a prototype for a many cities in Flanders as well as in Europe. The fringe has a kind of chaotic appearance, parts have never been completed to a finished urban fabric. As a consequence of this, the fringe has a high instability and because of that a high capacity for reconversion. The successes and pitfalls we got to know to work at the Lageweg, are useful for many other cities.

The aim for Antwerp is to create an integrated development that respond to the needs of the neighbourhood (lack of green areas and sports fields). We set ourselves the ambitious goal of enhancing the surrounding neighbourhood by creating a mixed urban area – affordable dwellings, manufacturing, more public amenities (green space, schools, sporting facilities and community services) – and enabling the transition of the present

2. Roesems, 2018

businesses to a circular economy. Therefore we have to encourage a cooperation across the plot borders with different private owners.

Why did we look for a new process?

In classic urban renewal projects, the authorities often own a large share of the land and can, as a result, weigh in on the project, the programme, the design, the public space, etc. In Lageweg, however, the city does not have that leverage. The land is largely privately owned, resulting in a heavily fragmented ownership structure. In a traditional "linear" process, the authorities would begin by expropriating the owners, then tackle the decontamination and lastly team up with a property developer who would redevelop the site and put it back on the market.

The aim of the Lageweg pilot project is of an entirely different nature. The project seeks to redevelop this hybrid area, not on the basis of a blueprint the city has drawn up beforehand, nor in accordance with strict regulation and zoning plans, but in collaboration with the owners of the plots and the established businesses. In a classic process there are often winners and losers. In this case we chose a co-creative process to make sure everybody wins. By ensuring that all stakeholders are co-responsible, the chances of one of the partners slowing down the process becomes smaller.

How did we engage the stakeholders?

Together with consultants (51N4E and Connect&Transform), we developed a set of consecutive instruments that would enable all stakeholders to work together. Starting with mind-opening dialogues and an exploratory kick-off discussion, we defined collective ambitions for the area. The first idea of a multi-plot development was born. Each owner started looking beyond his/her own plot, enlarging the spatial opportunities.

A second step was co-creating a design plan for the area and making it more visual by using an interactive scale model. This prompted one of the private partners to ask: "What is my financial gain?" In a classic process, providing the answer to that question would delay the entire process. In the Lageweg process, however, we started to work simultaneously on the financial aspect of the multi-plot development. Working on parallel tracks speeds up the process instead of blocking and delaying it. The financial question not only demonstrates the benefits of the process used in Lageweg, but is also a key in identifying the actual land owners. For example, at a certain point it was necessary to have a spatial and financial calculation model drawn up by experts. When it came to signing the declaration of engagement, we discovered that some land owners had representatives. This is crucial information because it revealed the identity of the true decision makers early in the process.

Another instrument was a safari tour of the site in the form of a guided walk with all the stakeholders. The brochure made for the walk showed the soil contamination and possible future development scenarios in one, five and twenty years' time. On the one hand, this information made the owners aware that the current land use plan needed to be changed in order to realize the long-term plan. On the other hand, it became clear that soil decontamination was an issue for more than one owner. One of the owners demanded that the land use plan (RUP) be altered or he would withdraw from the co-creation project on this site. At this point, the role of the city evolved from facilitating to regulating, denying the owner's demand in order to stress the importance of a joint plan and a common urban vision.

Stakeholders groups meeting.
Source: Integrated Action Plan of the City of Antwerp, 2018.

Private spaces in Lageweg, picture by Jasper Leonard.

51

Public value through temporary use

Meanwhile the area stays the Ugly Duckling of the neighbourhood. A huge part of the Lageweg is dominated by the empty buildings of a formal packaging factory. Since 2013, the plot of 30.000 square meters is empty and victim to vandalism. To avoid the buildings from further deterioration, the real estate developer wants to open up the area for temporary use. With a mixture of sports and socio-cultural activities the real estate developer wants to alter the negative image of the area and gather ideas for the final redevelopment from the start. The developer asked a communication expert to develop a way to promote temporary use at the site. The result is "De Blikfabriek". The name refers to the formal function as packaging factory. Since spring 2018 the first start-ups and creative workshops have found their way to "De Blikfabriek". In addition a place for urban sports, a co-working place and an urban camping will start soon to create a bustling area where people can meet each other. The city administration facilitated the process of temporary use with her knowledge of local organisations which are in need of space. A local civil servant brought together ietStof and De Blikfabriek. This textile workshop works with used textile but functions at the same time as a local social project where young people from the neighbourhood get taught in designing and sewing clothes. For at least 5 years the formal packaging factory will host temporary use.

What worked well and what are the pitfalls?

The Lageweg test case is a learning process, both for the city and for the owners concerned. The government has to assume the role of facilitator to get all stakeholders to support a co-creative vision and ensure that the owners make it happen. At the same time, it is necessary to guard the common interest. This balance is a continuous challenge.

Another possible pitfall is the tendency to relapse into a classic planning process, especially when there is a lot at stake and despite knowing that the classic process does not guarantee the best results. Lageweg is a test case, in which ideas are tested through trial and error in a contained setting. Another challenge is to capture the learning points and share the knowledge and lessons learned.

The test case is in that sense a search for a way authorities and citizens can work together on the future of the city. We are convinced that this will lead to a more sustainable form of urban renewal.

Temporary use design in Hoboken (De Blikfabriek).
Copyright: Marketing & Communicatiebureau Reputations.

The base of success for flexible planning

The basis for the success of a flexible, processes-oriented approach to planning (Flexible Planning) is the competence and energy of the people working in municipalities (city administrations). They have to be able to operate effectively in more flexible processes, to work together with private stakeholders and take up new roles. Governments need to move from a traditionally passive regulatory role, to a more active, initiating and facilitating, matchmaking role. URBACT stimulates administrations to experiment with these roles.

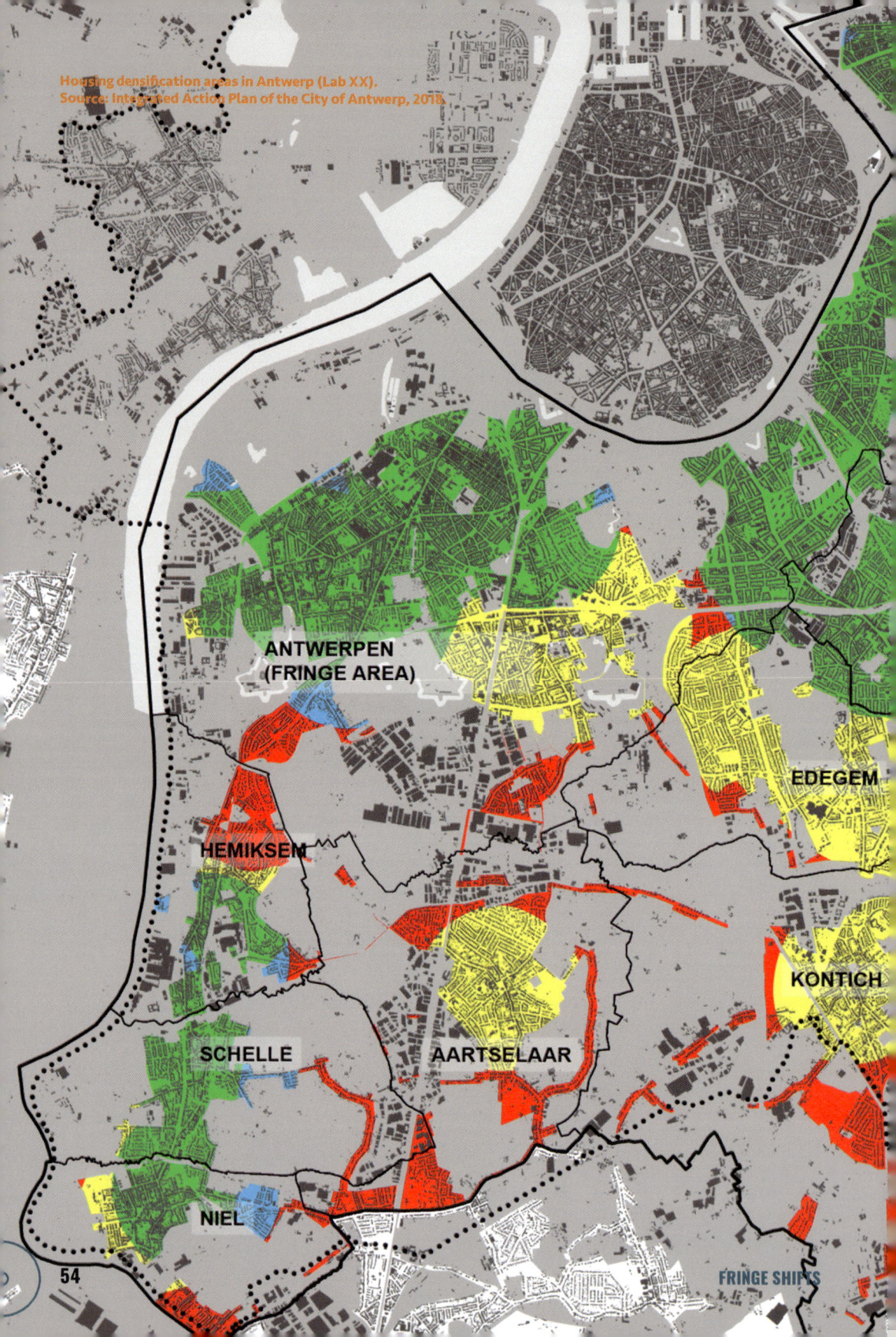

Housing densification areas in Antwerp (Lab XX).
Source: Integrated Action Plan of the City of Antwerp, 2018.

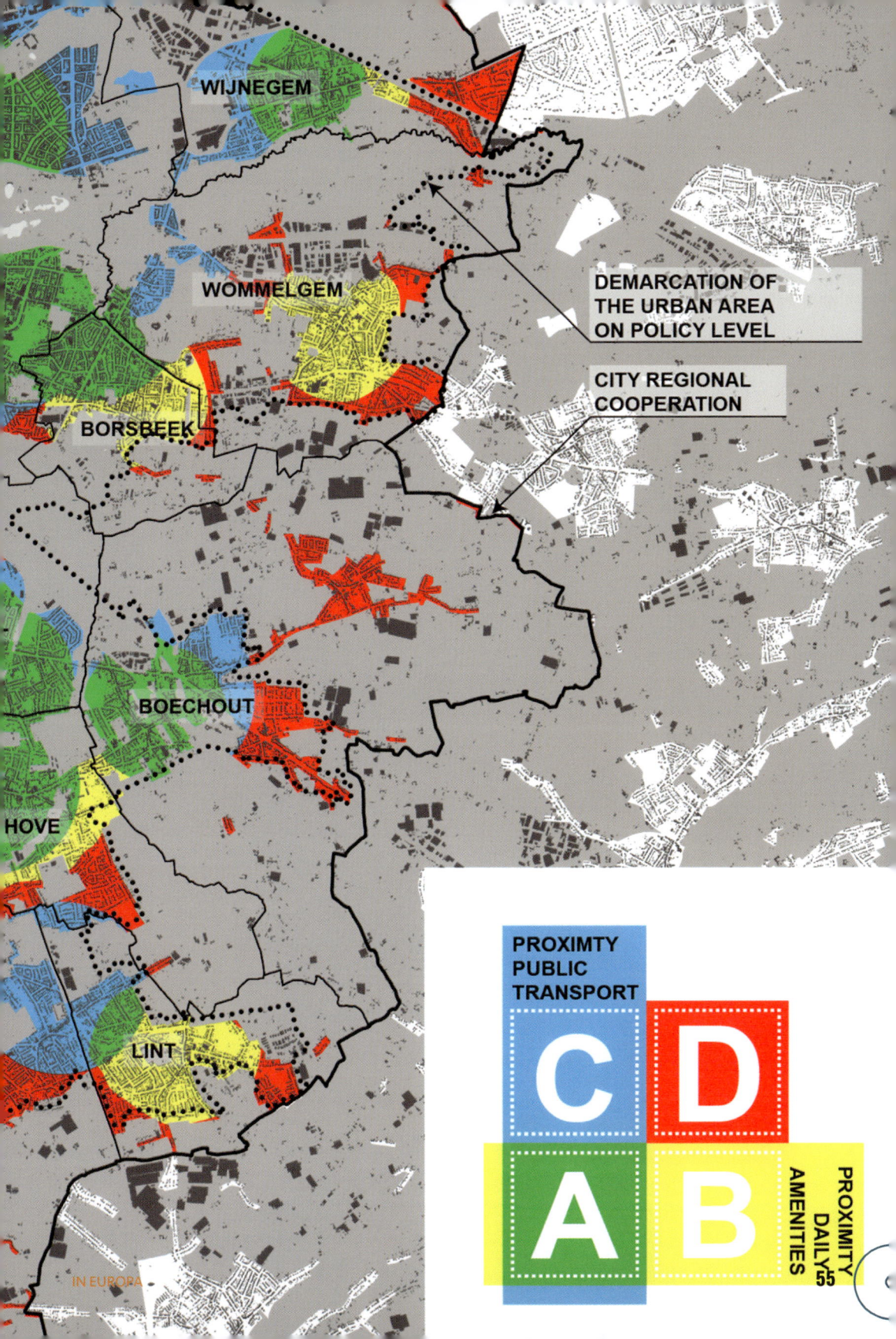

1.3
Oslo. Transforming for intensified use

Peter Austin
City of Oslo

REINVENTING THE FRINGE

Oslo worked in the EU-funded URBACT programme, looking at ways to achieve sustainable regeneration of existing urban areas. This work was driven by the twin policy goals of stimulating markets in weaker parts of our cities, and trying to reduce the pressure of urban sprawl. Cities need more housing and modernised homes, jobs and public functions for a growing population, preferably located close to public transport. These opportunities can be found in areas that surround our inner cities, that can be called the fringe.

What could be even better, would be that these new compact urban areas have such high quality that people would choose to live and work there. Seen as a whole, the benefits should compete well with other housing alternatives, such as villas in neighbouring villages.

The URBACT project *Sub>urban. Reinventing the fringe* was about transforming the complex periphery of cities into more attractive and high-quality areas for living and working, and thus giving alternatives to urban sprawl. Through flexibility and focus on implementation, there is the need to find new ways of thinking in urban planning.

Where is the fringe located?

There is of course some discussion about what this "urban" or "city" fringe really is. The details of defining this vary from place to place, and between different researchers and observers.

The starting point is recognising that this is related to existing urban areas. The question then is: When does it risk reinforcing sprawl, and when does it reinforce the city? This is not always easy to answer.

The first question to be answered is what is urban? And what is the urban fringe?

Urban areas do not usually fit exactly into municipal borders. To be able to get a common vocabulary and compare all the cities in *Sub>urban* network, there is the need of a good definition of urbanity. The OECD and the European Commission defined urbanity on the basis of density, and not by municipal boundaries.

The OECD uses two terms to define urbanity:
1. The morphological urban areas (MUA): this is the urban area, recognised as a continuous built city when flying above.

Pilot site of Hovinbyen.
Source: Integrated Action Plan of the City of Oslo, 2018.

2. The functional urban areas (FUA): This is the area that depends on the core settlements. This area is usually defined by commuting data.

Then the difference between either reinforcing sprawl or reinforcing the city can be considered on the basis of two criteria:

1. The fringe areas are within the existing morphological urban areas.

2. The fringe areas are, or will be, connected with public transport.

In all cities which participated in the project, the selected fringe areas lay outside the historic centres, but within the morphological urban areas. Each of the participating cities had chosen not to widen the spatial coverage of their built areas, but rather find ways of intensifying the land use with a wide range of functions and in a sustainable way.

In some of the partner cities these fringe areas were inside the municipal boundaries, in Antwerp and Oslo. In larger urban agglomerations with high densities, like the Barcelona Metropolitan Area and the Naples region, the fringe areas were municipalities outside the core city boundaries. But Badia del valles and Casoria are still contained within the morphological urban area.

WHAT ARE THE CHARACTERISTICS OF THE FRINGE?

The fringe areas in URBACT partner cities were largely built during the latter part of the 20th century, after the Second world war. The areas have lower density than the inner city developments, and are more fragmented and look more like a patchwork on a map.

The buildings are more or less 50 years old, and therefore often in need of renovation or ready for adaptation for new functions. This can be seen as an opportunity to take this momentum of change, to regenerate and rethink entire areas.

If there are low-density housing areas in the patchwork, there is a high maintenance cost for roads and other infrastructure, and the quality public spaces can suffer.

Most fringe-areas are dominated by car traffic, which results in extensive parking spaces above ground, traffic congestion and a non-sustainable environment.

Fringe areas are often divided by barriers, with highways, pipelines, cables and railtracks, mostly directed to the historic centre.

As a result, there is often little activity and even less human interaction in the streets. Even the open spaces are organised in a monofunctional way.

WHAT IS THE POTENTIAL OF THE FRINGE?

The fringe areas in the URBACT Sub>urban project are at a convenient distance from the historic centres, relatively close to the main concentrations of amenities and jobs. This meant that they still have a potential benefit of proximity, which is a basis to promote alternatives to the car.

Sub>urban fringe areas are in need of renovation and modernisation, and are often at the moment of resale. The fringe areas will in the end be changed on their own, but the Cities have a responsibility to take this momentum to rethink the processes and directions of change as a whole.

These fringe areas often still have larger plots. There is more space than in the historic centre and the 19th century urban fabric. Sub>urban had tried to rethink how cities will look and work, by combining positive elements of dense urban living with good access to green spaces. The fringe areas hold the potential to combine the best of both worlds, also attracting residents who would otherwise be expected to move out of the city. This will be an alternative to urban sprawl.

To do that Sub>urban also worked to help create an environment with good choices for both living and working close-by. The new building structures – including housing choices - should open up the benefits of compact urban living.

The transformation of the fringe is a new subject for research in Europe at the moment. So this is not a conclusion. But Sub>urban already succeeded to show some of the interesting examples and good practices from partner cities, as a way to move forward.

Introduction to the Oslo case

Oslo's fringe areas are similarly close to the city centre and have low-density land-use, including industry and warehousing, at the same time as having good public transport service. These areas represent a major potential for enabling sustainable development for the anticipated population growth.

The expansion of Oslo stops at the fjord-coastline and the protected forest. Therefore, it is natural to plan for an incremental conversion of today's monofunctional and fragmented sites, to become part of the multifunctional, compact urban fabric.

Looking more closely at the Hovin City area, is it possible to find that this is not a dead, depopulated urban zone without any modern functions. In fact, the area has a central role in the way the city of Oslo works today. Services and manufacturing, with production and distribution, are all part of the local scene, as they have been for centuries. More than 55,000 jobs and 40,000 residents already make up a thriving community, night and day.

The City of Oslo is cautious about rapid redevelopment, which could risk destroying part of Hovin City's identity and character. It was therefore searching for new ways to redevelop the area, filling the gap between a long history and an exciting future. Well functioning, attractive and inclusive urban living, was its main aim, working to follow the overall strategy for revitalising the area over the foreseeable future.

The City of Oslo aims to become a driving force for innovative and sustainable urban development. This means that Oslo must also learn from the experience of other cities, where they have similar challenges, so that it can enlarge its toolbox for urban planning and development. The participation in the URBACT Sub>urban project has been a major step for Oslo, where the city has gained substantial new knowledge, experience and a network of experts and colleagues throughout Europe. Oslo focused on five pilot areas, which are all closely linked to the overall strategy for Hovin City.

The working-method of URBACT includes sharing knowledge, testing and collaborating across and between the participating cities. This has given Oslo an invaluable opportunity to step aside and use the time and space and new colleagues to think in new ways. The strength of the pilot projects lies in precisely their untested starting point. A lot can happen, and has already happened, as the varied groups of stakeholders have worked together with a clear mandate to think about developing the areas in new ways.

This process has been valuable in itself, and has stimulated creative thinking, new perspectives, mutual respect and maturation of ideas for the future of Hovin City.

One of the most exciting cases is the pilot site of Bryn Station – one of the earliest stations along a mainline railway, which has remained underused and is now surrounded by warehousing and a major road junction. The developers around this site are now more prepared for redevelopment than ever before.

In the old industrial sites of Vollebekk and Hasle, the stakeholders have contributed to a whole set of new ideas for what the sites could be used for. Seen together, the pilot-studies have given important input to the overall strategy for the Hovin City area. The City of Oslo is now looking more closely at ways to integrate the existing functions into a new and compact urban structure.

The national centre for tennis and gymnastics is currently located at Hasle. The City of Oslo has looked into ways for this to become more closely integrated into the local area, so that these functions can also help to meet local needs. This centre is on municipal land, so there is the hope that the City could take a lead in this particular case.

In Sub>urban was also very clear, from local discussions and together with colleagues from other cities in the network, how small, carefully gauged steps today can make big differences in the long term. This means to keep discussing about visions and long-term results alive, in order not to lose track and to support an environment that can motivate the developers. URBACT has been central for Oslo in developing this approach.

Urban change in a challenging context

Hovin City is in Oslo's fringe. This area will face major changes in the decades ahead. Oslo is one of Europe's fastest growing cities, but expansion beyond the coastal fjord and the forest belt is impossible. So it's essential to work to continually find ways to accommodate growth through recycling, updating and modernising the city in new and more sustainable ways.

The very name «Hovin City», was introduced as part of the previous revision of the City Strategy in 2015, and has become adopted as a term for the extensive area lying between the inner city and the Oslo's eastern corridor of Grorud Valley.

The area comprises low-density build with industry, warehousing and retail, as well as scattered residential areas with little contact between each other and the rest of city.

The combination of low density and physical and mental barriers has given an impression of Hovin City as an area which is cut off from the rest of Oslo. In fact, the central parts of Hovin City are just as close to Oslo's main railway station as Majorstua, at the end of one of the most attractive and trendy retail streets in the inner city.

Concept for temporary uses in Haraldrud tower, by a-lab arkitekter.
Source: Integrated Action Plan of the City of Oslo, 2018.

(next page)
Einar of "Tårnet AS" presents the project of Haraldrud tower during the international workshop of URBACT on February 2017 (photo: Jonas Aarre Sommerset).
Source: Integrated Action Plan of the City of Oslo, 2018.

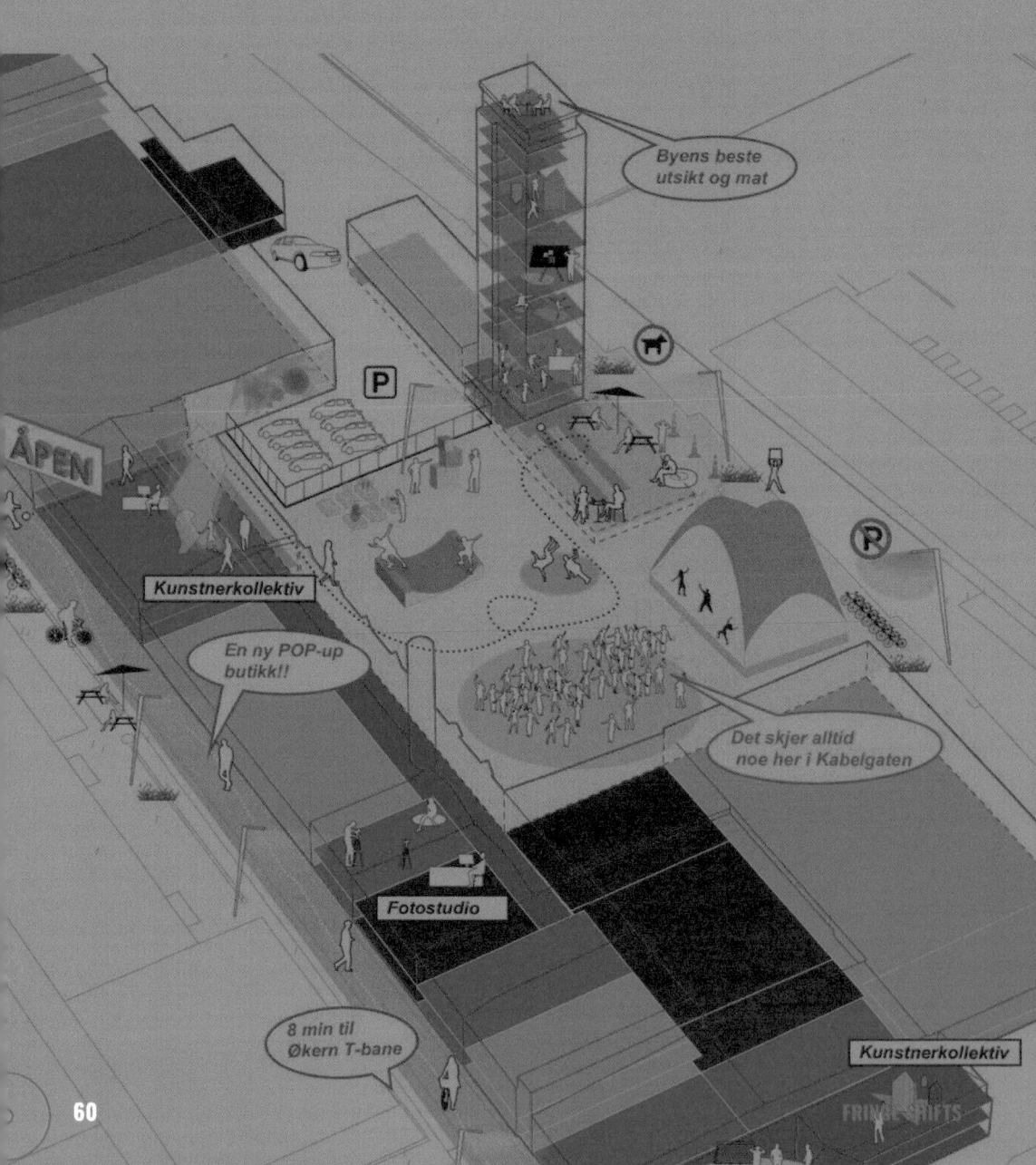

Accessibility by public transport is good in most parts of Hovin City, with two metro-lines crossing through the area.

Seen as a whole, the City considers there to be a big potential for developing Hovin City one step at a time, from being a sub-optimally used and monofunctional barrier between the city and the suburbs, to becoming a dense, mixed-use and continuous part of the urban fabric; a bridge between the city core and the Grorud Valley.

Being close to the inner city, and with under-used green space and waterways, together with the potential for densification and transformation, the Hovin City area represents one of Oslo's most important locations for urban development in the years ahead.

Strategic Plan for Hovin City

A proposal for the Strategic Plan was presented in 2016. The aim is to transform the area for 100,000 new residents and a similar number of jobs. Oslo hopes to rediscover its urban fringe. Not by replacing everything that is there today, but by improving the connections and relationships with the rest of the city and facilitating a variety of mixed land-use with higher densities.

In a European context, Oslo is far from alone in seeing the potential for densifying the urban fringe. Most European cities have under-used land somewhere in the zones between the historical inner-city and the suburbs, many of which were carefully designed and built in accordance with the contemporary theories and design trends of the post-war period.

However, due to today's knowledge and new requirements (e.g.: reduced climate-gas emission), the process of redefining the urban fringe is underway; taking part in the URBACT project Sub>urban was an important step forward.

One of the key points in the Strategic Plan for Hovin City is that the City should have a more active and inclusive role than today. To achieve this, the City must take more initiatives that would normally be the case, for collaboration between public agencies and departments, and with other local stakeholders. The City will then have the opportunity to both initiate and facilitate processes where other groups can take part in creating new pilot-projects, which can become models for participatory and sustainable development. By involving local residents in creating ideas, the City aims to achieve more social inclusion and widen the scope of local democracy.

Temporary use is an important new tool

As a primer for more permanent change, temporary projects can be a useful tool for stimulating urban development and involving local communities.

The way this is organised will influence success. Developers must take responsibility for these processes. Some kind of network should be in place to receive ideas and initiatives, and to guide stakeholders through the procedures.

The city's tenancy agreements should be reviewed so that temporary use can be adopted in a fair and correct way, which means that clear policy support is also needed. A possibility is to invite NGO's to present their ideas, as a way of stimulating the required policy agreements.

Strategic frameworks to be adopted

The city should first adopt its strategy for temporary use, which will include everything from short-term events to long-term / temporary use. Regardless of the length of activity expected, temporary use must always have an exit plan from day one.

Therefore, the city will look further into the possibilities to planning for multi-functional land-use, which would allow for a wide range of types of temporary use. The possibility of conditional approval should also be considered, so that the specified sites and areas will use temporary activities as a precondition for approving final, regular types of development.

Preferred and non-preferred types of temporary use must be defined in some way, perhaps mainly focussing on activities that are non-desirable. Dependency on car-usage, or environmentally damaging activities may fall in the category of non-desirable.

Rules and regulations/guidelines need to be in place to allow and encourage temporary use. Issues that could be included in such guidelines would include:

A) Activities which would not require special permits;

B) Waiving of charges for temporary activities – a kind of "urban living" rebate;

C) Specified areas for prioritising temporary land use;

D) Universal approvals could be considered, assuming that strict criteria would be met.

Guidelines for temporary use should be produced, which would help stakeholders in applying and giving illustrations from real examples.

The strategy for temporary use must be based on an overall analysis of the project as a whole, to include both indoor and outdoor activities.

Conclusion

The *urban fringe* represents one of the biggest underused potentials in Europe's cities today. But making these areas more sustainable and attractive is a huge challenge, due to reluctant markets, big public investments and a complex relation between private and public stakeholders already in the areas, and often fragmented ownership patterns.

The URBACT Sub>urban project has given inspiration to the City of Oslo, together with partners across Europe, in finding new, lower-cost and innovative approaches to stimulate change. Among the many approaches, involvement of local stakeholders in creative discussions, and encouraging temporary-uses to create new images and activities, are among the most exciting and novel.

Translated and adapted from:
Peter Austin & Isabelle Verhaert, presentation URBACT Sub>urban mid-term review, 13 June 2017, Brussels

City of Oslo, Planning and Building Agency, final report "URBACT Hovinbyen", 22 May 2018, Oslo (articles by Ellen De Vibe and Silje Hoftun)

City of Oslo, Planning and Building Agency, working notes from a workshop on Temporary Use, 2018, Oslo

Street festival in Kabelgata (site of Haraldrud).
Source: Integrated Action Plan of the City of Oslo, 2018.

OASE urban ecological festival, organized in 2017 in Kjelsrud, within the activities of URBACT (photo: Anne Cecilie M. Sølvberg-Louison). Source: Integrated Action Plan of the City of Oslo, 2018.

1.4
AMB (BARCELONA).
Transforming for social inclusion

AMB URBACT Team

INTRODUCTION

The growing complexity of cities is a great challenge. The Metropolitan Area of Barcelona (abbreviated in AMB, from *Area Metropolitana de Barcelona*) is not an exception. The urban processes of the last decades have transformed completely how the metropolis was planned in all its dimensions: spatial, social, economic, and environmental. In 1976 the PGM (*Plan General Metropolitano*), an urban masterplan that englobes in one plan most of the municipalities of the metropolis, was approved and has been a key tool to fulfil this transformation. However, it is essential now to reconsider AMB look and analyse the territory and update the planning instruments in order to intervene more effectively.

To face these challenges, the AMB is drafting a new metropolitan masterplan (PDU - *Pla Director Urbanístic*). This strategic document should integrate the urban diversity into a unique urban project, environmentally sustainable, economically efficient and socially cohesive and, at the same time, transform the planning instruments, with the core objective of improve the quality of life of its inhabitants.

The ambition of the PDU, its complexity and the premises of its predecessor plan imply a very complex drafting methodology. How to involve all the relevant stakeholders in its multiple faces and dimensions is a big challenge. One of the approaches that was decided (taking advantage of the Sub>urban network opportunity) was to work in detail on one municipality (Badia del Vallès) with very specific circumstances. The objective was double: to land and test metropolitan strategies but also, from the bottom-up perspective within the URBACT Local Group, to scale up local strategies and instruments that could be tested in the metropolitan scale.

The following chapter exposes the main findings of the Integrated Action Plan (IAP) for Badia del Vallès under the URBACT program and, at the end, how this experience shapes the design of the metropolitan fringe in the PDU.

Strategic Plan for Av. Pirineus, Ajuntament de Santa Coloma de Gramenet.

BADIA DEL VALLÈS

Badia del Vallès is a municipality which is part of the Barcelona Metropolitan Area. Built in the late '60s on a large plot split in halves between Barberà del Vallès and Cerdanyola del Vallès, the town was established as an independent city in 1994.

Originally, Badia was built to allocate civil servants from the central government that were moved to Catalonia to reinforce the postal, railway and police services. However, problems arouse in the allocation of flats for different reasons, one of them was that people had to move in before the housing estate was ready, and another one was that their salaries were good enough to afford a flat in Barcelona so they refused to live in the suburbs. Therefore, finally a great portion of the flats were allocated, with a controversial process, to non-civil servants, mostly immigrants from southern Spain.

BADIA DEL VALLÈS IN THE METROPOLITAN FRINGE

The metropolitan area of Barcelona has 3.2 million inhabitants. 60% of the population is clearly located in the compact and central fabric of Barcelona, 5% in the urban sprawl located at its edges and the remaining 35% is located in a string of midsize cities which draw an urban continuum in between both of them. This in-between territory is a kind of conurbation that has its origin in several historical small towns. Initially, they were isolated one to each other, and mostly dependent from Barcelona. Over the last century, although, they have been growing to almost connect one to each other, mainly through emerging monofunctional urban fabrics, which have become metropolitan fringes in many senses.

It is a puzzle of residential and economic activity areas, developed between the Second World War and the '80s, which were built in between this intermediate conurbation, in parallel with the large metropolitan road and railway infrastructures. As a result, in many cases, this pieces of the metropolitan puzzle have been segregated from its surroundings and hasn't been allowed to mature and reach proper "urbanity" in terms of functional mixticity and social cohesion. However, these fringes still have a great deal of potential to enhance its metropolitan role.

In this sense, Badia del Vallès is a paradigmatic case since its problems of physical integration have kept it isolated from its surroundings and lead the city to a kind of stagnation of its urban functions, which have been greatly reduced to the residential ones. However, its proximity to large metropolitan centralities, but at the same time its disconnection, put Badia in a privileged position for the future.

For this reason, the drafting of the IAP can clearly help Badia del Vallès to combine big scale challenges with a deep knowledge of the urban environment on a local scale in order to solve out its problems; a double scale strategy that has revealed to be very effective in order to reverse urban dynamics.

POTENTIALS & CHALLENGES

POTENTIALS

The citizens of Badia have a positive view of their own city. Some of the points they value the most are related to open areas (quality and quantity, green areas, sense of openness, etc.), attitude of people (sense of community, neighbourhood quality, safety, etc.) and facilities and equipment (services, proximity, etc.).

Badia is located in an area with a high metropolitan centrality. Its proximity to the Autonomous University of Barcelona (UAB) gives it a huge potential in terms of services, such as student residences, research and innovation centres, etc. The Sec River provides access to a territorial natural connection. The nearby mobility infrastructures, like motorways, Sabadell Airport and train stations, provide a good access to the region and the city of Barcelona. Moreover, a new area including a new high speed train station, offices and economic activity, that should be built nearby, could benefit Badia in many ways (urban integration, jobs, services, housing…).

CHALLENGES

The main challenges that Badia is facing are:

Spatial and mental isolation/ Low permeability

Two motorways, a river, an airport and a low density neighbourhood act as physical barriers that isolate Badia from their surroundings and leave it in a cul-de-sac position (you can arrive to or leave from Badia, but you cannot cross it). On top of this, its overwhelming and not friendly image has developed a stigma that isolates even more citizens. Therefore, breaking these physical and social barriers is crucial to integrate Badia to the urban continuum.

Mono-functional and mono-typological land and buildings

Badia is almost 100% residential neighbourhood with only one type of flat (three-bedroom flat). Introducing work areas and services to reduce the dependence on the surrounding neighbourhoods (high commuting rates, high dependence on private vehicle…) is a great challenge. Also, providing other housing types to match the demand is a request.

Too rigid housing tenure/ Rough liberalisation in 2023

The housing estate was originally 100% geared towards affordable housing, with low, fixed market price and important restrictions on buying, selling and renting. This tenure status has three main consequences: first, a fossilized population that favours the maintenance of social dynamics (social reproduction); second, an ageing and declining population that is shaping the need for and type of public facilities, upsetting the usual supply and demand balance (Badia has lost almost half of its original population) and finally, a paternalistic relationship between citizens and administration that disempowers the former (since Badia was developed by public bodies, there is a collective expectation that they will keep on solving all the problems in the city). However, the protected affordable housing regime will end in 2023. For the first time it will be possible to rent out the apartments, which are all privately owned. In consequence, new challenges will emerge, such as a rapid turnover of residents through gentrification or filtering processes; declining building maintenance as owners rent out the apartments and go to live elsewhere; a diminished sense of belonging.

Un(-der) used open spaces, buildings and resources

Badia del Vallès was planned as an isolated entity with public facilities and green areas adjusted to its size. However, the social fabric changes due to ageing and population diminishing, require new types of facilities and open spaces that don't match with the current ones. Transforming and maintaining the existing ones, and providing and financing the new proper ones is a challenge.

Ageing and decreasing population

The fossilized population, as explained before, has a direct impact in the increasing ageing rates. How to deal with this demographic change and, at the same time, how to attract younger population to compensate is a great challenge.

Unsustainability of the municipal public funds

Main municipal income comes from taxes related to housing and economic activities. However, the housing taxes for subsidised housing are very low, and there is almost any economic activity in the municipality. Besides, rates of open space and public facilities per inhabitant are higher than the average. Consequently, the combination of low tax revenues and high surface of public facilities and open spaces compromise the balance of municipal funds.

Large externalities from mobility infrastructure

Badia limits with two motorways with housing buildings facing to them. Mitigating their main externalities (air and noise pollution) is a great challenge.

Poor reputation from the outside

Badia has a bad image from outside. Reshaping its image is a requirement.

Petrification of social and economic problems

As was explained before, most of Badia's neighbours are still the pioneers, and their descendants. This fossilized population has favoured the maintenance of social dynamics with associated low incomes. Breaking this dynamic is a great challenge that the Municipality has been facing for the last years.

OBJECTIVES OF THE TRANSFORMATION

The vision that emerged from the Imagina Badia process to jointly draw up the IAP for Badia del Vallès is to reach a more connected, healthy and inclusive town. This vision is the outcome of a shared diagnosis at the local level spearheaded by the central debate group made up of citizens and staff from the Town Council and the AMB, which compiled the contributions from

Aerial views of AMB.
Source: Integrated Action Plan of AMB, 2018.

the expanded group (municipal government, political parties with representation in Badia) and from citizens, collected through an open session and the website.

Connected city

Badia del Vallès was designed and built as a housing estate connected in a friendly manner to the river and the open space in front of it. However, due to a coordination problem with the Ministry of Transport, two motorways (C-58 and AP-7) were built tangential to the river. Thus, in the middle of the construction process, streets had to be redrawn and buildings relocated, and Badia became what it is today, a cul-de-sac totally disconnected from the river. This physical isolation, coupled with the town being almost 100% occupied by immigrants from a similar background coming from outside Catalonia to serve in the public sector, also raised mental barriers that emphasised its isolation and increased the distance that Badia residents feel in relation to their surrounding cities.

The vision aims at reconnecting the city with its urban continuum in a simple, natural way, breaking its physical and mental isolation. The main objectives are to limit private mobility and to improve public transport, accessibility and supramunicipal connectivity.

Healthy city

As explained in the previous section, two motorways run very close to residential buildings in Badia, causing serious problems in terms of excessive noise and air pollution. In recent years, there have been attempts to alleviate the effects of noise with sound-reducing screens, but results were not as effective as expected, especially in the upper storeys of the buildings. As an additional problem, many constructions have elements that contain asbestos.

The facilities and public spaces undergo many of the problems typically found in this type of residential fabric: low-quality, poorly defined public spaces, some of them with clear signs of deterioration. Furthermore, the facilities are underused and no longer fit residents' current needs, since the population has decreased (almost by half) and aged.

This is why one of the visions for the IAP is to create a healthier city, primarily seeking two main objectives: first, a better environment by reducing the sound and air pollution and asbestos, and secondly, high-quality public spaces and facilities which better meet current and future needs.

Inclusive city

Badia is a city with 100% affordable housing, most of it privately owned, built in the 1970s for public servants and finally occupied by migrants from rural areas, either families with children or couples in their reproductive years. When children reached the age of leaving home, it was virtually impossible for them to keep living in Badia for different reasons. First, there was a shortage of housing, since many homes were privately owned and there was little rotation; and secondly, for those that have progressed in social terms, they were not eligible for subsidised housing and, therefore, were unable to buy a home in Badia. This expelled the second generation and prevented people coming from the outside, causing 3 main consequences. First, a petrification of the original population (most of the inhabitants are still the first residents or their descendants) that led to perpetuate the original social dynamics over time hindering the social progression (social reproduction). Second, an ageing and declining population is reshaping the need and type of public facilities, as Badia has lost half of its original population–initially there were 3-4 residents/dwelling, and now just 1 or 2. Finally, there is still an underlying paternalist relationship between citizens and administration, which disempowers citizens (a consequence of the origin of Badia as a town promoted by public bodies, which, in the social imaginary, is still supposed to be responsible for solving any problems in the town).

The vision is to attain a more inclusive city in terms of housing, civic life and peaceful coexistence, education and culture, and economic promotion. The main objectives are a more diverse and well-maintained housing stock, in order to provide different housing types to respond to the needs of the current structure of the population, improve the education and cultural offer and quality, promote the economic activity and reinforce the sense of community.

The affordable housing status will end in 2023. For the first time it will be possible to rent out the apartments. Completely new dynamics might suddenly appear. It is difficult to predict which dynamics will show-up with this sharp tenure change: a gentrification or filtering processes with their challenges associated. In any case, the main objectives should be to have instruments to control the process and diminish their externalities. Allowing new people to come to and live in Badia, such as students from the university or families with children, and at the same time keeping the actual neighbours within the municipality.

MAIN STRATEGIES OF THE IAP

As mentioned above, the IAP was drafted together with the central design group (GCD). At the 6th GCD meeting, it was decided to divide the actions according to whether they were geared towards open spaces or built spaces. Priority was placed on spending all the remaining time of the URBACT calendar to further examine the open spaces, rather than trying to deal with everything and running the risk of ending up with overly general actions. This decision was grounded on two reasons: first, the Town Council was highly focused on buildings and already had several programmes underway, while it was not quite as sure about how to deal with the public space. Second, when evaluating the objectives emerged from the shared diagnosis, it was determined that public space could meet a larger number of objectives. Nonetheless, GCD, and especially the Town Council, pledged to complete the IAP once the URBACT programme was over by defining and scheduling the actions referring to the built spaces.

Actions are grouped into four main strategies: connectivity and relationship with the region; structuring of mobility; intensifying and programming the use of public space, and showcasing the cultural and natural heritage.

These planning strategies are supported by the double scale approach: on one side, the large scale challenges (that involve the coordination of big actors AMB, regional government and central estate) that need a deep local knowledge; and, on the other side, small scale challenges that could easily be solved involving a large scale strategies and knowledge.

Connectivity and relationship with the region

This strategy responds to the vision of the connected city, and specifically to the objectives related to private mobility, public transport, accessibility and supramunicipal connectivity. The goal is to break the physical and mental isolation by stitching together and reconnecting Badia with its neighbours. It should be no longer a cul-de-sac city and instead become a networked city.

Mobility structure

This set of actions responds to a more connected, healthier city, and specifically to diminishing private mobility, increasing accessibility and environmental objectives. The actions can be divided into three main packages:

- Improving mobility and internal permeability and/or permeability with its most immediate environs.

- Developing a hierarchy of the road system to enhance the city navigability, intensify the use of open spaces and diminish private vehicle occupancy of public space both on roads and in parking places.
- Promoting more sustainable transport modes, like public transport, bikes and walking.

Intensifying and programming the use of public space

This set of actions responds to a healthier, more inclusive city, and specifically to the objectives of improving the environment, facilities and outdoor areas, civic life and peaceful coexistence, and economic promotion. Actions can be divided into three sets:
- Programming public spaces so that they can be adapted to the changing needs at any times via shared decision-making processes, without losing their global, structuring purpose.
- Facilitating a more intensive use of these spaces.
- Carrying out ongoing monitoring to mediate in the problems inherent to public space and better exploit its potentiality.

Showcasing the cultural and natural heritage

This set of actions responds to a healthier and more inclusive city, and specifically to the objectives of improving the environment, open spaces, education and culture, and economic promotion. The actions can be divided into three sets:
- Showcasing the cultural heritage.
- Showcasing the social assets that Badia has.
- Optimising the natural resources.

SYNERGIES BETWEEN THE METROPOLITAN AND LOCAL SCALE

The development of the IAP is framed within the efforts of the Urban Planning Department of the AMB. From this metropolitan vantage point, the definition of a proposal to transform Badia del Vallès pursues a threefold objective:

To define the territorial fit of this large residential complex within its metropolitan environs.

To define an internal spatial structure that is coherent with this fit while also articulating and showcasing the local elements.

To design, plan and manage the urban transformation strategies needed, in constant dialogue with the different stakeholders in the region: the departments within the local administration, citizens, entities and/or groups with economic interests in the zone.

Yet at the same time, methodologically speaking, the development of the IAP has been an interesting testing ground for the main tool of urban reflection and planning over which the AMB holds authority: the Metropolitan Urban Master Plan (abbreviated PDU in Catalan for Pla Director Urbanístic).

On the one hand, some of the most innovative transformation strategies that have been designed for Badia will be used to define the new rules to intervene in housing estates, being included in the PDU drafting and extrapolated, if appropriate, to the rest of the metropolitan fringe. On the other hand, those urban development proposals that came up from the effort of drawing up the PDU in its reflection on metropolitan large residential complexes are being "tested" in Badia and might be the way to implement improvement actions in the future.

After 40 years of planning according to one same master plan, the PDU is a new urban planning tool that reconsiders how to formulate new urban paradigms, most of them helping to transform the metropolitan fringe into spaces of opportunity. And, what are these new paradigms?

A new taxonomy to create a common language for the metropolis of the future

One of the most important approaches of the research carried out as part of the PDU is the study of residential urban fabrics. This is a sweeping analysis which proposes categorising residential areas from the morphological standpoint, combined with a social description of their residents. The result is a map with 4 main groups of residential areas which can be subdivided either into 14 morphological categories or 21 morpho-sociological categories. This generates a new taxonomy to be used to explain the physical and social complexity of the urban residential fabrics in the AMB area.

Within this new taxonomy, Badia del Vallès is included in a pattern made up primarily of zones of working-class apartment buildings. These metropolitan fringes are mostly located on the periphery of the urban continuum and composed of tall, freestanding, multi-family buildings with little diversity in the use of the ground floors and without much activity in the public spaces. Its social composition is marked by the lower middle-class status of the population living there, who are mostly affected by a high unemployment rate. With regard to the housing, what stands out overall is the sound state of conservation of the housing stock and the large proportion of owners as opposed to renters, with some of the highest homeowner rates within the housing stock of the AMB area.

New rules for assembling the new body of metropolitan regulations

Bearing in mind the aforementioned taxonomy, the PDU suggests showcasing the qualities of all 14 morphological categories by defining new regulations which specifically have to take into account the capacities of each of them in order to get its suitable strategy.

Furthermore, the PDU will also define specific areas with similar characteristics in terms of their accessibility to public transport and their degree of centrality within the metropolis. For each of these areas, it will set the physical and functional intensities for every morphological category which will be determined based on a complex indicator that combines compactness, functional heterogeneity and typological diversity of housing.

Badia del Vallès, like many other fringes, is an area with low accessibility and centrality, but also very little compactness and a great homogeneity in terms of uses and housing types. That means that, on the one hand, its physical capacity to be intensified could be quite high, but on the other hand, accessibility level could restrict or moderate densification strategies at the same time. In this sense, PDU should consider both facts, in order to determine the specific intensity range (minimum and/or maximum values) to be addressed in the future.

General views: infrastructures, parks and public spaces.
Source: Integrated Action Plan of AMB, 2018.

Housing

IN EUROPE

75

AMB urban fringe: pilot site of Badia del Vallès.
Source: AMB URBACT team.

New approaches to prioritise transforming actions in the metropolis

The third major challenge of the PDU is to identify areas of "special attention" in the AMB region which have to be addressed preferentially with priority action strategies, either because of their potentiality in terms of opportunity or because of their urbanistic and social complexity.

In this sense, it is essential to clearly establish the criteria to be used to identify both kinds of areas and ascertain how to relate them to each other so that the gains in the most economically viable ones can be used to finance the costlier ones. That is, the concept of urban solidarity should be applied at the metropolitan level.

In the case of Badia, from the local perspective, resources for transforming its urban environment are limited in terms of the town opening itself up physically and socially to its closest environs. Nonetheless, through the PDU approach, a shift in scale enables major metropolitan centralities to be identified nearby and Badia to be situated within their direct sphere of influence. In this way, we will be able to expand the spheres of intervention of the neighbouring metropolitan centralities to include the large residential complex, thus allowing it to benefit from its potentialities.

In short, the AMB has approached the increasing complexity of all the urban residential areas through both an understanding and recognition of their particular values and capacities and its role within the metropolis. That's why AMB is seeking effective tools for the future which guarantee balanced transformations that attend to the diversity of urban fabrics without losing sight of the metropolitan area as a whole.

(at the top of the page) Regeneration layout for Badia del Vallès fringe.
Source: Integrated Action Plan of AMB, 2018.

(at the bottom of the page) Perspective in Av. Burgos ad Badia del Vallès.
Source: Integrated Action Plan of AMB, 2018.

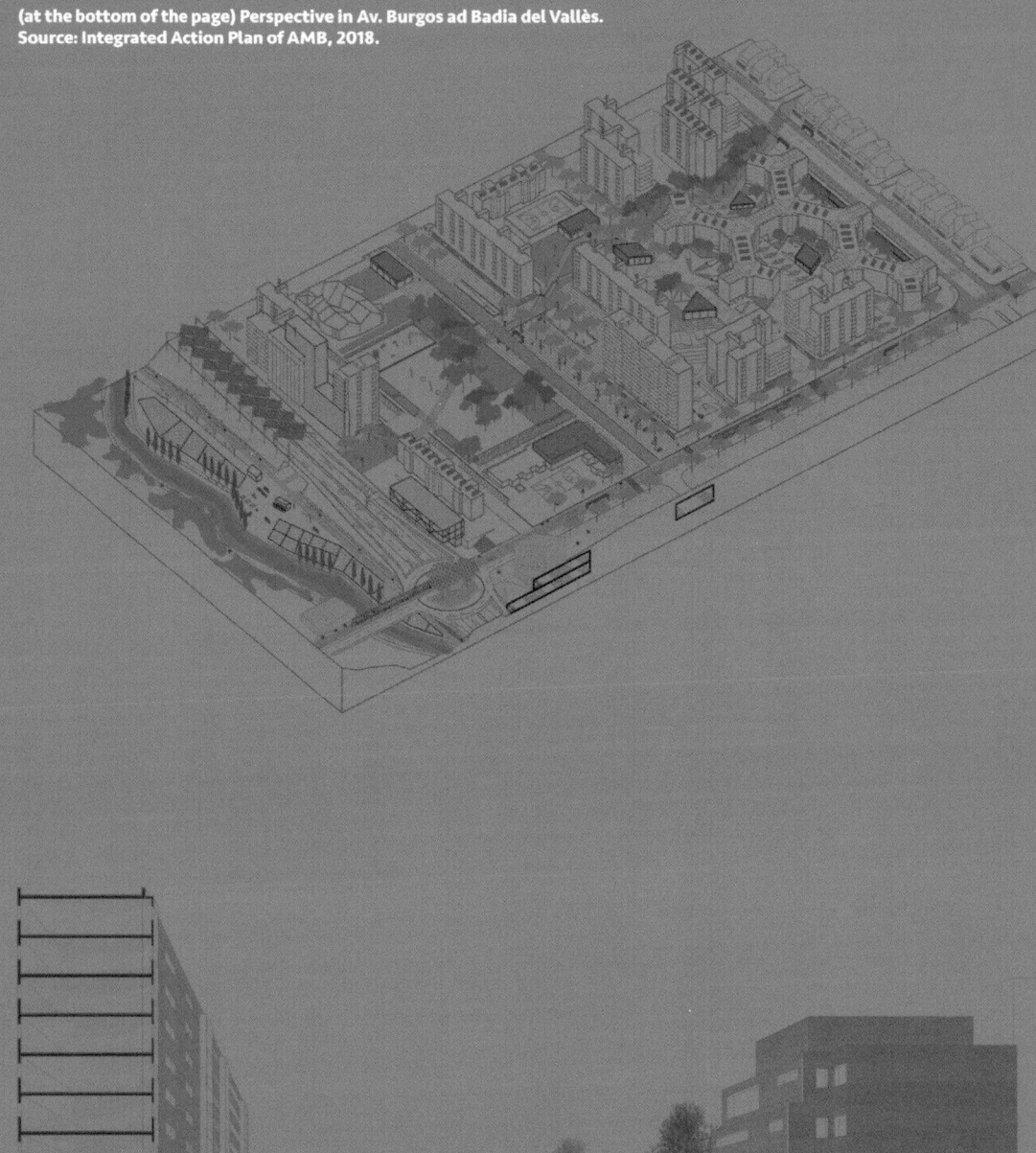

Cultural and natural heritage in Badia del Vallès.
Source: Integrated Action Plan of AMB, 2018.

1.5
Five Cities

BAIA MARE (ROMANIA)
STRATEGY FOR THE TRANSFORMATION OF THE FRINGE IN THE NEIGHBOURHOOD OF SĂSAR*

"The urban fringe in Baia Mare used to be the edge of the city, subordinated to the historic city centre. Unlike the classical urban fringe definition, Săsar neighbourhood (which is part of the entire fringe of Baia Mare) is not defined by a logistics area characterised by oversized public space, many single-storey buildings, large parking lots and vacant buildings and land, intersected by major infrastructures linking the city centre to peripheries and other areas in the outer city, but more likely, a low-density dormitory neighbourhood (between 51100 inhabitants/ hectare, according to the Integrated Urban Development Strategy for Baia Mare). Although it provides loads of opportunities (in terms of land use, green areas and underused public space, as well as transport infrastructures) between the low-density suburbs and the high-density city centre, the connectivity and identity of the urban fringe needs to be re-examined according to the following general challenges:

- reshaping new economic and residential areas in the context of urban regeneration, to incorporate business premises/ housing into a safe, sustainable, healthy environment;
- reconverting mono-functional areas built during the 1960s, 70s and 80s, into mixed liveable areas (by increasing the quality of urban public spaces and the life quality). (…)

Transforming Baia Mare's urban fringe should start as an incremental process, aimed at mixing cultural and ethnic backgrounds, people of different ages, incomes and education levels, while providing multifunctional spaces to meet their needs and requirements. Consequently, the challenge equally lies in spreading the benefits of growth and regeneration, as well as providing affordable housing, jobs and facilities for all over the fringe. Intensifying and making a better use of the existent urban structures and public space, likewise vacant and underused buildings and land will contribute to achieve a more compact, accessible and attractive city. (…) The vision for 2025 in relation to the urban fringe claims a process of reinventing Săsar neighbourhood which does not require major interventions and radical changes in its urban structure, but rather punctual and integrated actions to mobilize the community and promote active citizenship and to valorise its identity towards a mixed-use area with large housing offer, attractive and safe public spaces as well as multi-functional facilities and equipment. (…) In this respect, the overall mission is *to intensify the use of inefficiently used space, while increasing the quality and availability of houses and amenities and to find effective and transparent ways to deal with private and fragmented ownership to improve the quality of the existent functions and to provide new services for different typologies of residents.*"

* Extract from "English Summary of the Integrated Action Plan", City of Baia Mare, retrievable at the following link: urbact.eu/sites/default/files/media/baiamare_gebundeld.pdf

Urban fringe in pilot site of Baia Mare: collective housing and private garages.
Source: Integrated Action Plan of the City of Baia Mare, 2018.

Aerial view of Baia Mare.
Source: Baia Mare URBACT team.

BRNO (CZECH REPUBLIC)
STRATEGY FOR THE TRANSFORMATION OF THE FRINGE IN RED HILL*

"The fringe" represents chaotic and unbalanced used territories, flanking the city's borders, which emerged especially in the second half of the 20th century as vast, rather mono-functional zones and for which it is desirable to find new multifunctional utilizations.

Within the city of Brno, we focus on the areas between the existing contiguous, so-called compact inner city, large housing estates and a relaxed settlement in the neighbourhood of the city of Brno (Sub>urban hinterland of the city). (…)

During June 2016, the employees of the Department of Spatial Development and the Department of Development Localities processed so-called passports of locations potentially suitable for new development in the outskirts of Brno.

(…)The area lies between a contiguous area close to the city centre on the one hand and large housing estates on the other, neighbouring a rapidly developing university campus and related science and research centres. The area of all three parts together covers almost 70 ha. The area is intended for development according to the existing local plan, we respect the local plan and we want to help it gradually to be fulfilled, not to change it completely. (…)

For the Red Hill area the internal URBACT Local Group predefined these goals during the project phase:

- Create a stable network of stakeholders - involve all main internal and external stakeholders, harmonize their intentions and actions in the area within an established network of stakeholders;
- Get the representatives of the local government involved in the preparation and realization of Integrated Action Plan;
- Establish the common vision of the area development based on the spatial study and the Integrated Action Plan that will be shared by all stakeholders (maybe possible basis for a new Spatial Plan);
- Create new Urban Study for the Red Hill area (the completion of the study in spring 2018);
- Create a basis for systematic transformation of allotment garden - open the discussion about the allotment gardens with all partners;
- Incorporate the natural protected area of „Red hill" into the overall territory concept as an important landscape element enabling the improvement of the quality of life;
- Explore the possibilities of temporary use before the big development will take place;
- Prepare the site for future realization of transport and technical infrastructures, which is conditional for the development of the area – creating the foundation of the backbone network (investment of the city). Then it will be easier to develop the area;
- Help to stimulate the property settlement of the land ownership in the area.

In a long run (long term goals by 2030+) the location should be ready for the construction of housing so that there will grow an adequate multifunctional part of the city (continuation of the nearby university campus development area with following housing and free time activities, public amenities, public transport and road connection). The area should become an integral part of the compact city."

*Extract from "English Summary of the Integrated Action Plan", City of Brno, retrievable at the following link: urbact.eu/sites/default/files/media/brno_gebundeld.pdf

Urban fringe in Brno:
collective housing from '70s till today.
(Enrico Formato)

Urban fringe in Brno:
collective housing from '70s till today.
(Enrico Formato)

DÜSSELDORF (GERMANY)
STRATEGY FOR THE TRANSFORMATION OF THE FRINGE WITH THE EXAMPLE OF GARATH 2.0*

"Düsseldorf will continue to attract newcomers in the future. New housing will remain an urgent topic. Düsseldorf has been transforming for many decades from an industrial to a serviced based city. And the population growth will dynamically change the city even more. The urban planning objective will be to find an equilibrium between old and new. Not only the city centre and the inner-city quarters can provide new opportunities. The fringe is uniquely equipped for innovative urban projects. It connects the urban and the green space. It also intertwines the city with the region.

Düsseldorf's fringe is very diverse. That implies that our urban planning policy such as the integrated neighbourhood development has to be flexible. The aim is to make sure that all areas benefit from growth. The integrated neighbourhood development and the pilot areas are strategic projects that are aiming at making the fringe more attractive for new investments. (...) Our strategic concepts are always taking the entire city into account. We are convinced that the inner city and the fringe should be considered as equal parts of the whole city. (...) The on-going pilot Garath 2.0 will be the inspiration for new city quarters and we will continue to learn from our test site. Planning in built-up areas requires innovative planning tools for tailor- made solutions. That implies a learning process for all involved parties. The decision-makers need to take a risk and test new methods."

"It became clear, in the participation process, that in future planning in Garath the identity of the quarter must be paramount. Therefore, Neighbourhood Branding was conducted as a further step in involvement to find out through the inhabitants more about the identity and the reality of life there. (...) The results of the Neighbourhood Branding are recorded in core values. They connect the present to the future. They relate to the qualities that already exist today in the quarter and aim at a condition that should be reached in the future. They help to harmonize further planning with the character of the quarter." (...) "Based on a cross-sectoral policy and by means of a new tool – neighbourhood branding – Garath's identity was discussed during workshop sessions with locals. The results were evaluated publicly. The determination of local and shared core values has been important for the planning process. In an innovative planning process, we combined bottom-up and top-down strategies and worked in a cross-sectoral way with different stakeholders on an integrated action plan. The local action plan focused on housing, living, environment, participation, local provisions and public transport."

*Extract from "English Summary of the Integrated Action Plan", City of Düsseldorf, retrievable at the following link: urbact.eu/sites/default/files/media/dusseldorf_gebundeld.pdf

Aerial view of pilot site.
Source: Integrated Action Plan of the City of Dusseldorf, 2018.

Urban fringe in Dusseldorf: collective space and services. (Enrico Formato)

SOLIN (CROATIA)
STRATEGY FOR THE TRANSFORMATION OF THE FRINGE IN SREDNJA STRANA-SVETI KAJO*

"Solin is one of several small cities within Split's functional area - the second largest urban agglomeration in Croatia. With numerous archaeological sites and monuments, it holds a significant place in national history. (…)

Being a small city with nearly 28 000 inhabitants, composed of several smaller settlements, Solin doesn't really have a fringe in the usual sense of the word (…) Solin was planned as an industrial and infrastructural zone of Split. (…)

The chosen pilot site for implementing programme activities and future transformations is a strip cutting through three different layers of Solin's urban tissue: the settlement of Srednja Strana with lots of illegal and unplanned private housing and poor public spaces and facilities; part of the archaeological site of Salona; and the industrial and infrastructural (brownfield) zone that is preventing the connection of the city to the sea. (…)

None of the parts of the pilot site were unplanned; they were defined and articulated by different influences over time. Since there were no urban and design directions, the fringe area has no public spaces and poor infrastructure and public facilities. There are also areas and buildings that have not been in use for the past few years. The aim for the transformation of this site is to improve everyday living conditions, to increase the number of facilities and to make use of the overall potential of the (under)used spaces. Working on the pilot site together with Urbact Local Group, we detected two main goals for the transformation: better connections with the wider area and re-evaluation of Salona's importance, presentation and potential of urban transformation. Although these two goals exist on different scales and time scopes, they influence each other and must be considered as a common issue."

*Extract from "English Summary of the Integrated Action Plan", City of Solin, retrievable at the following link: urbact.eu/sites/default/files/media/solin_gebundeld.pdf

Plan, implement and organise management simultaneously

Beach in Solin.
Source: URBACT team for "Urban Challenges: Fringe Solutions" (Bruxelles, June 2017).

Solin beach

Archeological site in Solin.
Source: Solin URBACT team.

VIENNA (AUSTRIA)
STRATEGY FOR THE TRANSFORMATION OF THE FRINGE IN VÖSENDORF SIEBEN-HIRTEN*

"In the Sub>urban project area Vösendorf – Vienna-Siebenhirten you find different kinds of interesting spots in terms of transformation. Here you see and feel the different layers of urban development of the last decades. What they left behind is a fragmented urban landscape – small scale industrial enterprises (in many cases vacant), huge wastelands, abandoned buildings, a huge outdated retail park, industrial and commercial zones, historic villages, farmland facing highways, wilderness, ponds and new residential areas – and this in the middle of a vibrant, fast growing region. This all makes it an urban lab for future solutions. An additional challenge is, that the project area is crossing the city border, which is the border between Vienna and Lower Austria in the same time. This means different laws, land use regulations, responsibilities, competences and planning approaches. (...)

The project area has many identities at the same time and this means that development cannot follow "traditional urban principles". (...) The "reinvention of the fringe" cannot be done with conventional means. It demands experiments and new pictures. And that is why as many local stakeholders as possible are involved in the process. Important political representatives, experts from the planning departments, representatives of institutions and organizations, owners, committed citizens as well as international partners from the Sub> urban network wrote together future stories for the project area. These were discussed and enriched during the process. The future stories are visionary as well as ready for implementation and give space to already running projects. (...)

The current overall strategies set a vision that focuses on the entire city-regional issue. The Urban Development Plan Vienna "STEP 2025" defines Regional Cooperation Areas as an essential instrument of city-regional cooperation. The regional master plan for the district of Mödling defines target areas for integrated site and green planning in the Vösendorf-Siebenhirten area. And thanks to the binding organizational framework, international exchanges and financial support provided by URBACT III, it was possible to lay the foundations for a cooperation routine that will enable the implementation of the ideas developed in the project."

*Extract from "English Summary of the Integrated Action Plan", City of Vienna, retrievable at the following link: urbact.eu/sites/default/files/media/vienna_gebundeld.pdf

Density, Vienna.
Source: Vienna URBACT team.

Porous public spaces and housing estates, Vienna.
Source: Vienna URBACT team.

1.6.1   Dossiers

Private Europe.
What's up in the fringe?

Exhibition at the Contemporary Art Museum of Casoria.
November 14th – November 30th, 2016.
Curated by Anna Attademo, Francesca Avitabile and Enrico Formato

In 2016 the Municipality of Casoria hosted the Transnational Meeting of the *Sub>urban* network. The theme of the meeting was *Transforming Private Spaces*. The Casoria URBACT group, in collaboration with the Department of Architecture of Naples, took the opportunity to organise an exhibition on the theme of private spaces, gathering a series of iconographic images (at least five per group) from each of the nine partners, along with a short documentary explaining the characteristics of the fringe area. One of the main objectives of the *Sub>urban* network is to place the fringe at the centre of the urban discussion as an area of great unexpressed potential. Often these fringe areas are neglected: the images are a way of putting these places in the spotlight.
The mayor of Casoria and the representatives of all the partner cities of the network attended the inauguration evening of the exhibition.

Private (adjective), *belonging to or for the use of one particular person or group of people only.* Space (noun), *a continuous area or expanse which is free, available or unoccupied.*
*source: https://en.oxforddictionaries.com

The exhibition was intended to place attention on the theme of private spaces in the fringe of European cities. In the title of the exhibition, the omission of the word "space" accentuates the sense of privacy and closure that the term "private" encapsulates, as if to subtend a sort of Europe composed of infinite tiny private distrustful worlds.
So, what's up in the fringe? In this Europe?
As is clearly shown in the photographs of the exhibition, the Europe which presents itself to us hides extremely different fringe areas: what happens in the outskirts of Vienna is extremely different to what is happening in Solin, which probably presents characteristics of the fringe common to those of Casoria, but different again compared to what is happening in the private spaces in the fringe of Oslo. Each partner city faces the issue of transforming private spaces in a different way, according to different historical contexts, differences in governing legislation and so on. Although, on the one hand, these differences represent a positive aspect in the view of survival of a prevalence of mass standardisation of global phenomena, on the other it generates difficulties in sharing perspectives.

ANTWERP

Copyright Dries Luyten.

All the cities were asked to select material inspired by these key words:

- interiors/ordinary life scenarios
- fragmentation of property
- density/rarefaction
- gentrification/ filtering down
- public space/fences
- legal/illegal settlements
- ongoing transformations/regeneration

IN EUROPE

BAIA MARE

Copyright Baia Mare URBACT team.

IN EUROPE

AMB (BARCELONA)

Copyright AMB URBACT team.

BRNO

CASORIA

Copyright Casoria URBACT team.

DÜSSELDORF

Copyright Herribert Börnichen

Copyright: Barbara Wolf

Copyright Herribert Börnichen

Copyright: Leif von Nethen

Copyright: Barbara Wolf

Copyright Herribert Börnichen

Copyright: Leif von Nethen

Copyright: Leif von Nethen

OSLO

Copyright Oslo URBACT team.

SOLIN

VIENNA

Copyright City of Vienna Urbact team.

FRINGE SHIFTS

IN EUROPE

1.6.2 Ownership, Commons and the Right to the City

Dossiers

Carmine Piscopo
Department of Architecture, University of Naples Federico II
Alderman for the Right to the City, Urban Planning and Commons of the Municipality of Naples

The Municipality of Naples, the first in Italy to have set up a Department for Commons, has an established history in identifying administrative paths aimed at giving strength to the ethical, civil, legal and environmental debate focused on forms of use of the urban heritage for collective interest. This principle is present in the Italian Constitution: the category of "commons" identifies assets subtracted from exclusive use or from lack of social use, in order to express the fundamental rights of the community. This is not an ideological framework, but rather the implementation of a fundamental principle (Rodotà, 2018), which affirms the prevailing social utility of the urban heritage, excluding any form of privatization or, worse, of patronage use, aimed at strengthening the potential of a collective subjectivation. If the Right to the City, in fact, includes access to the resources that regulate life in the cities, this also implies a new configuration and a new arrangement of the social, political and economic relations that define these relationships (Micciarelli, 2017).

In keeping with this approach, in 2011 the current Neapolitan administration modified its Municipal Statute, introducing, among the aims, objectives and fundamental values of the City of Naples, the legal category of the "commons", interpreted as accessible, usable, shareable places, available for the representation and realization of instances, designs, recognizable desires of local communities and commuters. "Commons", therefore, are a functional asset for the exercise of people's fundamental rights.

Still, in 2012, the Administration approved the *Regulation of the Commons*, as assets of collective belonging, and then in 2013 it approved the *Principles for the governance and management of the Commons of the City of Naples*, according to which "every citizen must contribute to the natural and spiritual progress of the City".

Furthermore, the Administration acted on public water regulation, through the transformation of the previously existing company into a one under total public control.

The Administration then established, in 2013, the *Observatory of the Commons*, whose work led to the launch of two new regulations concerning the procedures for the identification and collective management of public and private assets, clarifying which assets can be included in the full process of achieving civic uses and collective well-being. This is rooted in the approval by the Municipality of Naples of the Aarhus Convention, which later became an essential part of the Municipal Council Regulation. It condemns self-referential planning, and any other abstract form of urban planning that does not rely on the direct participation and on the democratic right to the use of resources and public space, as places where to express the authentic needs of the communities, the production of lifestyles and new economies. The key point is not the notion of "financial income", a notion that has historically marked the assignment of public assets, but, rather, the idea that the "social income", with its Civic Uses (Uti Cives), is an integral part of the "economic income", as an essential part of the social well-being and the desires of the local communities.

On 17 June 2013, the Municipality of Naples adopted the *Charter of the Public Space*, approved at the end of the II Biennial of Public Space, held in Rome from 16 to 18 May 2013, as an active and concrete contribution to the process of democratic enhancement and study of the ways of using urban public space. This was a fundamental act for the Administration, recognizing the democratic right to use and the transformative potential of the urban public space of the City of Naples.

In 2014, the Municipality of Naples adopted two regulations concerning the recovery of collectively-owned and privately owned abandoned assets, following an articulated process of collective participation in the identification of projects and methods of use. These regulations triggered a debate in Italy, putting the prevailing public interest at the center of administrative actions. In these documents, the Administration acknowledges the value of already existing experiences in the municipal area, carried out by groups and / or committees of citizens according to the logic of self-government and experimentation of the direct management of public spaces, demonstrating, in this way, to perceive those commons as places susceptible to collective enjoyment and to the benefit of the local community, experiences that in their factual expression have been configured and are configured as "people homes", i.e. places with a strong social potential, deeply rooted in the territory. When these experiences are aimed at satisfying general interests and without profit-making purposes, and if justified by the high social value created, the Administration defines the possibility of proceeding with the compensation of the management charges, providing for civic or other forms of regulation of civic self-organization to be recognized in special agreements.

Furthermore, in October 2014, the Administration approved a regulation concerning the possibility of "adopting" parts of the city, starting from a participatory process of citizens gathered in civic committees. The "ways of participation for the implementation of social policies" establish a further point for discussion with the "Charter of the Public Space", where the methods of democratic participation and their burdens are defined in the formalization of the proposed regulations, through the establishment of territorial assemblies in constant dialogue with the inhabitants, where the public space becomes a place where it is possible to respond to the projections of the desires and requests of the local communities.

With this same spirit, in 2014 and 2015, the Administration drew up and approved: 1) the feasibility study relating to the project for the redevelopment of the "Vele" residential settlement, by setting up tables and territorial assemblies; 2) the new urban masterplan, approved in the City Council, for the Site of National Interest of Bagnoli-Coroglio. A similar path has been followed for the definition of the new Masterplan of the former Nato area of Bagnoli.

These actions unveil a modality of direct citizens participation, which the Administration has also tried to experiment in the transformation of large urban areas, interpreted as "commons", linking together direct participation, the right to democratic choices and the enhancement of the landscape, as a primary asset of the community. Through the actual engagement of the communities and then, through the definition of assemblies, the Administration has thus made itself the guarantor of the institutions' requests, formalizing their collective potential.

In the case of the former Italsider area of Bagnoli, the project presented by Invitalia in 2016, during the period of commissioners nominated by the so-called "Sblocca-Italia" Law, was remodeled as part of the "Interinstitutional Agreement" signed in July 2017 among Government, Campania Regional Authority and Municipality of Naples, to find space for long-debated principles: public beach and waterfront, creation of the park, recovery and regeneration of industrial archeology, enhancement of the marine and coastal landscape.

In the case of the former NATO area, the desire to start using the place, which has always been denied to the city for its function of extraterritorial national security, gave rise, on the basis of a long process of territorial assemblies, to the signing of a Protocol with the Municipality of Naples, aimed at identification of the area as social facility: a formal act with which the Administration, by guaranteeing a complex process of participation, has been able to highlight the shared will to return the original social function to the complex, recovering its public usability, reintegrating it in the urban life and reopening it to the city.

In line with this spirit, there are two regulations (in 2015 and 2016, matured over a long period of time), relating to the approval of the *Declaration of civic and collective urban use of the Filangieri Asylum*, and to the identification of seven spaces of civic significance ascribable in the category of commons. These are regulations that have crossed the borders of Italy for their ability to return a potential to collective subjectivity, as an anonymous subject who lives in the breath of the city and informs it. It is not a system of "assignments" to communities, but more a "restitution" to the collectivity of a place that belongs to it, in the full recognition of what the community expresses.

The last act in chronological order is the approval of the no. 458 regulation (10 August 2017) for the temporary use of discarded public equipment, without modifying the urban destination, aimed at the enhancement of the unused public assets or those in a state of abandonment.

Significantly it identifies and approves the lines of action for the enhancement of municipally owned assets for social purposes, the addresses for the temporary use of open spaces and buildings owned by the Municipality and the actors for the implementation of the projects. The regulation therefore establishes guidelines and actions relating to the creation of urban civic communities, the testing of temporary uses, the use of churches no longer used, the creation of temporary agricultural communities for young people and social and neighborhood educational gardens, the creation of new forms of collective living, for low-income families.

The territory of commons holds together the non-self-referential planning, the overcoming of the concept of property for new civic uses, the prevailing public interest, the need to link boundaries and social distances, putting new actors in front of the institutional and administrative entities. Not as an axiom that exclusively links the territory to its project (in a subject-object relationship), but rather as a challenge that urges us to overcome the given concepts and actors, in recognition of the existence of a process. In this regard, the resolutions of the current Neapolitan Administration for the establishment of democratic collective places, starting from the acknowledgement of existing realities in the territory, must still be remembered. This, in full respect of the "European Landscape Convention" (Florence 2000), where it is stated that the identity of a place is not given by abstract values, but rather by the recognition of the values in the local communities.

This principle will find greater strength when all the institutions involved will define a path capable of giving concrete shape to the relationship that links the landscape, as a "legal domain in the strict sense", to the civil and social rights of the people, to the right of citizenship, as "Right to the City".

In Naples, even if there are still many problems to be solved, the debate is spreading, clearly indicating juridical, ethical, civil, administrative, political principles that identify in the "commons" the overcoming of the notion of property. At the center are the democratic use of our assets and the preservation of our environment. And with them, the future of the generations to come.

Scugnizzo Liberato, Common asset of the city of Naples.
(Enrico Formato)

1.7.1

Antwerp 2003-2018: 15 Years of Work on the City

Interview with Paola Viganò
By Bruna Vendemmia and Anna Livia Friel

Interviews

Studio Secchi e Viganò, and then Studio Paola Viganò, were leading figures in the urban transformation of Antwerp: from 2003 to 2007 thanks to the drafting of the Structure Plan, and from 2003 to 2009 with the planning and construction of the Spoor Noord park and the urban plan for the whole area, from 2011 to 2012 with the masterplan for the Nieuw Zuid area and then, since 2016 with the Over de Ring (OdR) project for the Zuidoost zone.

The importance of this interview is evident for various reasons: above all Antwerp, the cornerstone of the project, is the main player with eight other metropolitan areas presenting great changes due to the development of new and unexpected urban dynamics; Paola Viganò has a vast experience as an urban planner and designer and she has worked on the implementation of the Plan through urban projects on different scales, and just as importantly, she is an internationally renowned urban theorist and practitioner.

The story of the *Over de Ring* project describes a complex project which shifts from an urban to an international scale (the Ring is an infrastructure of great importance for Europe and fundamental for the traffic of the Port of Antwerp). Many relevant cues for the innovation of planning, already highlighted in the drafting of the Structure Plan, came to light and are now in active use in different types of circumstances: urban culture as the background for the project ("Belgian pragmatism"); the political situation which affects the construction in the city; time, seen in a non-deterministic light, to consider the processes directed towards the improvement of urban quality.

This conversation reveals themes which are precious for a general reflection on the planning practices linked to a city: the actors, the different scales of the project, the legitimacy of several relevant choices in terms of accessibility and spatial justice. Underlying this is an open question: the legacy that the experience of Paola Viganò and Bernardo Secchi's project offers to the new generations of planners.

In 2003 the urban design firm was commissioned by the city of Antwerp to map out the

Structure Plan which then went into force in 2009. At the time the development of the plans was a way for the city to reinvent its organisational structure: the activity carried out by the city of Antwerp, defined as "active" urbanisation[1], constitutes an example of the management and implementation of the Plan. Such a large project always presents a margin of the unexpected insofar as spatial consequences are concerned, changes also happen within the relationships with the institutions and social and political transformations. How did the plan interact with these changes?

The city of Antwerp, its administration and its politicians played a truly active role, firstly in the definition and then in the implementation of the Plan. This is also thanks to Patrick Janssens, mayor of Antwerp from 2003 until 2012, who used the Plan as an instrument for reorganising the administration of the city, particularly in the urban development and public spaces sector.

The political implications involving the Plan in more recent years, when neither myself nor Bernardo Secchi were working in Antwerp, were described by Katlijn Van der Veken, at a conference in Florence several months ago.[2] When the plan was being defined, the Studio was commissioned as an external team[3] in collaboration with an internal team belonging to city administration. After an initial phase fraught with difficulties and conflict with the Flemish team, Katlijn Van der Veken was nominated as coordinator of the internal team and since then the collaboration with the city has been much simpler.

The main themes of the plan, in a collection of spaces and strategic projects and "generic policies" (meaning general issues involving the whole territory), gave rise to the formation of two working groups within the public administration. Once the plan was approved the two groups split up as follows: the first group, starting from indications supplied by the single areas, worked on the assigned strategic spaces without the intention of enclosing them into a single model, the core theme of the work, reinstating the tradition of draft standards from past plans. This group was dedicated to the implementation of spaces and strategic projects, putting into action actors, funding, and numerous opportunities for transformation, many of which were then carried out.

The second group worked more on background issues, examining situations and places that, while not being urgent, played a strategic role and were connected to important themes for the future of the city. This work led to reflections on a wider scale, and to the defining of new themes requiring research that the plan hadn't been able to carry out. In this way, even after approval of the plan, several research trajectories remained open, keeping alive the interest of the project for the city as a whole and leaving doors open to return to the reasoning which had led to its drafting. (Fig. 1)

I believe that it is important for a city to be endowed with these two instruments. The first involves practical action which carries out the developed strategy. It deals with the resources of the city and it mobilises capital and players. The second involves a different level and reflects the values, not just collective but general, regarding public well-being, beyond events and occasions. Secchi and I were enthusiastic

---

1. See Fini G., Pezzoni N. (2010) Il Piano Strutturale di Antwerp: *un nuovo dispositivo di convivenza per la città contemporanea*. Interview with Bernardo Secchi and Paola Viganò.
2. The event in question was the international conference *Shaping Regional Futures*, held in Florence 18/19 May 2017.
3. Studio Antwerpen Ruimtelijk Structuurplan coordinated and directed by Bernardo Secchi and Paola Viganò. For a complete list of the team see (Secchi, Viganò, 2009).

Structure Plan for Antwerp: Strategic spaces
(Studio Secchi Viganò).

(Fig. 1)

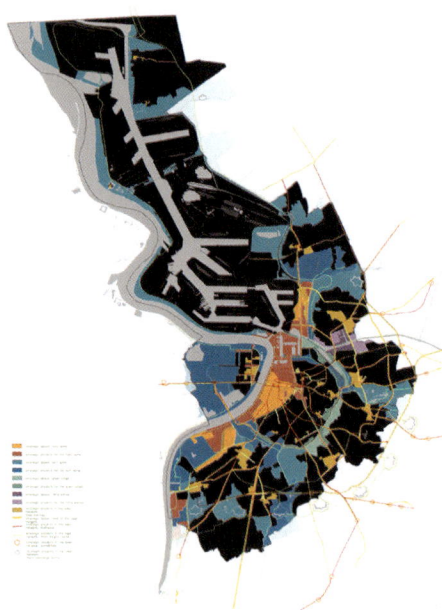

about it. It involved two levels of analysis and planning capable of working simultaneously and nurturing different types of energy. The group working on strategic projects was slightly larger and the other smaller, but still capable of focusing on themes and crucial questions and attracting the attention onto fundamental places, while not considered strategic at that time, and thus not included in the more urgent plans of operations.

This formula brought about great energy: each strategic project was backed by a team led by a young architect, urbanist or landscape designer who took up and maintained a dialogue with the actors, paved the way as far as issues of ownership or technical difficulties were concerned, and set up calls for proposals. At the same time the second group dedicated their time to rebuilding a more general large-scale reflection: on the theme of green spaces, on urban language, on the Ring and other extremely interesting issues.

After Janssens had served two mayoral terms, Bart De Wever, an important candidate of the Flemish right-wing and a leading figure who carried great weight nation-wide, won the elections.[4]

This marked a break, a very strong political and ideological change that had repercussions even within the two work groups.

Katljin (Van der Veken, ed) described how the new Mayor intended to release himself of the plan that he considered far from his ideology, and how he realised that in actual fact that plan could still be useful for the city: its structure still worked well, it was widely recognised and the public was aware of the proposed images, some of the strategic spaces could be modified without challenging the whole process, the positions taken and the general vision for the city. Consequently, after an initial ideological conflict, and in the name of "Belgian pragmatism", the plan that dated back ten years stayed in place, despite there being the opportunity and legitimacy for a change. The new administration examined the issues in this regard and decided to confirm the Plan, only making some slight modifications which didn't compromise the whole underlying rationale.

Framework, Episodes and Legitimacy

"Plunging" into some points by building a mesh of understanding anchored in the urban fabric is a strategy often used by Studio. Even in the research for Grand Paris the sections that were examined more closely for several parts of the territory are fundamental in understanding

---

4. The current mayor of Antwerp, whose term started in 2013, is also the leader of *Nieuw-Vlaamse Alliantie*, the New-Flemish Alliance, a moderate right-wing political-nationalistic party with origins from Volksunie which disbanded in 2011.

the complexity of the context of the work. You yourself, in a recent interview[5], highlighted the importance of "dealing with different scales" and in regards to the Antwerp Plan, Bernardo Secchi refers to a strategy of *renovatio urbis* based on the restructuring of the city from a "multidimensional and integrated" viewpoint.[6]

In parallel with the development of Antwerp, Studio was working on the project for SpoorNord Park, also known as "one of the points in which the two-scale process of change, the single project strategy and the whole city-system process, was activated in an evident manner". This plan aimed to interact as a framework that was capable of accommodating "new dynamics of self-organisation" while being structured by precise elements ("soft spine", "hard spine", "green Singel", "living canal").

In 2016 the city of Antwerp drafted a project to cover the Ring road that encircles the city (the same ring was once made up of defensive walls). Studio, together with five other teams was selected to reflect on the theme, in particular in the Zuidoost area.

How does a project like *Over de Ring* position itself in regards to the methodological strategy of the Structure Plan?

In defining the *Over de Ring* plan we insisted on three things: the construction of a common framework, the definition of an urban language, and lastly a collocation of projects formulated over time. The framework required the recognition of basic elements of a project conceived from its core: coverage of the entire Ring of Antwerp. This was a complex, costly, uncertain project that could, paradoxically, remove the attention from the longstanding practical problems experienced by inhabitants living along the Ring. It was fundamental to us to insist on the immediate need (before carrying out the entire coverage process) for interventions connected to public transportation (along the Singel which runs parallel to the Ring and improving the railway system to provide a metropolitan service), to air quality and noise barriers (with protection systems included in the project for a "longitudinal park"), to pedestrian, cycling and biodiversity continuity which is still poor today. The planning of the framework had to deal with several issues: we dedicated a great deal of time to redesigning the Singel, even though it hadn't been a theme we were supposed to tackle directly. We worked on water and water management, as well as the integration of different modes of transport and we insisted that all this be taken into consideration within the budget devoted to the cover of the Ring.

This constituted the framework: the idea that, even before putting our hands on the greater project, there would be a series of smaller less costly projects that would affect the transformation of mobility and liveability.

In order to define this framework, we tried to build an alliance with the other teams in a common discussion with the *intendant*[7]. This worked and enabled us to present ourselves as a compact unit with clear ideas on what needed to be done when dealing with politicians **(Fig. 2)**.

The second consideration which we made was that, in an operation of this size carried out by multiple individuals and architects, landscape designers, participation experts, it would be useful to think about the typology of the urban language and the types of spaces to be organised. This is also important in consideration of its time scale (about 20-25 years) and

---

5. *Horizontal Metropolis, les territoires prodiges*, published in A+ Architecture in Belgium 28.06.2018 ed. Elodie Degrave. Available at : http://a-plus.be/fr/actuel/horizontal-metropolis-het-beloofde-land-2/#.W0Uer9gzby
6. (Secchi, Viganò, 2009).
7. The *intendant* (Alexander d'Hoge) is the coordinator of the entire project of the coverage of the Ring. Each of the six international groups were selected to work on one segment of the project.

Grote Markt Berchem in Antwerp (Studio Secchi Viganò, Grafton Architects, MAARCH, Sweco Belgium, Idea Consult, Antwerpen aan't woord, Sertius, D2S International ODR).

(Fig. 2)

its uncertain outcome. The intervention had to be conceived not as a monolith, but as a series of episodes which would eventually join together in the great park imagined above the Ring. In order to prevent these episodes from fragmenting, we proposed a typological viewpoint: we envisioned new contemporaneous squares (as part of the cover and which could be built earlier). The *grote markt* is the large market square typical of Flemish cities. It is the most multifunctional space that exists – large enough to host any type of activity. We thought it would be interesting to use, even just symbolically, a unifying space which unifies *intra* and *extra muros* (Fig. 3). Another element that we identified were the boulevard bridges which were to be protected from noise and pollution without having to wait the twenty years for the total coverage of the Ring, or the ecological valleys. So this is how to build an urban language made up of a series of projects conceived as a sum of the elements and not as a grand gesture to be put into practice at one time.

Onto the third point. Even though the budget allocated for the entire operation was very large, the teams and the coordinator were worried about the risk that all the projects as a whole would have greatly exceeded the allocated figure.

Some therefore pushed for a predetermined selection of the projects, despite the fact that no team had made unreasonable proposals. According to a broad assessment the budget would have to be doubled to carry out the proposed projects. The preventive selection seemed to be the only feasible option, with the risk of losing out on valuable contributions and ideas. I maintained that it would be more appropriate to think as if we had planted a forest: you can't do it tree by tree, you sow seeds and you plant smaller plants close to each other, more than those needed to survive. The point is that today we can hardly say which projects will be easily achievable: there are technical and financial uncertainties, we don't know precisely how some hitches will work out, the people involved and timeline are also unknown factors. In our

The team for the Noord area is composed of BUUR, LATZ, S333 e GREISCH i.s.m. Levuur, Tree Company, ProFlow, 3E, Eld and Anno offices.
The planning team for the Nordoost : ORG i.s.m. ARUP, Common Ground and Deltares offices.
The planning team for the Oost area: 51N4E, NDVR e H + N + S.
For the Zuidoost area: STUDIO PAOLA VIGANO, GRAFTON ARCHITECTS and MAARCH i.s.m. Sweco Belgium, Idea Consult, Antwerp, Sertius and D2S International.
For the Zuid area: AGENCE TER, TVK e ARCADIS i.s.m. Interboro / Marleen Goethals, IBM, Deloitte and Crepain-Binst.
For the Zone West: DE URBANISTEN, ENVIRONMENT and COBE i.s.m. Ney, SBE, D + A Consult, Yellow Window, Mint, ABO and Copenhagenize.
EU. source: https://www.overdering.be / original text in Dutch.

Over de Ring Project: division of project areas.
Source: Over de Ring official website (overdering.be).

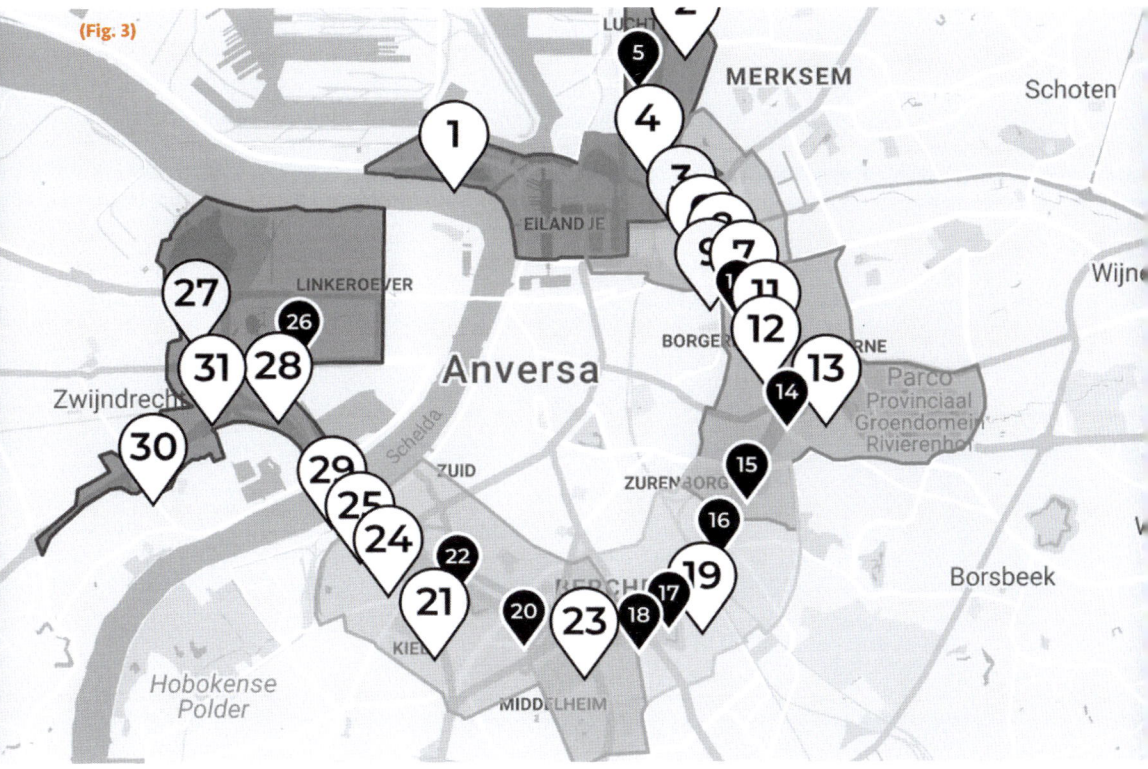

(Fig. 3)

case, for example, the south-east segment along which the Berchem station is located involved dealing with the Belgian railways and we were not sure that they would have supported our choices regarding the project, similarly to the De Leien public transport company, with whom the collaboration was more transparent and fruitful.

Why make a selection? Since many interventions can be achievable immediately, and others need further discussion, examination and reworking, and the whole picture is cohesive and the projects are interesting, it is worthwhile to conserve and place it all on a timeline – short, mid and long-term- enabling each to be carried out. In the mid/long-term it is reasonable to imagine a new budget and more participants in the financing for the different works. For this reason, it is essential that all projects be taken into consideration: some will be carried out, others will need further analysis. But it is above all fundamental to organise them over time: in 25 years transportation will be different and so perhaps some of the ideas proposed today will not need to be realised. It would mean that each project will be given the chance to adjust according to the evolution of the masterplan as a whole, constructing conditions which offer richer opportunities to the different parts of Antwerp that the Ring passes through. **(Fig. 4)**

The multi-scale character in this case is connected to the use of specific conceptual instruments: the typological innovation to deconstruct the idea of a single project, but at the same time to propose a non-literal continuity, made up of recognition and legibility of the infrastructural intervention within the city.

Project Area of Antwerp (Studio Secchi Viganò, Grafton Architects, MAARCH, Sweco Belgium, Idea Consult, Antwerpen aan't woord, Sertius, D2S International ODR).

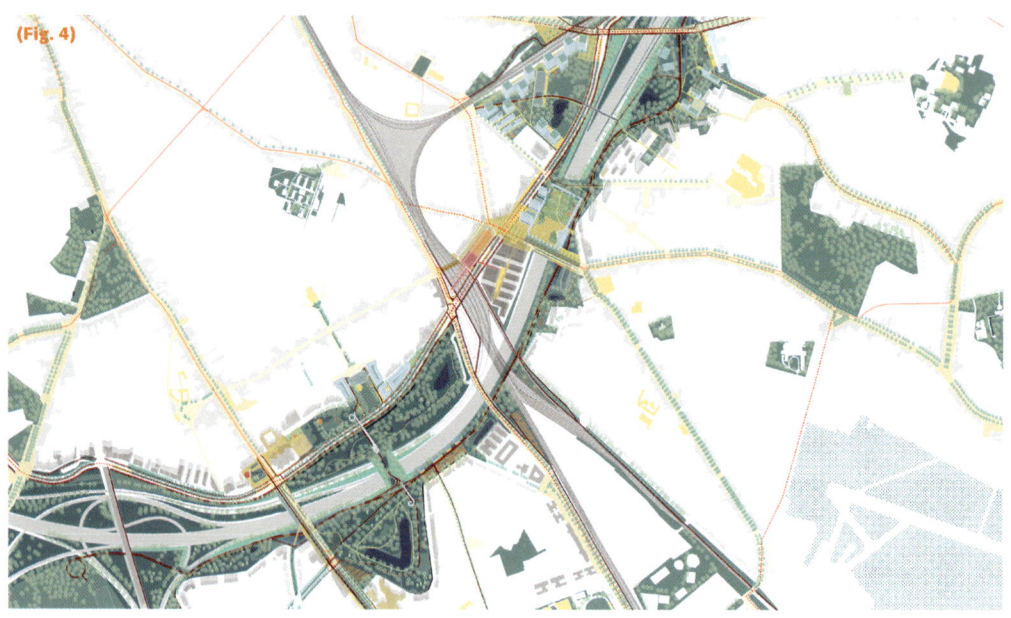

(Fig. 4)

Time – The new Over de Ring and its connection to the Structure Plan

Whereas the Structure Plan was drafted as a flexible and inclusive instrument, working on *Over de Ring*, seven years after submission of the Plan, forced you to re-examine and verify its adaptability in the face of the emerging needs of the city and its inhabitants.

How did the Structure Plan of Antwerp, 11 years after its approval, respond to these transformations?

When we began working in 2003, it was clear that the city needed a plan: Antwerp had long lost its hopes of being the object of an overall project. There was the need for a plan that could organise the transformation of the city in its various parts, but also for a vision of the possibility of imagining the future transformation not within a formally decided framework but in an open way. This is suggested in images[8]. I believe that the use of images was taken into serious consideration by all those involved with the plan and the images endowed them with the skills to position the discourse of the city on levels differing from contemporary Belgian urban planning: some images were comprehensible to all, like the city of water (Waterstad), others were less immediate, like the porous city (Poreuzestad). These were, in any case, assessed carefully and considered crucial for the future of Antwerp.

The plan was understood by many, not because we used an easy language, but because

8. The Structure Plan for Antwerp was built on three main categories: images, scenarios and strategies. According to the Plan the images that interpret the city are Waterstad, Spoorstad, Havenstad, Megastad, Villages and Metropolis, Ecostad e Poreuzestad. In Fini G., Pezzoni N. (2010) *Il Piano Strutturale di Antwerp: un nuovo dispositivo di convivenza per la città contemporanea*. Inteview with Bernardo Secchi and Paola Viganò, Secchi states that the work conducted by Paola Viganò on images and collective imagination was inaugurated with the Plan for Jesi (1983-1987) and he highlights the importance of a project composed of images in contrast to the disregard for "skills of foreseeability" on the part of urbanists.

that language was capable of interpreting and collecting, in that decisive moment, the expectations of a city that had been suffering from conflict and paralysis for too many years. Sometimes, in observing plans, one gets the impression that they are totally disconnected from the real city, that they are for another city. Working on the *Over de Ring* project I felt that the plan was still very close to the city, its themes and its problems. It seemed to me that the city of today was still contained within the plan for Antwerp, as well as many of the city's still needed goals, in as much as, obviously, some things have changed. For this reason, again, I thought it was a reasonable idea to put the project into action and not abandon it.

Although the *Over de Ring* project offers the chance to reflect on some of the themes dealt with in the Plan (for example the idea of "green Singel"), one could say that the proposed vision by OdR is in contrast with the *imaginaire* of the city included in the plan. The OdR establishes itself as a large-scale project that blocks urban development as self-enclosed actions; on the contrary the structure plan suggests that the project for the territory – in favour of a continuity over time capable of including its elements of unpredictability as needed – should make use of a bottom-up process which is all about the people and that can adapt itself as needs change. How did you handle this contradiction?

Recovering the plan during the work on the south-east segment of the Ring was the opportunity for a real exercise in reinterpretation, in the light of the idea of total coverage, towards which I felt some doubt. Why would we participate in a competition if we didn't totally share the proposed vision? Firstly, the grand-scale theme directly related to the Plan and it seemed strange to not be a part of it. In the Plan we had described the Singel in terms of *green Singel* and among the projects there was that of in-depth work on areas connected to the Ring. This was the space that once had been occupied by defensive walls and then became the site for the motorway in the Seventies. The *Singel,* on the other hand, is closer to the city and is an asymmetric boulevard bound by buildings on only one side. Together they constitute a vast and very congested area: The Ring is the route connecting the north and south of Europe and it is where all the traffic directed towards the Port of Antwerp merges. The bottleneck of Europe, as it is defined. But along its space there are residents, businesses and activities – it is not only an open space. All in all, it's a clear case of spatial injustice. And this also led to several citizens' movements supporting a campaign for the realisation of the extensive coverage.

For these reasons, despite not being fully in agreement, I decided to participate in the *Over de Ring* selection process, and during this phase, obviously, the issue of picking up and rereading the Plan came up. I found that it was still full of questions and suggestions, it still presented interesting themes and it could still serve as a flexible base for this new reflection.

We decided to bring a constructive but critical viewpoint by acting within the dialectics between the various actors involved.

At the time the Plan had already included these parts of the city, proposals for coverage were already regularly being made: a problem between internal and external areas existed, there would be a 200-250-metre-wide strip separating them. No one was against the idea of covering some parts of the Ring, but there was the risk that an entire coverage, at enormous cost, would become the alibi for not considering alternatives that would decrease road traffic, facilitate other types of mobility, reduce pollution and so on.

Besides, carrying out a project like that would require an extremely long time, probably a genera-

Public discussion (Studio Secchi Viganò).

(Fig. 5)

tion, and the problems experienced by the densest part of the city are mainly related to air and noise pollution, along with difficulties in urban mobility, since the city is divided by the infrastructure. These problems could not wait twenty years to be solved. On the contrary, they need concrete solutions which can be carried out in a short time, while awaiting the completion of the project as a whole. Nevertheless, the process of defining the OdR project also brought to light numerous technical difficulties. For example, covering a highway for a such a large number of kilometres means creating breaks in tunnels and guaranteeing exchanges with the outside. This improves liveability along the covered areas but pollution is concentrated around the break sites. These aspects were not initially known to the citizens who participated in the different phases of construction of the project.

Being cautious regarding the hypothesis of covering the Ring allowed us to understand, perhaps more clearly, the limits and potential of its realisation.

The Actors

The *Over de Ring* project was characterised by very active citizen participation. The Antwerp Structure Plan had been able to involve many actors and combine top-down and bottom-up models, and to communicate constructively with the public administration.

How did the different actors contribute to the construction of the project? Can we say that in these projects the citizens were an active part of the planning process?

During the drafting of the Antwerp Plan the fundamental images were in part suggested by the actual inhabitants of the city. In drafting the *Over de Ring* masterplan this participatory component revealed itself in a more mature and effective form.

During the drafting of the masterplan of the eastern segment we had at our disposal a space in which to build a relationship with the city: a row house with a shop front window on the high street in the centre of our project area. This and in surrounding areas was where we organised many meetings (Fig. 5). The participation of the citizens in the project took place in different ways which included small municipal administrations, organised groups, actual movements and between individuals.

The citizens' movements were born before the selection process and were opposing the idea of closing off the Ring (still incomplete today) via a long overpass. These movements achieved the construction of a tunnel and over time they became quite important and autonomous. These are movements that are progressively becoming active political forces within the city, and that include many influential figures (many urban planning lecturers, for example). They can count on the support of thousands of people[9] and are capable of financing surveys to verify their hypotheses. Aside from the movements, even single citizens participated very actively in the meetings, together with the administrations of the districts included in the city of Antwerp (Berchem,

---

9. The importance of these movements for the urban development of the city becomes even more relevant when considering the urban dimension: Antwerp numbers approximately 500,000 inhabitants.

for instance, has its own mayor and board). They were particularly involved in the discussion and presented proposals, asking that part of the total budget be allocated for their realisation.

It was therefore a participatory process of great complexity and very challenging, not only for the activities (field trips to get to know the area with its inhabitants, building a large-scale model to explain the functioning of the infrastructures and their relationship with the different parts of the city, etc.), but also the complex relations between citizen and strong movements, institutional and non-institutional actors at different levels and covering different roles. Their participation generated numerous debates and was a great asset to the project. The *intendant*, by blending North-American and European traditions, gave great importance to an evaluation procedure of the project whereby citizens could write in letters in support or against the proposed projects.

Belgian Pragmatism and Liberalism

In 2003 after being selected for the Spoornoord Park and the Structure Plan, Studio opened a location in Belgium – in Antwerp and then in 2010, in Brussels. The Hoog Kortrijk selection is only one of a long series of projects selected and realised in Belgium: the main square and the new cemetery in Kortrijk, The Structure Plan for Antwerp, Spoornoord Park and then the Theatre Square, the Hoge Rielen masterplan, with the Hostel Wadi, the territorial vision for Brussels 2040, the Over de Ring project. You are actually a lecturer at the Catholic University of Leuven. All of these experiences have allowed you to develop a privileged viewpoint into Belgian political culture. How has this culture influenced the construction of the city and shared urban space?

There is one characteristic that I recognise in the Flemish administrative system: pragmatism. This was made clear to me when we met the new mayor of Antwerp and his urban planning commissioner in occasion of *Over de Ring*. Bernardo Secchi immediately saw the risk of blind pragmatism, a pragmatism that is blinding and leads to "blind" action: however, during the many professional commissions carried out in Belgium, we had the chance to experience *able pragmatism* which can overcome ideological close-mindedness and bureaucratic inflexibility and is able to realise, for the good of all, improvements in the spaces of the city.

It was by virtue of this pragmatism, I believe, that Bart De Wever managed to put aside any ideological contrast and decided to keep the Structure Plan.

The masterplan for the Schelda riverside has a similar history: after the mayor's election the project, drafted by Proap, winner of an international planning competition[10], was first halted in favour of new intentions of building more parking space than previously planned. Later, the need to protect the city from the rise of water levels drove the city council, despite their diverging views on the solutions proposed by the previous council, to promote the realisation of the project.

10. The call for projects for the regeneration of this area of the city was necessary due to the daily variation of water levels by approx. 5 metres. Five international groups were selected to participate: West 8, from Holland; SSS3, international group based in Holland; Secchi e Viganò, from Italy and creators of the Masterplan for the city; BAU Studio, Jean Busquets, from Spain; and PROAP from Portugal as coordinators of an international team (Servillo L.A., *"Antwerp: riqualifcare il lungofume"*, in Planum, October 2009). This was the winning project, drafted in 2006. It proposed the reconstruction of a dynamic landscape that could vary in the case of exceptional flooding, by constructing, on one side of the river, floodable areas to be used temporarily. On the other side were "dry" platforms for permanent activities. For more info: http://www.proap.pt/project/antwerp-quays-waterfront-1/

These examples clearly demonstrate that in Flanders the culture of pragmatism, joined with a close sharing of values connected to quality of life, guide the choices that are the cornerstones of construction in the city. Ultimately, what we imagined to be an extremely strong political rift ended up being continuity based upon pragmatism and in this case supported by the ideal of extreme individual freedom. The individual is placed at the centre of politics, the individual must be free to choose and to act. For this reason, for example, although political orientation is slanting towards the direction of no-car territory, through the construction of new generation cycling lanes and new pedestrian areas, parking areas were maintained and consolidated, so the individual is not forced into this transition, but chooses it spontaneously. The cost of this approach is high and only wealthy territories can afford to do so, posing, in my opinion, enormous problems to democracy, to our ideas of democratic relations with space and building in the city.[11]

Legacy[12]

In a 2010 interview with Studio, in regards to the Structure Plan for Antwerp, a clear desire to transform the dictates of planning practice emerges. In first place, the crisis which affected European urban planning from the seventies, and later, the growing lack of "predictive skills" in urban planners.

Have the years since the drafting of the plan served to show its effectiveness and assess its legacy: can we say that this plan paved the path for new ways of working on the city?

In the plan for Antwerp we brought the experience of plans developed in Italy, elaborating planning models which we had already used in plans for Brescia, Pesaro, Prato. In our eyes the Antwerp plan never seemed to be a completely different plan; on the contrary, it was an opportunity to try out an approach elaborated in Italian cities in a different setting, with some adjustments. However, in the plan for Antwerp the role of imagination took on an even more important and explicit role: images were brought to the discussion, analysed both close up and from a distance: there are some close up images that everyone understands and some more distant and conceptual ones that offer a renewed viewpoint.

The aspect of the plan that I consider important today and I don't think appears very often is its ability to hold together a reflection of the structure, city and territory, and a reflection on the strategies of transformation: the presence of both, neither one nor the other, nor does either overpower the other. They are both crucial. A structural understanding of the territory is absolutely essential, even though strategies are then worked on for the following five years and vice versa. The Antwerp Plan is a structure plan. By structure plan we generally mean a plan that does not define strategies, but that identifies the major stable long-lasting elements of the territory. From our point of view, however, Antwerp has always had a strategic value. Even Jef Van den Broeck, honorary professor in the department of architecture, urban design and spatial planning at the University of Leuven, who oversaw the plan (in the role of 'coach' between the internal and external team) and had worked on the legislation for structure plans in Flanders, agreed with our approach. He shared our idea that the structure plan needed a consideration of strategies, exploring plans on different scales. This approach involved the ability to maintain a view of structure and to build, at the same time, coherent planning strategies, starting from a structural understanding of the territory, in order to face the theme of legitimacy of the projects and their potential selection- This ability, I believe, is one of the innovative aspects of the Plan that we developed.

This seems to be the point from which to restart: asking ourselves, once again, what structures urban and territorial space today and which strategies, positioned in time and space, can define a future open to choices and project.

11. In his volume *La città dei ricchi e la città dei poveri* Bernardo Secchi highlights that every city has always been "a space for social and cultural integration" (...) but also a "powerful machine for distinction and separation, marginalisation and exclusion" (Secchi). It is evident that, in the current political and economic conditions, an approach to the project which is based on laissez-faire policies will not guarantee spatial equality that translates into a fair supply of public spaces and services. On the contrary, it accentuates the already existing gap between wealthy and poor territories.
12. See. Fini G., Pezzoni N. (2010) *Il Piano Strutturale di Antwerp: un nuovo dispositivo di convivenza per la città contemporanea*. Interview with Bernardo Secchi and Paola Viganò.

1.7.2
The Time Scaling

Interviews

Interview with Michel Desvigne
by Francesca Garzilli

The step-by-step urban transformation tested by the Sub>urban network, recall several of your works, for instance Ile Seguin. Considering your past experiences, how did a temporary prefiguration garden start the changing process of the area? What were the consequences in the whole territory of the Boulogne-Billancourt municipality, and how have relations with citizens and administrations been managed?

Since the closure of the Renault factories in 1992, Seguin Island had been at the heart of vast development operations that had been postponed many times without anything being really done. From 2004 to 2010, we have developed and tested a general overview, initially with the urbanist François Grether and later with Jean Nouvel. As a matter of fact, a precise masterplan could not be established at this time. However, while waiting for the constructions to be programmed and designed, the site could not remain undetermined. It was necessary to conceive a project that would progressed by successive steps and changes, and that could give the abandoned area an immediate landscaped quality.

For this reasons, we decided to develop a quite flexible system of public spaces, conserving the memory of the island's construction, its multiple transformations, and accepting the indetermination of the moment. When industry occupied the island, it was often compared to a gigantic ship. Its beauty was linked directly to its scale, to a certain sense of "excessiveness". The foundation and artifice of this former construction served as the basis for the site's character and its quality.

We developed a very specific typology of public spaces, an intermediate one, between square and garden. The determination of a set of precise components allowed us to build a prototype. However, not only this prototype showed the way the components were supposed to be built, but it also showed the spatial compositions they could provide. A mosaic of components included pathways, gardens, lawns and functional surfaces, and allow for a broad range of uses and a flexibility in setting up numerous programs.

Fig. 1 - Ile Seguin © MDP

Finally, the mayor decided to let the public access the prototype, transforming it into a prefiguration garden **(Fig. 1)**. This first public space to open on the island (covering roughly two hectares of the overall eleven hectares), prefigures the central garden planned for the island's future comprehensive development. It serves as a foundation, a preliminary and temporary stratum that will evolve gradually as planning and development continue.

The garden succeeds in presenting and framing in a joyous and playful manner the construction taking place around it: immense sandboxes for children, experimental and participatory gardens, picnic areas. It is as well a place where outdoor events and a restaurant can easily be set up. But above all else it provides an access to the public into the heart of the Seine valley. From a new point of view, the expanse and beauty of the hills could be rediscovered. We tried to make a minimum intervention. However, after 10 years the garden still exists.

It must be acknowledged that this kind of interventions, even though apparently less important, in reality require a great effort.

Therefore, they must be politically supported. It helps to understand and study the aspects to be taken into account during the execution phase, and to estimate the budget necessary for the realization of the entire project. It is important to understand the importance and seriousness of this kind of projects. They may seem marginal, naive, but they are not. They represent a first stage, with a formally provisional dimension, but with an idea, an image, and an extremely consistent and decisive perception.

In the second half of the XX century, the radical change of Casoria's land use transformed the territory from rural to Sub>urban. The establishment of industries and commercial zones and the proliferation of entire abusive neighborhoods has determined, on the one hand, the fragmentation of the space with the spread of waterproofed plates, on the other, inadequate settlement systems from the point of view of basic infrastructures (for example: insufficient sewage systems, absence of public services, etc.). How can a good landscape project start change processes by acting on environmental components and by reconstructing ecological qualities in waterproofed lands? And what can be, if any, the concrete interest of a public or private investor to start from a landscape reconfiguration? (as the first step of broader urban transformations).

It is an important question and therefore we cannot be *naive*. In big areas like this one, where the territorial quality has to be exalted, it is difficult to think that a private person would be ready to invest. This type of projects generally require public investors. Long term public space projects rarely attract to private investors. But it sometimes happens. Novartis Campus project in East Hanover, for example, used to be supported by private investors. A double interest allowed to play on different but converging timing and objectives: on the one hand, the desire to give quality to the territory, which necessarily takes decades, on the other hand to reinforce and make open space available allowing people to work inside the campus immediately. Most of the time, projects dealing with a long term vision and a time management, concern public lands with public investments.

The Park aux Angéliques **(Fig. 2 and 3)** that we have been developing along Bordeaux's right bank is the product of a long process. Being well familiar with the Bordeaux territory upon which we have worked for over fifteen years, we have revised our usual approach in order to harmonize with the long gestation period of the city and its territory. The development of the park along the right bank was gradual. Its configuration is particular, benefiting from a landscape thinking more often used in the creation of large territories. It borrows a form of rusticity that gets straight to the point, structuring the future development of the site in a sustainable way by progressively adapting to its evolutions and transformation. As a result, through this creation of a very large park, we have contributed to the recomposition of the city center and to the transformation of how it is used.

The Metropolitan Area of Naples is strongly marked by large infrastructures. The airport has led to a radical change of north area of Naples and its provinces. The open space results fragmented by motorways, highways, and railways. Moreover, in the neighboring municipality of Afragola -2 km from the center of Casoria and 4 km from Capodichino airport- Zaha Hadid realized the new high-speed railway station in the middle of a completely agricultural area, disconnected from the city. Traces of fragmented agricultural past, faint residues of the historic rural past of Campania Felix, remain as residual spaces between infrastructures and urban spaces. Many of these rural land are no longer used and are returning on a state of neglect. As a result, could we look at the fringes around the infrastructures as Intermediates Natures? As buffer zones between the evanescent countryside and the city? How to maintain the natural character of these spaces? And how can we conceive alternative public spaces in these areas? (for instance slow mobility)

In our project for Paris-Saclay Campus **(Fig. 4a and b)**, the fringes prove to be one of the most structuring elements. It is emblematic in its concretization of an idea all the more meaningful in contemporary society: that of the powerful recomposition of peri-urban territo-

Fig. 2 - Parc aux Angéliques © G. Leuregans

Fig.3 - Parc aux Angéliques © Mairie de Bordeaux, T. Sanson

ries. The project site here becomes a magnificent laboratory for approaching the challenges involved in spatial transition, an area of investigation which relates in reality to a multitude of other contexts.

The edge of the South Campus is not a simple line, a demarcation boundary line embodying a temporary stabilization of the urban expanse. The edge area here widens and enriches itself until becoming the place where the reconciliation between two long opposed worlds, the city and the countryside, can take place again. We are developing an intermediate landscape located at the hinge between the large agricultural fields of the surrounding plateau and the heart of the city-like campus.

The proposal gives quality to the site without completely altering it. The focus lies in shaping the land with economic means, not orienting it towards the idea of establishing a nature to simply contemplate, but rather towards the creation of a space in which practices, activities, and exchanges can take place. The intermediate landscape is a small, domestic piece of countryside. Within a space today fragmented and experienced for the most part by car, it reconstructs a scale appropriate to the pedestrian. It can be easily strolled, facilitating connections by foot or bicycle between the towns of the plateau and the valley.

Through integrating the territory's uses in its design, chief among them being agriculture, the project establishes all its relevance. As a result, it includes an agricultural dimension adapted to the urban context of the campus. The use of techniques and methods borrowed from the sphere of agriculture introduces many technical requirements, such as the storage of topsoils, materials, and water, the establishment of nurseries, and the setting up of an ecological engineering capable of contributing to the transformation of the site. Its evolving character makes of the edge area a living and inhabited landscape.

It is important to know that, in the first place, no one wanted to invest in this Intermediate Nature.

The first step has been to identify the actors, find a strategy, and understand how to realize that. In your case, not too much different from Saclay, the actors could be the farmers, agricultural organizations and companies. Again, an essential point is certainly to take into consideration the environmental needs required in the territory. At Saclay we played with the storm water management. In Naples it rains a lot for short periods, and so this aspect could be the first step to take into account: considering the water as the first landscape layer, providing ditches, tidal, basins as supports, in order to enhance, to improve the existent ecological continuity in the territory which could be compromise by the new infrastructures.

Being able to keep different scales together is fundamental for a landscape project that brings together different stakeholders, with the ambition to repair and restore complex territories. The slogan of Casoria's Sub>urban Integrated Action Plan is: "think as gardener: combining vision and daily care, dealing with the unexpected, learning from the mistakes". The plan sets among the objectives the creation of neighborhood parks, starting from the identification of drosscape, marginal areas, abandoned industrial areas. These areas, could be bind together, working as green network, also through temporary uses. For example, in the Euralens project, there was a very precise proposal for an ecological reconnection based on the American parkways experience. We believe that this approach can also be used in our case study. However, we know that there are obstacles and risk factors. How to match different scales and times of intervention together? How to intertwine the fringe project and the whole general Plan with reference to the American

Fig. 4a - Paris Saclay, Lisières © MDP

Fig. 4b - Paris Saclay, Lisières © MDP

landscape movement (green network, parkways)? What are the limits and issues in the definition of a strategy that ties together different scales and times of intervention?

The territory has great potential for landscape connections. As in France, the dense infrastructural network, has determined limits to urban proliferation. Paradoxically, this is a great potential support that could give quality to the territory. For instance in Paris there is an underway project that will restore the quality of all the infrastructures around the city through the afforestation along the roadways. There are vast areas of cultivation, many abandoned areas, free spaces around the highway, so there are strong possibilities. Obviously you have to find investors, but also talk with the owners.

Our territorial projects developed at Paris-Saclay and Euralens define strategies and tools in a context that is similar in some ways. They shows that different answers are needed for the different scales of a territorial project. The neighborhood's scale and the territorial one related to the infrastructures will perhaps require different solutions: if the agricultural fringes could help on the urban and neighborhood's scale, they certainly do not make sense at the infrastructural scale. Here, we are talking about a totally different way compared to the agricultural project that we already mentioned. They are different scales with different tools.

The question of the different scales of intervention is a prerequisite. For example, the Paris-Saclay project simultaneously requires the following scales:
 a territorial perimeter of approximately 7,700 hectares;
 a campus about ten kilometers long;
 public spaces of a campus districts of about 250 hectares;

The simultaneity of variable scale on the same site obliges us to constantly accommodate our proposal. So that each new point of view informs or questions the previous one. There is no homothetic relationship between these different scales: what works for one does not necessarily work for the others. The systems of physical coherence are different from one another, and must be articulated between each other.

Perceiving the scale and providing the right answer to the right dimension is, in my opinion, the key to the success of a project to recompose a territory.

2. CASORIA, ITALY

2.0

Images and graphics in this chapter are by Enrico Formato (page 133, pages 146-147) and Alessandro Capozzoli (page 131). The collage at page 152-153 is composed of pictures by Alessandro Capozzoli, Enrico Formato and the Sbs_Lab (Francesca Avitabile, Ermelinda Clarino, Pietro Salomone, Bianca Senese, Pasquale Volpe).

Casoria is one of the densest municipalities of the Metropolitan City of Naples, a conurbation extended over about 1,200 square kilometers, with 3.2 million inhabitants and 92 municipal entities.

By the end of the '70s, Casoria was one of the most important industrial centres in the South of Italy, with chemical and steel industries, today in a state of abandonment. In the following years, a thriving tertiary sector was developed, with private facilities and commercial activities, but currently this sector is also in crisis.

The whole city is in a phase of economic and demographic decline, and has lost about 5,000 inhabitants in the last fifteen years. This phenomenon can only be addressed to structural conditions: the low level of settlement and environmental quality, infrastructural inadequacy and the absence of green areas, car congestion and housing pressure, the scarcity of opportunities working.

In 2013, the Municipal Administration adopted a highly innovative Municipal Urban Plan, consisting of a Structural Plan and an Operational Plan aimed at creating a large periurban public forest. The Plan was prepared by a public planning office, called the "Step by Step Laboratory" (hence abbreviated as SbS _ Lab), composed of municipal technicians and researchers of the Department of Architecture of the Federico II University of Naples. Based on this planning strategy, the Municipality of Casoria joined, from the first phase (2015), the URBACT "Sub>urban" network, led by the City of Antwerp. In recent years, the SBS _ Lab focused on the development of URBACT Local -or Integrated- Action Plan, within a wide participatory process.

The Action Plan takes up the concepts and methods defined by the 2013 Structural Plan, with the aim of implementing them in a specific urban sector. The regeneration is based on a step-by-step strategy that, starting from the realization of feasible interventions in the immediate, aims at a deep transformation of the settlements, in a sustainable and inclusive way. Starting from the reactivation of forgotten areas - underutilized, disused, marginal urban parts - we tried to create the conditions, in the future, for urban reconfiguration actions even in the densest and most complicated urban parts, characterised by low quality and in crisis, difficult to regenerate, with high ownership fragmentation. The key role is played by the reuse, also progressive, of disused industrial areas, placed between the compact urban centre and the periurban zone.

CASORIA, ITALY

2.1
Initial situation

GENERAL OVERVIEW

Casoria is a medium size city – 77,000 inh., 12 km^2 – located in the metropolitan area of Naples, close to the main city. After the Second World War, Casoria had a huge expansion, as a result of reconstruction programme and public aid for the economic development of Southern Italy (funds coming from the American so called "Marshall Plan"): in a few years – especially during the 50s and 60s - an impressive demographic growth changed the former rural village (20k inh. in 1951) in an important industrial pole, with about 80k inhabitants (2001). The urban growth was not guided by adequate public planning and policies: both the industrial districts and the new residential neighbourhoods were built disorderly, outside of any general framework. Only in the 70s, Casoria had a General Town Plan ("Piano Regolatore Generale" in Italian), and, however, thousands of buildings, both productive and residential ones, were built, during 70s, 80s and 90s, in contrast with the land use planning rules. The result is a dense and low-efficient urban settlement, car-based, characterized by low-quality of life standards. The systemic inefficiency of the urban growth did not help the permanence of industrial activities: since the early 80s all the main factories were dismissed. Today, five big brownfields, contiguous to the city core – "fringes in the city" - are still waiting for new uses and are nowadays colonized by wild vegetation (urban forest or "third landscape"). Moreover, with the financial crisis of the last decades, many economic tertiary activities – offices and shopping centers, particularly located along the main infrastructure – closed or reduced their business. The first consequence on the social structure is an impressive unemployment rate (30%) and the increase of criminality. Finally, during the last decade, Casoria lost inhabitants (3 thousands in the last decade) and several vacant apartments and services spread both into the dense XXth century belt and into the fringe (1,885 unused residential units, about 10% of the total amount). The shrinking phenomenon is not homogeneous, since mostly educated and wealthy inhabitants are leaving Casoria.

CASORIA, ITALY

WHY DOES CASORIA WANT TO REINVENT THE FRINGE?

Casoria needs to look at the future through a radical shift from its recent history. The initial spark of the change can burst right into the fringe, where many "forgotten" spaces can be more easily revived, reused and transformed right away.

The basic strategy of the IAP derives from the new Town Plan, approved by the City Council (2013 and 2015), that firstly addresses the goal of reversing the current, negative image of Casoria, from a "town of disposal" and a "landscape of concrete" to an innovative, bright, green, and sustainable city. The focus is on voids and unused areas (as agricultural residues, buffer bands of highways and railways, etc.), particularly widespread in the fringe.

The Plan proposes a large and continuous green area, a new urban forest characterized as a social space for public use and provided with collective facilities and common services. A new park of 3 square kilometres is planned as a complex green machine, a self-sufficient environmental assemblage, providing its own energy through photovoltaic & piezoelectric harvesting systems and small biomass power plants and fuelled by the life cycle of the urban woodlands and recycling of organic waste. The strategy intends to transform degraded spaces to push the urban transformation: the large open park – whose extension in the long-time-scenario (20 years) will amount to a quarter of the entire municipal territory – will change the urban structure.

The Plan is conceived as an adaptive and flexible "active device" working on space over time. It is composed of a general Strategic Framework (Structural Plan) and a first Operational Plan limited to the common-wooden-park areas (Operational Plan no. 1, titled "The big common park"). The deconstruction of the traditional, comprehensive and careless of time land-use-plan brought the Plan out of the stranded debate about the future of the large abandoned industrial fences located in the core town, close to the historical centre. Therefore, first of all, the Plan identifies the areas of the wooden-park to be realized in the short term as a form of topological continuity and hybrid metabolism. Only later the reform of urban city-core areas will be designed with further Operational Plans, when new contextual and political conditions gradually will rise. In order to overcome the obduracy of this settlements, the Plan needs large popular support and significant financial resources.

All this means starting from the fringe, by a plain spatial transformation – social and ecological oriented – harvesting the energy needed for more complex regenerations.

THE FOCUS AREA AND THE PILOT OF MICHELANGELO PARK

The Integrated Action Plan (IAP) developed for Sub>urban, tries to put into practice the strategy on which the Structural Plan is based. The IAP is focused on a district located between the city core and the so-called "Road of Americans" (a highway connecting Casoria with the Domitian coast, originally planned by Allied forces during the Second World War).

The IAP focus area is particularly interesting for several reasons: 1) it is composed of different morphological types of residential settlements: private dwellings and social housing neighbourhoods, with different densities and functional mixes; 2) a huge commercial and productive area is located along the Road of Americans, even if some shopping centres are in crisis or dismissed; 3) the larger brownfield in Casoria – the former Rhodiatoce chemical factory – defines the northern border of the focus area, in connection with the historical centre and the railway station; 4) large vacant public facilities are widespread in the area, e.g. the 7-story building of the former tribunal or the slaughterhouse; 5) two large former military areas are available for new uses today; one of them is occupied and used by squatters; 6) large infrastructures, highways and the national railway, pass through, in both directions (N-S and E-W) and they are surrounded by continuous interstitial spaces with large junctions and other unused and degraded buffer strips.

Generally, the spatial structure is porous, with many open voids – abandoned green areas and few rural fields – interposed between main infrastructures and built-up neighbourhoods. Large asphalt parking areas surround the productive and commercial areas, especially on the southern side.

Testing the step-by-step strategy in a so complex and representative sample is particularly interesting, since many types of planning actions can be tested.

At the same time, the area is interesting for the presence of large municipal-owned parcels. This initial condition, quite diffused all over the fringe, makes it feasible the implementation of the regeneration process, starting from the opening to temporary uses and basic improvements.

In parallel with the starting of the general debate, since 2015 until today, a first pilot is being implemented into the focus area: the new Michelangelo public park, the larger one in Casoria.

It is a former military site, which covers about 30,000 square meters, close to the viaduct of the Road of Americans, about 1 km far from the city core. As a consequence of a national law, the Italian Air Force has given this area to Municipality for free, some years ago. In 2015, the site was a perfect example of the so-called "third landscape", with wild vegetation growing in the large natural soil surrounding a little building where military radars were previously located.

The area has been opened to the public use for the first time during a "social gardening" event, during the URBACT Transnational Meeting in November 2016, to hundreds of young students and citizens with the participation of colleagues of the Sub>urban network. Previously, a large participatory process was developed with inhabitants, associations, other stakeholders, to establish functions, and the conditions to access into the area. Anyway, the co-design of the park was substantially defined during the public event, with the help of the landscape architect Miguel Georgieff (Atelier Coloco, Paris).

Nowadays, the site is open to temporary events, and the construction of basic infrastructures (toilets, and water well), designed for it, is in progress. The furniture has been co-designed during participatory events and tables, benches and other facilities, have been built for free as a result of a public sponsorship procurement. Moreover, the fence of the site will be restored by private investors interested in the renewal of a former shopping mall located in the district ("Euromercato", one of the first American shopping mall in Italy).

The implementation of the Michelangelo pilot area, and the co-management rules to be tested there, will be extended in all the similar sites of the urban fringe.

2.2
The Integrated Action Plan

TRANSFORMING THE VISION INTO ACTION

The main objective of the IAP is the promotion of local development through the creation of a network of abandoned and underutilized spaces – buildings and areas – of the fringe. This kind of vision can be considered as the establishment of circular economy principles into the practice of spatial planning.

The Structural Plan approved in 2013 recalls this strategy combined with a gradual implementation approach, triggered by the abandoned spaces regeneration in the periurban area. The strategy aims at a more ambitious perspective: to push even more complex regeneration processes in the medium term, which affect the central urban parts, congested with inhabitants and functions.

The public, social and ecological reuse of marginal areas - dedicated to the construction of a big periurban park (a sort of forest that develops from the great infrastructures to the dense city) - is aimed at two objectives: to increase the amount of green in a municipality characterized by very low environmental standards; to equip the Municipality with new public spaces and recreational, social opportunities, in order to improve the living of the inhabitants.

The new public green network, obtained through the rediscovery and connection of degraded spaces - is a fertile ground for the development of eco-innovation companies and for the creation of job opportunities, even low competence jobs, in the sectors of agriculture, plant nursery, maintenance and care of the city. The network of *"public woods"* will also reconnect private, marginal areas, where the Town Plan allows the construction of unbuilt services of public interest - as playgrounds, urban gardens, farmer markets, etc. – in return for rights of access and public usage. Even these activities can be helpful in promoting the creation of new job opportunities. In the field of ecological innovation, the socio-economic development represents a further considerable objective of the Action Plan.

The regeneration process starts from the fringe to extend to the city core, passing through the reuse of the large brownfields located in the crown of the dense urban area.

One more objective of the Action Plan is to foster the debate on brownfield, in order to start the negotiation with the ownership on public temporary use of some private areas, in the short term. On the other hand, in the medium-long term, the aim is to transform brownfields into new integrated high urban quality and energy efficiency districts; their urban rehabilitation will also allow triggering the relocation of some buildings located in disorganized and low-quality settlements in the dense urban crown and the city centre.

Finally, the parks network will constitute a public ecological element of reconnection on a regional scale, linked to the large infrastructures network and included in the Structural Plan as a program of the metropolitan city Plan. In the long term, the *"urban forest"* will be able to reconnect all the hinterland centres of Naples with each other and with the public hubs, as the High-Speed Train Station of Afragola and the future technological and service hub linked to that.

This is the reason why is desirable that the participatory planning SBS (Step By Step) laboratory, operating in Casoria since 2015 and composed by technicians, politicians, professors and researchers of the Department of Architecture (DiARC) of the University of Naples, environmental and social associations and stakeholders - will include Metropolitan Region, Campania Region and the surrounding districts.

The process described could be linked to the ongoing elaboration of the new regional landscaping Plan, in synergy with similar participatory and innovative experiences, such as Repair research, financed by EU Horizon 2020 program (GA 688920), led by the Department of Architecture of Naples and Campania Region with the involvement of the Municipality of Casoria.

The Action Plan covers an area of about 320 ha, located between the city centre and the so-called Road of Americans. A focus area that includes parts of the fringe and some important "nodes" between the fringe and the dense city.

In a strategic plan, the objectives constitute the conceptual junction between general vision and actions, ongoing and planned, to be placed in a roadmap with short (2 years), medium (10 years) and long-term (> 20 years) stages.

In our case, the objectives of the action plan have been defined in a "public arena" through the participatory process that is started in December 2015. They are closely related to the most relevant topics that local actors see as priorities to be addressed to improve the current condition. So, a "challenge zone" has been defined, as the result of the main critical issues to be faced to solve the problems that the urban fringe suffers today in Casoria.

In summary, the main objectives of the Action Plan are:

01. Increase of the natural areas.

In general, the goal is to increase the amount of permeable green areas, to improve current environmental standards and to increase systemic resilience. This will guarantee the improvement of the environmental standards with positive effects on the reduction of the air pollution (the trees produce oxygen and absorb the Co_2), the reduction of the noise coming from the infrastructures (the trees as sound barrier), and the improvement of the perceived image of Casoria (from concrete-city to forest-city). Furthermore, the compact presence of trees in those areas along the infrastructure and in abandoned lots, occupying the ground, constitutes a deterrent to the abusive abandonment of waste, one of the most urgent problems in the area north of Naples. Finally, the increase in permeable surfaces improves the behaviour of the urban system in the event of meteoric precipitation - currently the area is exposed to widespread flooding risk - and helps to reduce the summer heat island effect, counteracting the negative effects of climate change.

02. Increase of the amount and quality of space for public use

Casoria is today in a deep deficit of areas for sociality, sport, and recreation. Even the proper parking lots are very limited, causing a massive presence of vehicles parked along the city streets. The different urban parts – either low density, informal or not, either high density, private or public housing – are disconnected from public spaces. Therefore, the deficit of open public areas does not only concern purely quantitative aspects but also qualitative, relational aspects, as often the existing equipment and services appear as disconnected fragments, within a discontinuous urban fabric, with low pedestrian and cycle interconnection. For this reason, the creation of a large periurban park, both on public areas and with incentives for private owners, is a priority objective for the municipal administration. From the urban planning point of view, this means giving priority to interventions of public interest, trying to stimulate, subsequently, private and quality interventions. Furthermore, even on existing public spaces, action must be taken to improve comfort, security and liveability.

03. Creation of new job opportunities

Unemployment is one of the most relevant problems in the metropolitan area of Naples: Casoria is no exception with an average of unemployment rate at around 30%, which doubles itself if referred to the younger social groups. The reuse of waste territories – "wastescapes" (Amenta, Attademo, 2016; Formato, Amenta, Attademo, 2017; Geldermans et al., 2018) - even with temporary and instrumental uses - can be an opportunity for the development of new local economies and new job opportunities, both in the eco-innovation (with high skills required) and in the social economy fields, aimed at the maintenance and care of urban spaces, and at new forms of welfare.

04. Re-opening of brownfields fence

The abandoned industrial areas are located between the urban centre and the suburbs. One of the main abandoned areas of Casoria, the former Rhodiatoce chemical factory, is one of the places of greatest interest for the Action Plan: its positional value is very significant, also considering the proximity to the railway station.

Therefore, its at least partial re-opening would help to reconnect the urban centre with the city fringe and to ensure better integration with the regional context. Moreover, the area has been colonized in the last decades, by a wild nature - a "third landscape" - which today presents itself as a real urban forest. These are the reasons why it seems very important to reuse as soon as possible, part of this enclosure, anticipating the public use of some of its portions and the opening of sections of the enclosure wall of the area. According to the Structural Plan, temporary public uses are "traded" for the opening of the negotiation process with the private owners of the areas.

05. Renovate the brownfields

Among the ambitious objectives of the Integrated Action Plan is the regeneration of the large abandoned industrial areas of Casoria, extended for tens of hectares, and now partly reconquered by a flourishing spontaneous vegetation, awaiting transformation from more than thirty years. The realization of this objective must be included in a medium-long term perspective, and above all it requires the availability of private investments, given the nature of the areas and the ownership. The transformation of the brownfields is guided by the Structural Plan which also provides for the possibility of relocating in situ, as a "reward", the building quantities that are today improperly located in the historic centre or on its immediate margins.

06. Regenerating dense urban and periurban areas

To be realized in the long term. These areas are characterized by low quality standards, high density and low presence of green and public space, chaotic and car-based areas. In the short term, the redevelopment of the existing public space and promotion of cycle-pedestrian mobility can be carried out. In the long term, it is proposed to eliminate the concrete surfaces within some "corridors" and built-up areas - also through the potential demolition and relocation of buildings – to facilitate the construction of new public spaces. The process can be also stimulated by urban incentives coming from the transformation of brownfields (delocalization of volume). In implementation of the Structural Plan, the elimination of some buildings (or "de-concrete") project must be built over time - it is not in any way a device or an imposition, but it is built on a consensual basis, in collaboration with the inhabitants and investors; it can be stimulated with urban incentives offered by the transformation of brownfields (delocalization of volumes) or even by urban subdivisions of local reorganization with building types suitable to further realize density of the urban settlement, "freeing" ground surfaces (i.e. promoting height development).

07. Promoting the enhancement of the historic centre

It is a long-term objective, which takes account of the elimination of concrete surfaces of the dense urban crown (O6). Moreover, the urban planning incentives used for O6 can be used to promote the relocation of modern buildings not compatible with urban restoration. In the short term, the approval of the Restoration Manual contained in the new Structural Plan will be able to guide the building restoration interventions carried out by private individuals in the historic centre. The focus area does not properly include the historical centre of Casoria. However, the actions to be carried out in the fringe are structurally linked also to the achievement of this objective, as they favour the feasibility of actions planned for the future in dense urban areas.

08. Ecological and public reconnection on a regional scale

The scale of the challenges that Casoria have to face requires the involvement of the other municipalities of the district. The reconnection with different urban centres of the region, the establishment of a system of resources, as well as the coordination of some basic services, is as necessary as urgent. Although a real integration will take long time, it is possible to start to formulate some initial reconnection actions in the medium-short term, with particular reference to new public connections between the centre of Casoria and the new hub of the High-Speed Train Station of Naples-Afragola, which connects to Rome in 1 hour.

KEY ACTIONS

The following are the main actions (key actions) that can now be identified at the municipal scale, for the pursuit of the listed objectives. However, further actions, even of significant impact, may emerge in the near future, in relation to events and opportunities that are not entirely predictable today. Likewise, some of the actions listed below - in particular those that envisage medium to long implementation times - can be better clarified and partly modified as a result of the actual implementation conditions in which they will be deployed.

A0. Approval of the Structural Plan

The approval of the Plan would make it possible to have a flexible regulation tool within basic rules and procedures that are certain, transparent and valid for everyone. This is a preparatory action to all the others - therefore called "0" - since the Action Plan is strongly consistent with the provisions of the Structural Plan. The Structural Plan will be accompanied by the first operational plan of the "Big Park" to which all the specific actions envisaged in the Action Plan will be integrated.

Time: Action projected in the short time. The Plan was adopted in 2013 and 2015 by the City Council. The new administration is assessing the need to make some changes to the planning instrument before proceeding to its final approval.

Link with objectives: all objectives can be achieved more easily by having the plan fully in force.

Nature of the financing: the adjustment of the Plan requires modest economic resources, for the updating of the cognitive data and the eventual modification of the graphics, on the municipal budget.

A1. Realization of Michelangelo Park

The area - a former disused military site - has an extension of about three hectares and is located close to the Road of Americans.

In 2015, it presented itself as an example of a "third landscape", since the vegetation grew spontaneously for some years, on a vacant and not waterproofed land where there is only a small building where radar equipment was located. The "public conquest" of the site took place with a social gardening event, during the Transnational Meeting in November 2016.

Before this event, a large phase of participatory urban planning has been carried out with the inhabitants and the city associations, in order to establish the functions, methods of use and other issued related to the reuse of the area. The guerrilla gardening, conducted by the Coloco landscape designers, was intended as a proper "collective project", during which the pedestrian routes were traced, and the alignments and essences of the trees to be located on the site were decided; the elements of biodiversity spontaneously raised on the site were recognized to be preserved in the future. Some schools in the neighbourhood have been involved, as well as associations, ordinary citizens and politicians. In addition, all the representatives of the Sub>urban network attended the event, and each city planted a tree in memory of the day of exchange of the new future of the fringe of Casoria.

Subsequently, park cleaning and small movements of the ground were carried out, with funds taken from the municipal budget. Currently, the Via Michelangelo site is used for temporary events. Some infrastructural works are being completed (services and water well) while public facilities have been acquired for free, through a sponsorship invitation (in transparency, as part of the participatory process of the local action group).

In this park, the process of co-management will be also tested. The characteristics of the process have been debated too for some months and could be approved by the City Council for all other public areas not used in the city (action A2).

Time: Action projected in the short time.

Link with the objectives: O1. Increase the amount of natural areas; O2. Increase the amount and quality of space for public use; O3. Creation of new job opportunities; O8. Ecological and public reconnection on a regional scale.

Nature of the financing: The Municipality has allocated 120,000 euros from the municipal budget for the basic adaptation and renovation works, necessary for the public use of the space. The furniture was acquired for free through a form of sponsorship within the participatory process. Even the fence will be redeveloped by private investors who will place advertising panels on the high-traffic road in exchange for the renovation itself.

Note: all participatory planning, co-design and co-construction procedures tested in this first project will be applied to the planned actions that follow.

A2. Regulation of co-management and civic uses

In the participatory laboratory there has been a deep debate on how to regulate the use and management of unused public spaces, to be reconquered for public life, such as public green spaces and social spaces. Furthermore, it was considered that these spaces could offer new job opportunities, linked to the planting of productive woods and crops for the biofuel, the agriculture and the commercialization of local products, the plant nursery, the establishment of innovative start-ups in the fields of environmental sustainability.

The draft regulation provides for the opportunity to "divide in three" the abandoned / underutilized public property: granting part of the area to no-profit associations; leaving a portion of the park open and always accessible; a last portion, could be destined to sustainable production (for example to the localization of a plant nursery or agricultural gardens), asking in exchange the care of the public green spaces, in order to create job opportunities and local economic and sustainable development. The reactivation of this type of areas and buildings would be flanked - entering in synergy with it - by a parallel action of revitalization of marginal areas, mostly unbuilt, of private property. The rules for the social reuse of abandoned or underused private space are instead contained in the Operational Plan for the Big Park (to be approved with the Structural Plan) and provide for the possibility of modest service constructions in exchange for a public use and re-naturalization of the vacant and - sometimes - damaged lots, the increase of permeable surfaces and the planting of already grown trees coming from other sites

Time: Action projected in the short time.

Link with the objectives: O2. Increase the amount and quality of spaces for public use; O3. Creation of new job opportunities.

Nature of financing: no financing is required.

A3. Legitimation of the use of the Boccaccio park

The other abandoned military area, or Boccaccio Park, near the railway station, has been illegally occupied for some years by some political militants who have cleaned up the space and organized social and recreational activities opened to the neighbourhood and the inhabitants of Casoria. The area has the same configuration of Michelangelo park, by size (also about three hectares) and landscape, and it is also a largely vacant area. Two large kerosene tanks for military aircraft, completely buried, define a sort of soft hill, today largely covered with vegetation.

The occupants of the area carry out no-profit social activities and, moreover, the management of the area takes place democratically in assemblies opened to the public. However, this remains a situation of illegality that prevents the Municipality from supplying the park with drinking water or electricity. The squatters participated with a certain constancy and, in turn, URBACT local action group took part in some initiatives they organized.

The municipal administration of Casoria intends to resolve the current state of illegality, within a more comprehensive reasoning on co-management.

Time: Action projected in the short time. An agreement is required to be formalized, in compliance with the rules of co-management that will be valid for all areas in similar physical and legal conditions. Obviously, every decision belongs to the City Council.

Link with the objectives: O1. Increase the amount of natural areas; O2. Increase the amount and quality of spaces for public use; O3. Creation of new job opportunities; O8. Ecological and public reconnection on a regional scale.

Nature of the necessary financing: no funding is required to regulate the current condition of use. Modest funds are required to provide water and electricity supplies. Subsequent upgrading and infrastructure of the site: toilets, irrigation system, green areas and routes - can be financed by municipal funds or by drawing on the ERDF funds managed by the Region Campania.

A4. Public assembly on Rhodiatoce: start of negotiations

Rhodiatoce was one of the first chemical industries established in Casoria in the 50s. Since the beginning of the 80s, the area has been completely unused. The site, whose extension is 16 ha, is located in a strategic position, among the city centre, the railway station, and the southern fringe. For more than twenty years politicians have been debating the future of this area in which, with the previous urban plan, it was not permitted to build new houses or commercial activities. The new Structural Plan provides some basic rules that can be articulated in a flexible way by a transformation project that in turn must be participated and carried out with transparency. The basic rules are: at least half of the lot has to be allocated to public space; realization of mixed uses: residences, tertiary, commercial and services; creation of a social mix, with residences on the free market, mixed with affordable housing and social housing; possible increase of the building index if the restructuring of the area is connected to the decompression of a part of a dense city, or a relocation of buildings incompatible with the restoration of the historical centre. Furthermore, for the formal opening of the negotiations, the Municipality provides certainties on the timing of its definition in exchange for immediate public use of part of the lot, a "passage" in the green.

Time: A public assembly, preliminary to the beginning of the negotiation, can be organized in short time. For the formal start of negotiations, the Structural Plan must be in full force.

Link with objectives: Short time: O2. Increase the amount and quality of spaces for public use; O4. Reopening of brownfields; Average time: O5. Renovate the brownfields; O6. Regenerating dense urban and periurban areas; O7. Promoting the enhancement of the historic centre.

Nature of financing: no public financial commitments is required. The investment for the transformation will be entirely supported by the private sector.

A5. Plan for sustainable mobility, education and basic infrastructural adjustments

Today, Casoria is a city where it is very difficult to move by bike or on foot. The causes are so many and not only concern "bad habits". The poor quality of public spaces, both in urban and peri-urban areas, together with the absence of safe and comfortable cycle paths, contribute to encourage travelling by car. In this sense, it seems appropriate to draw up a Sustainable Mobility Plan, an instrument expressly provided for by Italian law, to try and reverse the above described situation. Before impacting with "hard" infrastructures, it is possible, in the short term, to carry out minimal and temporary measures on the most suitable routes, in order to create cycle-pedestrian circuits, introduce "zone 30" and limited traffic areas, promote sustainable mobility through new signage and through education especially for the younger generation.

In this sense, the "focus area" offers itself as a laboratory to test solutions and practice educational activities, to be subsequently transferred to other urban areas. The cycle network must be reconnected to the inter-city routes provided for by the Metropolitan City Plan. In addition, the avenues and paths of sustainable mobility can be characterized, over time, as green penetration axes, with new trees, hedges and - where it is possible - draining pavements.

Time: The approval of the Sustainable Mobility Plan can take place in a short time and starts with the educational activities (to be carried out in schools, in the new Parks, etc.), the reform of road signs, the progressive introduction of traffic restrictions driveway and private parking.

Link with the objectives: O1. Increase of the natural areas; O2. Increase the amount and quality of space for public use; O8. Ecological and public reconnection on a regional scale.

Nature of financing: modest funding are required for the drafting of the Sustainable Mobility Plan, the reform of road signs in the focus area (where to test the measures), the implementation of "light" appearance changes (painting of the road surface, planting of trees and hedges, etc.) and the educational process.

The infrastructural interventions can instead be realized over time, also in relation to additional public funds made available by the Campania Region or other bodies.

A6. Cycle-pedestrian loop

A first infrastructural work, triggering the strategy of reconnection and sustainability previously exposed, envisage the creation of a cycle-pedestrian promenade capable of "passing through" all the main priority regeneration sites to be implemented with the key actions of the local action plan. The route, which is about 7 km long, can be composed of segments that are added over time and progressively improved in comfort, with lighting, cooling, urban furniture, etc., in relation to the development of the A7 solution. In some places, the walk will take place at high altitude, so as to bypass the road arteries and offer unpublished landscapes.

Time: the closure of the loop should be projected over the five-year period (short-medium time). No expropriation of any private area is required, any passage in private areas of shopping centres (parking areas) can be negotiated on a case-by-case basis, in relation to the best accessibility allowed by the sustainable public path.

Link with the objectives: O2. Increased amount and quality of space for public use; O8. Ecological and public reconnection on a regional scale.

Nature of the necessary financing: funding is required for the construction of the new pedestrian cycle infrastructure (walkways, bridges, paths) and for the adaptation of existing roads. The necessary funds, estimated at € 1 million, will be partly charged by the municipal budget and partly included in the Community funds spending program, to be requested from the Campania Region.

A7. Park of the arts

Near the Via Michelangelo Park, it is planned the construction of a park dedicated to art. However, the project will have to be designed with prevalence of public green spaces, and it has to be considered as an integral part of the network of periurban parks designed in the municipal plan. The site where this function is located is particularly significant because it would allow to reconnect the two former military areas of via Michelangelo and via Boccaccio, with the Rhodiatoce and a district of affordable housing, now isolated within the first suburbs of the city. Furthermore, this area is already partly owned by the Municipality.

Time: the construction of the museum centre necessitates a time for the expropriation of part of the areas (while about 10,000 square meters are already public property), in addition to the construction time per se. The scenario of completion of the project is to be projected in the medium-short time (5 years).

Link with the objectives: O1. Increasing the amount of natural and wooded areas; O2. Increased amount and quality of space for public use. O6C. Regenerating pre-existing settlements (with attention to public initiative districts).

Nature of the financing: funding is required for the acquisition of the areas and for the implementation of the interventions. The intervention will be financed with community funds managed by the Campania Region. The cost is estimated at 3.5 million euros.

A8. No. Wall: s_New Openness.
Wide Accessible Local Life: Scenarios.

It is an integrated set of actions focused on an area characterized by public facilities (some of which are abandoned), and which is located between the city center and the fringe, along the link to the new Park of via Michelangelo. Currently, the area is characterized by large, waterproofed surfaces where each public building is enclosed in its own precincts.

The area is located in a district involved in critical socio-economic phenomena and concentration of poverty. Some buildings have been abandoned and then partially sublet to immigrants.

Because of the age of the drainage system there are flooding problems and collapse of buildings risks caused by water infiltration in raining periods.

The proposal was prepared - together with the University of Naples Federico II: Departments of Architecture, Engineering and Hospital University - on the occasion of the first UIA call of 2016, and is already approved by the administration. Overall, the No: Walls campus is a settlement aimed at being self-sufficient in terms of energy and recycling of the water resource. From the functional point of view, the existing public facilities will be joined by receptive structures and facilities for the training and promotion of social economic activities. Currently, some of the buildings included in the regeneration program are being renovated under the 2019 "Universiade" context.

The general purpose of the project is to foster integration of vulnerable social groups, such as the elderly, migrants and refugees, the new poors, by reducing cultural gaps and creating job opportunities, enhancing local resources.

Time: the realization of the program foresees a time of three years. An estimated investment of 3.5 million euros is required, basing on the European funds managed by the Campania Region.

Link with the objectives: O1. Increasing the amount of natural and wooded areas; O2. Increased amount and quality of space for public use. O3. Creation of new job opportunities.

Nature of the financing: funding is requested for the acquisition of the areas and for the realization of the interventions. The intervention will be financed with community funds managed by the Campania Region. The cost is estimated at 3.5 million euros.

A9. Car:men_Casoria Remix: Motion, Energy, Nature.

This is an integrated set of actions centred along the Road of the Americans (SP1) along which there are large "unaddressed" areas, mixed with dense parts, composed of shopping centres and production facilities.

The proposal - prepared together with the University of Naples Federico II and some innovative start-ups in the field of alternative energy sources - was developed during the second UIA call in 2017 and already approved by the administration. It envisages the construction of a systemic innovation, capable of transforming the kinetic energy produced by vehicular traffic flows along the main roads, into electricity, which can be used to support the development and care of a continuous linear forest.

This vision is complementary and not an alternative to that of sustainable mobility because road traffic can be concentrated only along the main infrastructural arteries, favouring instead soft mobility in urban and periurban areas.

The forestation - initially extended on public areas extended for about 15 hectares with a prospect of doubling on private areas during the five years - begins in public areas and subsequently develops in private areas, also thanks to the incentives aimed at the enhancement of surplus of electricity produced by the transformation of vehicular kinematics.

Time: the implementation of the program includes a three-year activation time (public areas) and a "five year" extension to private areas. An estimated investment of 4 million euros is required, available from European funds managed by the Campania Region.

Link with the objectives: O1. Increasing the amount of natural and wooded areas; O2. Increased amount and quality of space for public use. O8. Ecological and public reconnection on a regional scale.

Nature of the financing: funding is requested for the realization of the interventions. The intervention will be financed with community funds managed by the Campania Region.

The cost is estimated at 4.0 million euros.

A10. Agency for the management of Empty Dwellings & Productive Spaces

Many apartments remain vacant because the owners are not willing to entrust them to people with low income. The creation of a municipal agency that "guarantees" rents, and helps to bring together supply and demand, could help regenerate entire residential sectors in crisis. The same strategy is applicable to large disused or underutilized production halls that could host innovative start-ups, thanks to adequate guarantees that could be provided by the Agency.

Time: This is an innovative management experiment in southern Italy, to be built in institutional collaboration. The implementation time may be short but requires political support and increase of administrative staff.

Link with the objectives: O3. Creation of new job opportunities. O6. Regeneration of dense urban and periurban areas; O7. Promotion of the enhancement of the historic centre.

Nature of the financing: funding is required for the Agency's management activities and for providing adequate financial guarantees. The intervention could be tested in the focus area and financed with community funds managed by the Campania Region.

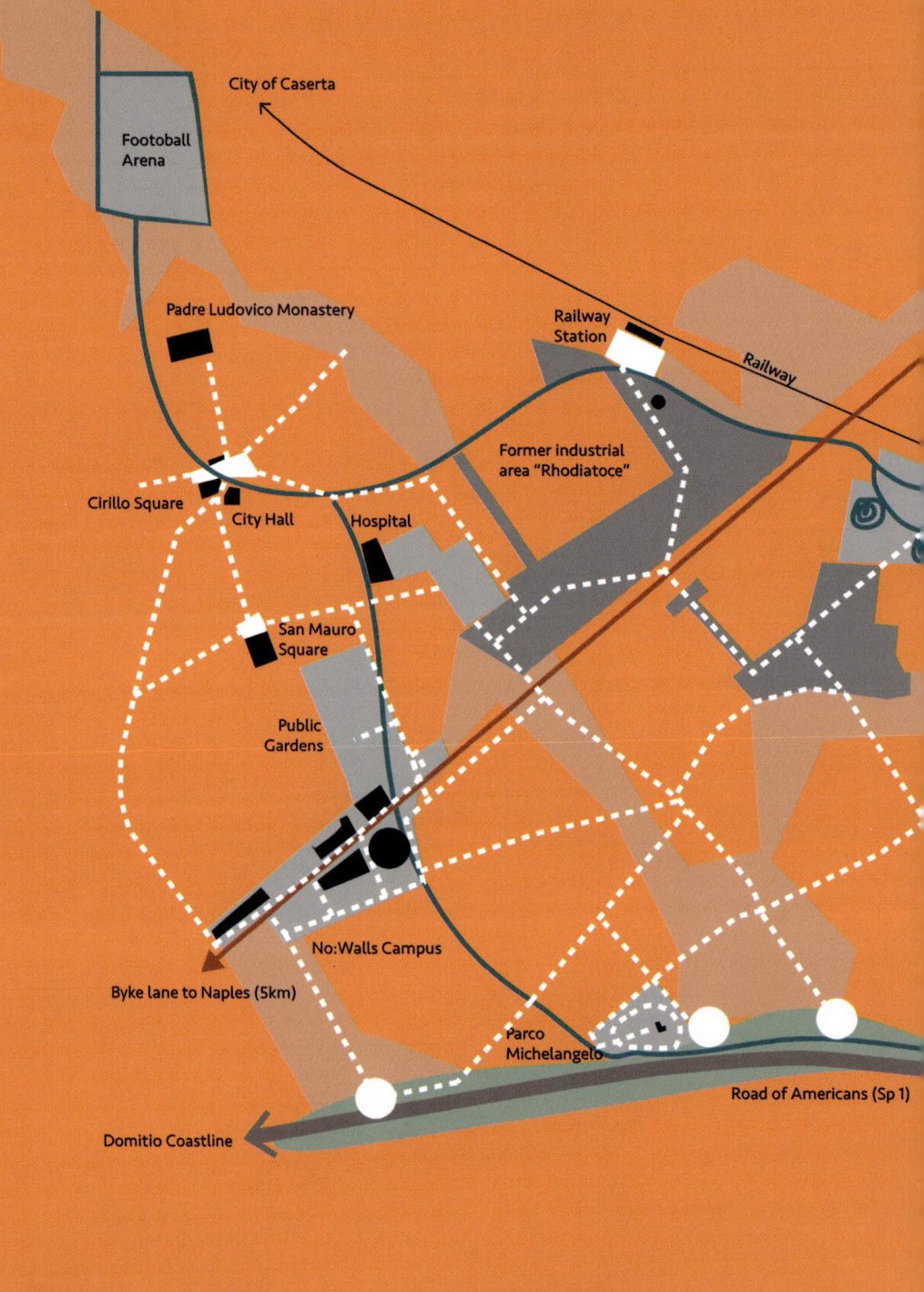

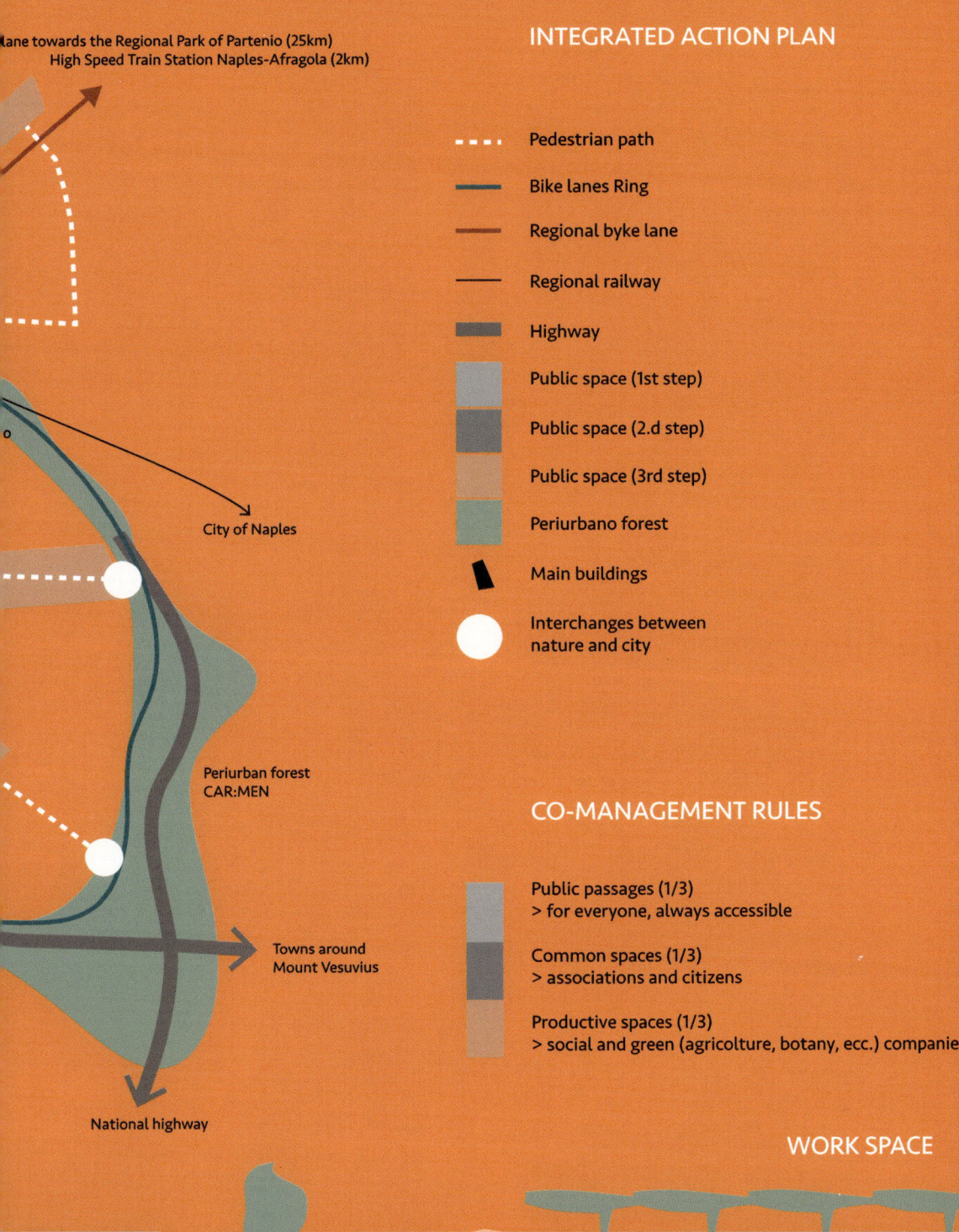

2.3
Principles, methods, new perspectives

THE ACTION PLAN AS A LABORATORY OF INNOVATION

The Integrated Action Plan developed for Sub>urban puts into practice the step-by-step strategy defined by the municipal Structural Plan: its focus area covers about 320 hectares south of the dense urban center, in an area characterized by the coexistence of residential settlements, areas production facilities and equipment, infrastructures for mobility and residual urban voids. Starting from the reactivation of "forgotten" areas - marginal, underused, disused - and their networking through public and ecological corridors, the Action Plan aims to create the conditions for regeneration that are compared with the complexity given by the presence of ownership fragmentation and coexistence of car congestion, settlements underuse and abandonment. A strategic role in this process will be played by the progressive reactivation of the abandoned industrial areas, placed between the most congested city centre and the external periphery. The actions tested in the focus area will be extended to the entire city fringe.

DESIGN OF HYBRID METABOLISMS

The Action Plan promotes feasible regeneration actions in order to promote a radical vision of change, in compliance with the principles of environmental sustainability and social inclusion. The gradual increase in trust between the population and investors, will be the lever for increasing the level of interventions as they can be implemented. The proposed approach is based on the ecology of Ian McHarg (1969), with an innovative focus on the hybrid dimension of the fringe, consisting of an inextricable mix of natural and artificial components. This approach is based on the theories of Landscape Urbanism (Waldheim, 2006) and on the experiments that were conducted between the 60s and the 70s at the University of Pennsylvania, on the impulse of McHarg.

First of all, with an emphasis on a multi-scale and adaptive conception of the urban project that "learns" from the landscape project, weakening the predictive status of the traditional urban blue-print (Corner, 2006). Furthermore, considering the importance that a scientific method and technical skills have in the project, overcoming the mere aesthetic research:

«...the landscape is transformed by layers. It is not the fix anticipation of a project. Each layer is new and transforms the previous one. The first layer entails nothing more than earth movement, ditches, meadows, sapling, stakes mainly, perhaps a road» (Desvigne, 2012, p. 25).

The idea of an urban nature, as a product of the interaction between different types of things and actors, plays a fundamental role in the study of urban metabolisms. In this perspective, there are no longer boundaries between the natural and the artificial world: the metabolic functions include human social life and production but also all types of non-human metabolisms.

The material interaction between these systems drives the real changes in the reality of the settlements.

In chemistry, two main metabolisms are distinguished: catabolic, which breaks down the organic matter into simple cells obtaining energy; anabolic, which uses energy to configure complex cells such as proteins and amino acids. By analogy, in a metabolic conception of urban systems, the different elements and actors (human and non-human, natural and artificial) generate assembly chains with effects on the energy balance: the planning activities thus determine the space-time conditions in which to give body to the reactions aimed at achieving certain strategic objectives, with respect to which to "dose" the use of resources. In Casoria, the strategy aims to create simple catabolic chains capable of producing energy to activate in complex anabolisms, through which the dense and contradictory urban structure can be modified over time. The real events of transformation, even if on modest scales and sizes, are essential for the success of planning activities as long as they are consistent with the general strategy. This is the reason why we start from the simplest actions, such as the introduction of temporary public uses, the massive planting of trees, the reconstruction of pedestrian and cycle paths and ecological corridors.

An important in-depth study is dedicated to environmental sustainability, with attention to the "circularity" of periurban resource flows (water, energy, waste): rainwater, adequately collected and purified, can be used for irrigation of the periurban forest and public parks; wood waste, released into the composting cycle, will produce soil conditioner for agricultural land and energy; additional electricity will be generated by vehicular traffic; the energy produced in this way vwill be used to sustain the life of the forest and encourage its extension, with positive effects on the CO_2 balance.

This green infrastructure, thus fed, is programmed to penetrate urban systems, deconstructing their compact structure through new spaces of ecological and public connection.

"NEW PACT" BETWEEN THE CENTRE AND THE FRINGE

The Action Plan proposes to reciprocally contaminate the different urban parts, with the aim of promoting new forms of integration. A "new pact" between the fringe and the city centre is hoped for, in order to relate the transformations that can be activated in each of these areas, amplifying the scope and implementing a positive effect. In practice, this can mean working on incentives, urban planning and taxes, such as to favour the transfer of dense areas from one neighbourhood to another, densifying the abandoned and dispersed areas and, on the other hand, promoting the infiltration of the public forest within dense and congested urban systems, often unplanned.

LEARN FROM THE CENTRE

With regards to the themes of functional mixity and density, the fringe should learn from the city centre, where urban life is dynamic and active also thanks to the coexistence of residence, services, offices and neighbourhood commercial activities. This mix can be a model for periurban settlements, where the functions are segregated and dispersed. In this perspective, it is not sufficient to intervene on functional hybridization within the built-up areas; on the other hand it seems necessary to regenerate the space between the abandoned or monofunctional urban parts.

LEARN FROM THE FRINGE

Conversely, the city centre could benefit from the "import" of some topological features of the fringe. In particular, a greater porosity could be pursued, obtained through the selective demolition of low quality construction pieces. The urban redevelopment of the residential settlements, characterised by demographic decline and at the same time extremely congested, could constitute a strategic move to restore values within the historic core and improve the quality of relations between the centre and the fringe. The thinning operations, in any case, are intended as the result of negotiation processes, planned over time, without any form of top-down taxation.

ISSUES OF SCALE

The last issue concerns the scale to solve the current critical conditions: this topic has to do with the institutional structure of the Metropolitan City of Naples, characterized by administrative fragmentation (92 municipalities, with an average land area of 1,200 square km). It is clear that the complexity of the problems and future challenges could benefit from a joint public policy. For the single municipalities, the issues are difficult to deal with, both for purely physical reasons (they are common to several administrative units), and because, taken individually, they do not have either the sufficient technical-administrative skills or economic resources necessary to trigger the reversal of current trends.

In this perspective, considering what happens in other European metropolitan areas (for example, in the Agglomération Parisienne), the formation of intermediate administrative units could be stimulated, through the aggregation of contiguous municipalities affected by similar territorial themes.

For example, Casoria could take advantage of the close connection and relation with the new high-speed railway station of the metropolitan city of Naples, which is located in the Municipality of Afragola, just 3 km from the focus area of the Sub>urban project.

CREDITS

The SBS_Lab is composed by:

for the Municipality of Casoria
Salvatore Napolitano: Local Coordinator
Francesca Avitabile: Assistant Local coordinator
Ermelinda Clarino: Assistant Local coordinator
Bianca Senese: Assistant Local coordinator
Pietro Salomone: Assistant Local coordinator
Pasquale Volpe: Assistant Local coordinator

for the Federico II University of Naples (Department of Architecture)
Scientific coordinator: Michelangelo Russo
Project coordinator: Enrico Formato
Assistant Project coordinator: Anna Attademo

Scientific consultants: Francesco Frulio and Francesca Scafuto
The Action Plan is a collective product of the laboratory, as, if not otherwise specified, all the images reproduced in this book. The text published here was written by Enrico Formato.

A special thanks to: Miguel Georgieff and Danilo Capasso of the Atelier Coloco (Paris), for the organization of the "social gardening" event of November 2016; Alessandro Capozzoli for the photographs; Fabrizia Ippolito for the lesson held at the Transnational Meeting in Casoria; Gennaro Alfano, Chiara Menchise, Marika Miano and Michele Moffa for the friendly collaboration and participation.

Special thanks to the Prefect Silvana Riccio, without whom this work would probably not have been possible. Thanks also to Mayor Pasquale Fuccio and Councilor Marianna Riccardi who supported the continuation of the URBACT project activities.

Finally, we thank all the citizens and associations that have actively participated in the process, in particular: Teresa Blasotti and Tommaso Arcella (I'Mobility); Daniele Marino (ArkLabor- Association of Architects), Giusiana Russo and Teresa Scialò (Legambiente); Millipede Cooperative; Filomena Simonelli and Annamaria Casolaro ("Mauro Mitilini" School); Maria Cira Ferrara (A.S.D. Volley Casoria). "Immobiliare Rosy srl" for Michelangelo Park's wooden equipment, "Cosmo spa", which owns the "Globo" brand for the construction of the path in the Park and other redevelopment works, "Centro Garden sas di Vincenzo Maisto" for trees in the Park.

CASORIA, ITALY

2.4.1

Dossiers

Casoria: the new Municipal City Plan

Enrico Formato and Salvatore Napolitano

Until the early eighties Casoria counted many important industries and it was an important production hub. For at least the past two decades the city has been facing the hefty phenomenon of abandonment. At first the industrial areas were dismantled, and then other areas were abandoned: space which was once agricultural, fragmented by infrastructure and today largely unutilised; residential buildings in the dense city that, also due to the decrease in population (4,000 inhabitants in five years), are underutilised and dilapidated; retail spaces, having collapsed over the past five years due to the recession and the competition of more modern shopping centres further from the cities (Vulcano Buono, Campania, La Reggia, etc.).

Under these conditions – contraction and urban crisis, further worsened by a national economic recession – the new municipal city plan[1], designed to face the current trend, was drafted in 2013.

The new plan benefitted from the recent regional urban planning reform, and it proposes a regeneration on different scales and centres on the key factor of 'time', the space between the general instruction and the specific plans.

The plan is new in its content and its form. It is articulated in structural outlines (valid indeterminately), and operational plans which are strategic for the governing administration. This plan is not a map (of interest, of transformations, etc.) but it aims to become an instrument, based on the protection of the territory and the use of resources in a network, to be specified, as needed by the situation, into "actions" (public, private or mixed initiatives) whose context of transformation, with a five-year time limit, allows for verification and flexibility in relation to the socio-economic circumstances, the political orientation, and the real availability of public and private investment.

The flexible and process-oriented imprint of the plan requires a public planning office that is efficient and well-equipped for the challenges and role of a medium sized city such as Casoria. In this sense, it is fundamental to pursue the experimentation launched by the drafting of the plan and carried forward with URBACT: the municipal planning committee, in drafting the 2013 *Puc* (municipal urban plan) defined a new organisational model including the involvement of young

---

1. The pro-capita income of citizens of Casoria is €7,800/y. Unemployment is reported to be around 30% with peaks among youths of 65%. The Urban Plan, drafted on the basis of guidelines issued by the administration through the Resolution of the Council (*delibera di giunta*) n. 32 of 25 March 2013, was first adopted on 19 September 2013 with Council Resolution n. 111. Successively it was adopted in 2016 by the Commissioner nominated by the Prefect, Resolution n. 9 of 28 January.

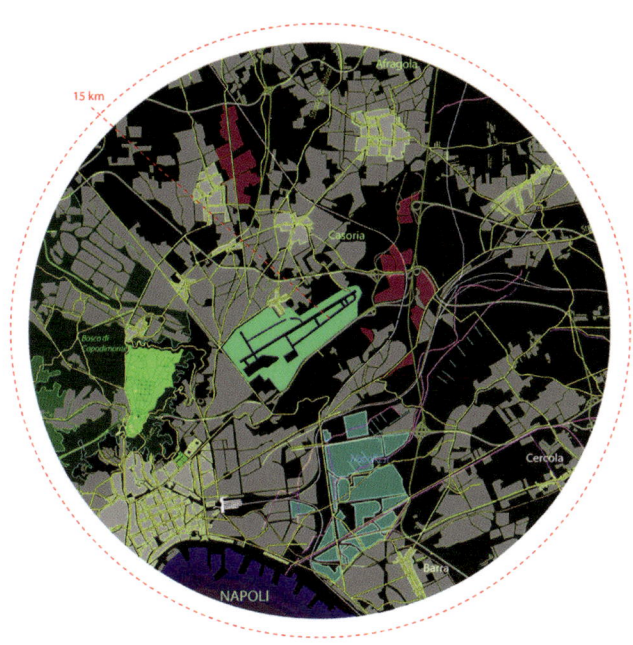

The photographs and images presented in this volume are part of the Municipal Urban Plan (PUC 2013) for the City of Casoria, developed by the Planning Office, coordinated by the supervisor of Planning Salvatore Napolitano and the scientific consultancy of Enrico Formato (Department of Architecture of the University Federico II of Naples) and by Michele Moffa and Paolo Sacco (Suburbia Mode architecture firm).

(above) Layout of the Municipality of Casoria, in the area north of Naples

(below) Brownfield sites in the Municipality of Casoria.

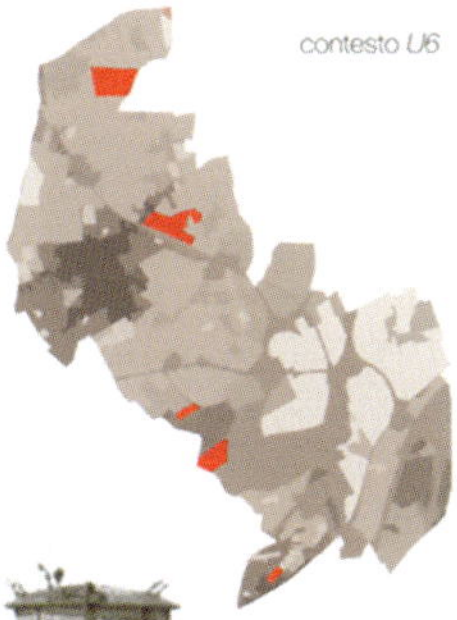

graduates to form a permanent working group along with the municipal staff members of the sector, in close collaboration with researchers and experts from the University of Naples "Federico II" and external professionals.

The urban development proposed by the Plan (structure plan and operations plan) starts off, also symbolically, with founding a large city park (approx. 3 sq. km, a quarter of the municipal area), a wooded area with vegetable garden and isolated public building which will change the imagine and role of Casoria over the next decade, restoring ecological and public continuity (the park is part of the provincial ecological network and will connect new metropolitan lines currently under development: the high-speed Naples Afragola station, the eco-urban Naples-East system, and the park along the Asse Mediano planned by the Province administration).

The first operational move of the Puc 2013 was designing this park, to progressively "infiltrate" into the more compact low quality urban systems. This was a choice that, apart from the obvious symbolic value, and vision (starting from green space and not from buildings, as has been done traditionally), assumes a characteristic of necessity in relation to the need to recuperate spaces for facilities and services which fulfil at least minimum standards, defined in regional and national regulations (currently Casoria only just reached 10% of minimum amenities established by the law if we also consider private facilities[2]). This choice aims to not just stay on paper and for this reason it was modelled to find synergy between private initiatives and public interest: facilities and services can be used by private citizens as long as they respect certain conditions allowing public use (for example: building a swimming pool with controlled prices, cultivating land to use for educational activities etc.)

The network of redeveloped public spaces of the urban fringe has the task, in the short term, of reconnecting the areas of peri-urban green spaces with the historical settlements for which the plan proposes, with a detailed plan (to the scale of each building), a complex operation of urban renovation. The foundation is *integrated conservation*[3]:

The city centre exists as an environment, not as a mere sum of products: it is the historical setting, for example, but not only: the relationship between things and inhabitants – the object of conservation. On the basis of this principle Casoria also presents fabrics to conserve; the alterations, while heavy, were carried out extremely recently compared to the time taken for the historical setting to define itself. Fifty years of atrocious urban and construction operations haven't cancelled out the millenary history which indeed still survives in the sense of belonging on the part of the citizens to their area: Arpino and the centre of Casoria.

Casoria still exists as a municipality and not just as the fringe to the capital city of the province. For this reason, furthermore, conservation – through the recuperation of what has survived and the reconfiguration of intrusions and modern alterations, is a current theme and it assumes a strategic

---

2. The existing equipment and services, compliant to standards issued by Inter-Ministry Resolution n. 1444/1968, are estimated as 290,116 sq. m, approx. 4 sq. m per inhabitant. Particularly lacking are public and green spaces, both per quarter (57,000 sq. m) and on a general level (non-existent). The new urban plan counts, in total, approx. 3 million sq. m of areas for general and neighbourhood services (see. Explanatory Report, Puc2013, p. 187 and following.). On the other hand, the city is profoundly marked by the phenomenon of illegal construction. In total, in occasion of the three building sanction laws, 9,500 applications for amnesty, of which 6,000 are still to be processed (data: centro studi Sorgea, 2016).

3. This concept was defined in the Declaration of Amsterdam approved by the European Council in 1975.

role in carrying out the orders approved by the Regional Territory Plan that includes each single Province's territory plans. For historical settings, therefore, the plan outlines a long term process (not coincidentally included in the structure plan, valid indefinitely), which details, on a morphological basis, the models for restoration and proposes incentives for the upgrade and relocation of modern volumes.

The modern city is provided with models targeted towards the reclaiming of undeveloped land, the regeneration of public networks, improved energy use and a reinforcement of anti-seismic precautions for the buildings. These policies are flexible and articulated in relation to the context and are intended to undergo further planning, to be examined in relation to the knowledge of the details and developed with the participation of the citizens in the choices to be made: transformation interventions on what already exists (not mere maintenance) are more difficult than new construction, they have to be felt positively by the population, based on real financial availability and benefit from a solid social consensus.

The general morphological model is based on the clustering of the shapeless twentieth century city in micro-quarters, interspersed with new green public spaces obtained from the appropriation of existing spaces, and based on a strong reassessment of the system of infrastructure for local mobility, with attention paid to developing the network for sustainable mobility which is practically inexistent today.

For previously industrial brownfield sites (or those which will be become such) the plan outlines a role of "trigger" for more organic urban regeneration, but only after the great park becomes a reality and the pollution levels left by the dismantling and the remediation processes are definitively contained. Conceivably, in areas that present appropriate environmental conditions and through public initiative, residential estates may be introduced, but only on the condition that half the intervention sites be equipped for infrastructure and services, and one third of the potential residences (in a process connected to regeneration operations on other city areas, and especially in the centre), be allocated for social housing.

It is very important to identify temporary uses during the remediation stages (compatible and in synergy with these) in a concrete and short-term approach to bring the citizens closer to the previously inaccessible great barriers which remain in the fabric, especially in the centre, of the city: the temporary and permanent public uses, the definition of remediation processes, the use of brownfield sites as driving forces for the transformation of entire urban sectors.

The organic inclusion of brownfield sites in the process of regeneration of wider urban settings is therefore the main guideline of the plan.

Conservation, recuperation and reuse of existing building stock, the use of open space and its ecological and productive enhancement, describe, lastly, a process of great transformation which is not only that of the perception of the territory. They aim to outline the concrete opportunity for an alternative development of the economy, one which attempts to start from what exists, to the local resources, environmental sustainability, and the desire to marry economic well-being to liveability.

Vision for the regeneration of open spaces in Casoria.

Complete plan of opens spaces in the Municipality of Casoria: Plan of the Park.

2.4.2

Dossiers

NO.WALL:S
New Openness. Wide Accessible Local Life: Scenarios

Anna Attademo and Enrico Formato[1]

Current condition

NO.WALL:S was a collaborative effort by the Municipality of Casoria and the University of Naples Federico.[2] The proposal, presented in the 2016 "Urban Innovative Actions" Call, promoted by the European Commission, was the occasion to experiment with the topic of urban and periurban infrastructure, in a "recycling" perspective. In this sense, the proposal can be interpreted as a demonstration of how and in what way the rules, the methods, and the techniques to transform the landscape are being corrently modified.

---

1. This introduction was written collectively by the authors following extensive discussions, however paragraph 1 was written by Enrico Formato, paragraph 2 by Anna Attademo.

2. The research was conducted and coordinated in 2016 by Anna Attademo, Enrico Formato, Marika Miano and Michelangelo Russo of the Department of Architecture of the Federico II University of Naples, with professors and researchers from the Department of Industrial Engineering and University Hospital (Policlinico) of the Federico II University, with the support of the SBS_Lab (Public Works and Urban Planning Office of the

The project focus on the urban centre and the XX century belt of the Municipality of Casoria. 1) The city centre is inhabited by populations with low-income and poor education, in addition to the growing quotation of migrants. The unemployment rates reach 30%; 2) The environmental quality is very low, with high concentrations of fine particles; elevated soil sealing produces summer heat islands; the buildings are characterized by poor living comfort, lacking in common areas that should be dedicated to activities such as study, sport, lifelong learning; the HVAC systems are responsible for high energy consumption; the housing is inadequate in terms of living quality and energy efficiency standards; 3) the city centre reports the highest level of metabolic disease incidence and this aspect implicates low life expectations 4) the quantity and quality of public spaces is critical and also the equipments (such as schools) are isolated from the public space. In addition to this, the public space itself is experienced by residents as 'foreign space' and often is vandalized.

The proposal-addressed area consists of: the former municipal slaughterhouse; the former detached Naples courthouse; school buildings and their surroundings; the municipal public park; a large set of underutilized public open spaces.

NO.WALL.S project

The project provides the definition of an "eco-sustainable campus for social integration" composed of park areas and cycle-pedestrian greenways, pre-existing buildings now equipped to accommodate support activities for local development, assistance and health education. The purpose of the project is to foster integration of vulnerable social groups, such as the elderly, migrants and refugees, the new poor, by reducing cultural gaps and creating job opportunities, enhancing local resources. The proposal aims to improve the quality of life in the city centre, characterized by traffic congestion, lack of public spaces and green areas and low-quality housing. The proposed solutions are intended to meet the challenges of energy transition by means of: renewable energy sources; energy efficiency; new permeable areas; promotion of walking and cycling tours. The target area is on the edge of the city centre, in the nearby of the train station, and involves abandoned public buildings and areas. This area is next to under-construction public parks in the Urbact III program and to the sports facilities, locations of the Universiade of 2019. This proposal is meant to offer a "pilot project", which could also be considered repeatable in other similar neighbourhoods, both in urban and international context. The innovation concerns not only the participatory planning process, which is widely inclusive, but also the working co-management between the municipality and associations.

Project intended challenges: 1) the inclusion of weak subjects in production activities, reducing unemployment; 2) the implementation of a Health Integrated Program and ICT literacy, focused on the improvement and the adoption of a healthy and active lifestyle, the promotion of the social and multicultural inclusion; 3) the enhancement of the environmental quality through the creation of permeable spaces, buildings retrofit, improvement of living comforts in terms of indoor air quality and its own adequacy, promoting energy efficiency, reducing climate-altering emissions and wastefulness; 4) the creation of collective aggregation places identifying specific activities and specifically customized to target society sectors; 5) the empowerment of local community in the use of public spaces, thanks to the co-management with the associations and the increase of the occupied percentage in social services and in the health sector.

The social policies in Casoria correspond often to social welfare policies. The support measures frequently translate themselves into modest subsidies, which are directly distributed by the municipality. This action does not solve the unemployment problem and, moreover, may favour illegal labour. The public housing programs, promoted and achieved in the 70s and 80s, contrary to other European countries, have produced neighbourhoods with high levels of social segregation, widespread criminality and inadequate housing for recently settled immigrants, or for the elderly and young families with low-income. Even from a sanitary point of view, public structures play their role in assisting "the sick", providing very low level of health education and welfare. The lack of public spaces dedicated to the sport practice and fitness worsens this condition. Very low, in addition, are levels of health care for migrants.

The NO.WALL:S project intends to completely transform the current approach, transforming the welfare device in a collaborative process, using the economic resources to create jobs opportunities: financing associations will multiply the positive effect of public funding through the employment increase in the third sector. Another important element of innovation is linked to the participatory nature of the project and the "public arena" created on the occasion of the URBACT Local Action Plan may constitute a valid basis: both the planning, interventions and implementation phase can take place in a public context, in which potential conflicts between the parties can emerge and be collectively faced and discussed.

(next page) Proposal for 2016 Urban Innovative Actions Call: masterplan and visions. Graphics by Enrico Formato, Flavia Donatella Esposito, Sandra Fico.

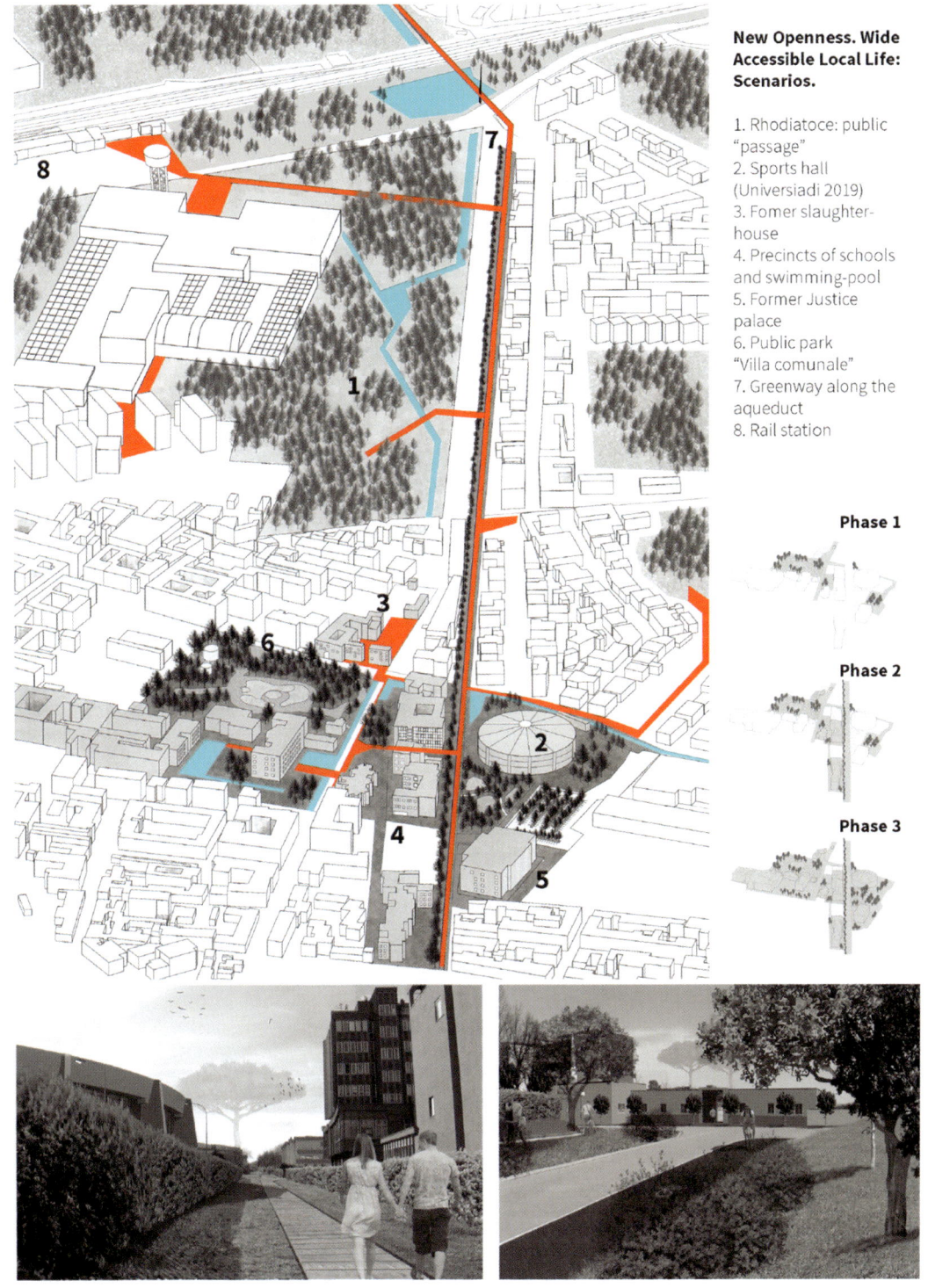

New Openness. Wide Accessible Local Life: Scenarios.

1. Rhodiatoce: public "passage"
2. Sports hall (Universiadi 2019)
3. Fomer slaughter-house
4. Precincts of schools and swimming-pool
5. Former Justice palace
6. Public park "Villa comunale"
7. Greenway along the aqueduct
8. Rail station

Phase 1

Phase 2

Phase 3

2.4.3   Dossiers

Motion, Energy, Nature for rethinking Wastescapes CAR: MEN: Casoria Remix

Libera Amenta, Anna Attademo and Enrico Formato[1]

Current condition

CAR:MEN project is a research developed by the Neapolitan Unit of the Horizon 2020 REPAiR project "Resource Management in Peri-Urban AReas: Going beyond urban metabolism"[2]. The proposal was prepared by the Municipality of Casoria in collaboration with the University of Naples "Federico II" and with some innovative start-ups, operating in the field of environmental sustainability and alternative energy sources[3], and was developed to participate in the 2017 Urban Innovative Actions (UIA) call.

This project aims to repurpose the underused areas along the infrastructure network system of the municipality of Casoria. Specifically, the idea is to envision a systemic Eco-Innovative Solution, in line with the European ambitions related to Eco-Innovations (EC, 2012), for the sustainable regeneration of the Wastescapes, along the Road of the Americans (SP1).

Wastescapes (Amenta, 2015; Amenta and Attademo, 2016) are buildings as well as open spaces, in complex socio-economic and environmental conditions (e.g. abandonment, pollution, and so on). They are mixed with dense built areas, composed of shopping centres and production facilities.

The Road of the Americans, object of this study, is the first highway of the Neapolitan area, traced by Allied Forces in 1944. Today, this is one heavily congested road, characterized by constructions on the edges of the so-called "street-market". These quarters are reached everyday by car, even from close neighbourhoods.

The main idea of this project proposal is to transform the kinetic energy produced by the flows of vehicles, passing through the main road axes, into clean electricity. In particular, through this systemic innovation, the project aims to use the clean energy produced to support the development and the maintenance of an ecological network in the form of a continuous linear forest, replacing the existing Wastescapes.

---

1. This introduction was written collectively by the authors following extensive discussions, however paragraph 1 was written by Enrico Formato, paragraph 2 by Anna Attademo, paragraph 3 by Libera Amenta.

2. The proposal was developed in collaboration between the Municipality of Casoria and the Department of Architecture of the University of Naples. In addition to the authors of this chapter, the group was composed by: Francesca Avitabile, Danilo Capasso, Maria Cristina Majello, Chiara Menchise, Francesca Scafuto, Bruna Vendemmia.

3. Proposal partners: (private companies) Luche Ltd; Underground Power Ltd; Italyeas Energy Environment Sustainable Development; (associations) I'Mobility, Legambiente, Panta Rei.

In Casoria, Wastescapes are specifically abandoned or underused areas, large parking lots, and storage areas for production activities. These marginal spaces ask for new solutions following the principles of a more Circular Economy (Ellen MacArthur Foundation, 2013, 2015; EC, 2014; EEA, 2016), where everything is upcycled, and the loops of resource flows are closed for a better quality of life, in urban and peri-urban areas.

With the actions of this project, Wastescapes are included within a wide territorial recycling vision and in the perspective of a better spatial integration with the surrounding areas. In addition, they can become engines of transformations, capable of affecting positively the metabolic flows of urban systems, towards a circular urban metabolism (Girardet, 2010).

CAR:MEN project

In fact, the project is exploring the new technologies capable of transforming existing traffic roads towards more sustainable networks. To do so, it investigates the possibility to generate electricity, that can be useful for the nourishing system of new urban forests (hydraulic pumps, irrigation systems, etc.). As a consequence, forests that, as we know naturally function as lungs of the planet, are able to absorb the produced CO_2 from cars, transforming it into valuable oxygen necessary for life. This vision is complementary to the implementation of a sustainable mobility network: the traffic roads are concentrated only along the main infrastructural arteries, and the soft mobility is organised in urban and periurban areas.

This solution is made possible by the recent development of technologies capable of transforming the kinetic energy into electrical energy (first prototypes are in Italy since 2016). Considered motor vehicle traffic and pedestrian movements around facilities, we estimate that these devices will be able to produce 2,500,000 kwh/year totally clean energy. The proposal, prepared together with the University of Naples Federico II and with some innovative start-ups operating in the field of alternative energy sources, has been developed to apply to the second Urban Innovative Actions (UIA) call for tenders in 2017. Even if it has not been selected for funding in the UIA program, it has been anyway approved by the local administration of Casoria. In fact, the municipality aims to start realising it in the short term; to do so, this green network can be implemented firstly in public owned areas.

This is, in fact, a step-by-step process, starting from feasible solutions guided by a more ambitious strategy feasible in the long term:

1. today, in the short term, the energy produced by the vehicular motion feeds the water phyto-purification and irrigation systems. Moreover, the clean energy produced can provide charge for electric bikes,

2. water basins to collect the rain-grey-water could irrigate the forest and public parks; the first rain water is recovered from roads, parking lots, air conditioning systems, and can be recycled and purified thanks to electrical and electrolytic systems. After a process of enrichment with natural fertilizers, compost of organic waste (produced in the urbanized areas), this water will nourish the linear woods and the adjacent park areas,

3. a sustainable mobility network is designed for the cycle lane, as a further mitigation tool for the impact of the vehicular traffic. It is a compact forest, with high visual, sound and environmental mitigation value of pre-existing driveways,

4. in the future, with the decreasing of the use of fossil combustion and the prevalence of electric or hydrogen propulsion cars, the cycle kinetic-energy/electric-energy will become completely

circular: in fact, with the clean energy, produced by the kinetic energy of the vehicles, the realization of points for recharging batteries will be possible, with the recovery of potable water which will foster hydrogen-powered vehicles.

The whole green network is crossed by the cycle-pedestrian ring; the ring takes advantage of summer lighting and cooling systems powered by clean electricity.

Afterwards, the forestation subsequently develops in private areas, also thanks to the incentives aimed at the enhancement of surplus of electricity produced by the transformation of vehicular kinematics.

Systemic innovations and Living Lab approach to regenerate Wastescapes

This project proposes an integrated work that leads to the construction of a green-infrastructure with multi-functional values, developing several service functions for the population. The idea is to create more comfortable public spaces, and paths for the sustainable mobility, reducing, in this way, the impact of road networks through the realization of transpiring surfaces: woods, rainwater accumulation with phyto-purification systems of waters leaching, and so forth.

Hence, this project proposal presents innovative contents both as far as the project management is concerned, as well as for the decision-making processes. It develops a "system thinking" approach to the territory and its possible re-uses, both for advanced energy harvesting and for the regeneration of the Wastescapes.

In particular, for the production of clean energy, on the one hand, the proposal requires the experimentation of slowdown of vehicular traffic systems, by employing a technology capable of recovering the kinetic energy produced by the flow of vehicles on the main road axes; on the other hand, it includes the testing of piezoelectric flooring for recovering kinetic energy generated by the passage of persons in correspondence with the access to the station of Casoria-Afragola trains, and other facilities. In a first phase, this solution will be implemented in public buildings (e.g. schools, sport facilities), then also in private buildings, especially shopping malls. Internationally, these technologies have never been used in a systemic key, where environmental and urban regeneration are realised simultaneously, but only in specific cases, according to business logics.

The innovative decision support tool proposed by the project integrates the perspective of urban metabolism with the regular planning processes in the fields of resource management and sustainable development of fringe areas. One of the key challenges is to reinterpret the fringe, highly infrastuctured urban areas, often leading to the emergence of Wastescapes and uncontrolled urbanisation with high waste production, environmental risks, and thus missed opportunities for a more Circular Economy.

In addition, the proposed project promotes the inclusion and empowerment of all stakeholders, and especially of the vulnerable population groups, which are usually excluded from decision-making processes.

Therefore, it can be implemented following a Living Lab approach (Leminen, Westerlund and Nyström, 2012; Innovation Alcotra, 2013; Steen and Bueren, 2017) that considers the continuative participatory process of "co-creation" as based on five phases: Co-exploring, Co-design, Co-Production, Co-decision, Co-Governance, methodologically defined in the REPAiR project. The Living Lab is intended as a physical and virtual environment, including a series of meetings with the involvement of all stakeholders. Moreover, it ensures the installation of a transparent process that involves

Proposal for the 2017 "Urban Innovative Actions" Call: eco-innovative solution for the re-use of kinetic energy. Drawings by REPAiR (Horizon2020-GA 688920) unit of the Department of Architecture of Naples.

Public-Private-People-Partnerships (PPPP) (Innovation Alcotra, 2013, p. 9). Living Labs have also monitoring functions, and they aim to ensure the co-management of certain common goods, such as: resource-water (recovery water), resource-energy, resource-ground, as new soft-connection areas for public use among neighbourhoods, and other different parts of the city. This integration needs to be intended as the mutual synergy between physical actions and "social" interventions, and between technical skills and collective identity.

CASORIA, ITALY

2.4.4   Dossiers

Participation and Empowering. The GOPP Method for the Co-management of Common Property

Francesca Scafuto

> *"Until secrecy, prejudice, bias, misrepresentation, and propaganda as well as sheer ignorance are replaced by inquiry and publicity, we have no way of telling how apt for judgment of social policies the existing intelligence of the masses may be"*
>
> John Dewey, The Public and Its Problems, 1946

Citizen participation for the purpose of the regeneration of neglected areas in the urban context is a method and also a good prospect to pursue in order to endow a project with an efficient and feasible imprint, as well as responding better to the needs, the aspirations and the perceptions of the inhabitants and those who are familiar with it. The space is not seen simply as a physical space to be defined (Gustafson, 2001), but as a perceived symbolic representation. This includes a sense of belonging, safety and roots: a space for the prefiguration of the uses and functions in which the interests and the needs of the community are represented.

The process of participatory planning in the *Sub>Urban. Reinventing the fringe* project for the city of Casoria required an interdisciplinary approach: urban planners worked alongside a community psychologist in the hope of promoting more effective and empowering participation. Results were observed both in terms of citizens' engagement and in their personal and collective interest and growing empowerment in achieving common objectives, as well as in their proposals to be used as a starting point for the regeneration of the area.

Participation and Empowerment

Participating is "taking part" (Cotta,1979): acting in the community one belongs to voluntarily for the benefit of all (Pellizzoni, 2008; De Piccoli, 2005; Mannarini, 2004). The factors which hinder participation are diverse: they vary from the perception of personal cost, to a threatening context with numerous risks for oneself and one's safety, to one's sense of identity and sense of strength and power in collectively affecting change in problematic situations (Scafuto and La Barbera, 2016; Scafuto et al., 2011, 2018).

Empowerment is seen as a process which aims and succeeds in applying pressure and influence on choices for the common interest. This is carried out through the critical awareness of social, political, economic factors of the system which is inhabited, and the action on the part of the citizens in the so-called intermediate structures (associations, committees, informal organisations). Part of empowerment is believing to have some collective influence, and an empowered community realises its power through activism and participation. When the participation is effective it coincides with a process that promotes psychological empowerment (beliefs and faith in being able to change the unfavourable situation), and material empowerment (achievement of desired results and objectives). Within the context of community psychology empowering participation is aimed for both as a method and as an objective.

The specific objective of the co-planning lab conceived by the *Sub>Urban* project was to involve the citizens in direct participation as consultants through a collective elaboration of ideas, aspirations and proposals in reference to the areas to be regenerated, destined for green parks. The long term aim has not yet been achieved – it depends closely on the political and institutional "macro" level. The aim is to reach a higher level of participation than consultation, and implies a sharing in the area of decision-making, a common action and a partnership between institutions and citizens. This could perhaps be expressed in the form of co-management of the areas involved in the regeneration project, considering them, as the participating citizens wish to do, as "common property".

The epistemological paradigm that accompanied the research was action research, wherein knowledge is constructed and is, by nature, very dynamic. It develops and evolves through action, acting on the phenomenon itself that is the object of intended change. In this paradigm, research planning and intervention planning go hand in hand and follow a circular process, requiring constant feedback and eventually producing co-constructed knowledge that essentially has an ecological value and is useful for those who produce it in the living contexts, it is valid for that community in that historical moment. The researcher cannot be neutral, but aware of the values, the principles and the theories, they become an enabler who knows the complexity of the systems, plans strategies and methods, builds relations and facilitates the process of self-awareness on the community.

In the co-planning process, the project called for:
- a phase for planning action that was flexible according to the feedback provided each time by the participants;
  - a phase involving promoting initiatives and listening to the concerns of the citizens;
  - a phase of interactive community consulting where the voluntary participation of the citizens, even single or non-residents, was fundamental. These citizens interacted in an informal setting, characterised by pleasant and spontaneous dialogue, with plenary sessions alternated with smaller group discussions;

(right side page)
(above) Problem Tree (Enrico Formato).
(below) Proposals from the citizens for the Via Michelangelo public Park in Casoria (Alessandro Capozzoli).

- a phase of *outreaching*, in which even the citizens who were harder to engage in the discussions were involved in town walking and biking in the areas surrounding the parks. These meetings were organised more directly by local associations, and served as a reconnaissance tour of the abandoned areas to be reused, as well as to increase the numbers of participants with whom to spread information about the project;

- a phase of discussion, monitoring and assessment of the results, viewed as outcomes, achieved or not yet achieved.

The specific themes of the citizens' meetings, which were facilitated by the author in the role of community psychologist, were the following:

1) planning: starting from the identified problems and objectives;
2) use and usability of the parks: equipment, activities and sustainability;
3) the parks in the city: accessibility and infrastructures;
4) public parks as "common property": models of allocation and community co-management.

The fourth themes led to a phase of assessment of the results regarding the discussion with the "informal" experts (who had experience in managing parks and in some cases came from neighbouring territories), members of associations, local experts and administrators for the guidelines for the regulations for parks as common property. The methodology utilised for co-planning was Goal Oriented Project Planning (GOPP, the model outlined in PCM - Project Cycle Management). This dictates planning that starts from objectives and not actions, in a structured method and in the presence of facilitation in which the participants are actually the stakeholders and beneficiaries of the project in question.

The group was led through the logic of the planning with the help of various especially designed or adapted instruments provided by the author (like planning forms, essential questions during meetings, world cafes, charters of common property). Some instruments required physical movement and space and were adapted from social theatre (Boal, 2005).

The project brought about results as far as output is concerned, namely data produced by the citizens, and in terms of outcomes, namely for the beneficiaries of the project, the citizens and the stakeholders who had participated.

The first noteworthy output is the fruit of the elaboration and so-called problem tree (see side image): starting from the examination of a specific problem, the associated problems were identified and then put in order on the tree, according to a linear cause-effect principle. The specific problem examined, around which the project intended to centre, was the following: "the citizens of the city of Casoria participate sparingly in the care of common property in their city".

The citizens were facilitated in the formulation of problems starting from their knowledge of the territory, and encouraged not to confuse "current negative situations" with "missing solutions". The diagram in the right side page illustrates the problems reported by the citizens in relation to the central issue: on the top are the effects, and below as one moves towards the roots of the tree, are the causes from which the problems first originated.

This logical-rational segmentation perspective allows for a more pragmatic approach to the issues and protects from the sense of impotence that derives from facing enormous problems outside one's control. The use of the problem tree led to the collective elaboration of objectives viewed as possible transformation of the "current negative situation" into a more desirable "positive future situation".

In short, the specific objective of the co-planning lab was thus "making the citizens of Casoria more active in the care of common property, in particular the green spaces that will be future parks" and the final aim became "regenerating and adding value to the residual green spaces as common property/spaces, starting from the ex-military areas in Via Boccaccio and Via Michelangelo". Using this as a starting point, the other problems were also transformed, according to their level in the process, into mid or long-term objectives or results to be achieved.

Community consulting continued with the elaboration of proposals for the use and usability of parks by brainstorming in relation to the priorities on the tree illustrating objectives, to be used as a stimulus for further research and review in following meetings. In this way, the elaboration became process-oriented and the citizens had control over what they produced: individual and small-group proposals were sifted through collectively, in a further meeting, to examine the feasibility and critical aspects of controversial points.

Among the interesting outcomes we find:

- "minimum equipment", to be produced, even made by hand, by the citizens themselves, in order to accelerate the immediate public use of the areas recognised as currently having intrinsic natural value;

-accessibility in terms of ease of access, with the use of pathways and public transport as an alternative to car use (bike sharing, shuttle services). The citizens requested spaces reserved for cycling paths with the planting of rows of trees;

-the overriding of barriers, with free access to green spaces, possibly free from material fences or providing a surveillance service for the prevention of the defacement of property, in a logic of protection, but also openness.

The Regulation of Common Property, therefore, will require a commitment on the part of the citizen regarding: surveillance, maintenance and monitoring. These actions are considered as support to cultural, didactic and social actions that citizens could put into act. The administration, on its part, must make a financial commitment as well as deal with accessibility (e.g. upgrading public transport towards the park areas), security, and communication of the initiatives being carried out by the citizens' groups and associations).

To illustrate the results in terms of outcomes, namely the benefits (skills acquired by the participants, and the impact of the project on various levels of the context), an ecological perspective was adopted (Peirson et al., 2011). This framed the system in the various subsystems it was made up of; individual, group, community, institutional and political.

On the first level, feelings of pleasure and hope in the ability to improve the socio-political situations which impede public access to the care of common property were reported.

On the group level, participation was embodied in the presence of a rather stable number of citizens, varying from a minimum of 20 to a maximum of 60, who built a favourable collaborative and interactive environment.

On the community level some descriptors of empowerment can be considered: the self-organisation of several organisations regarding participatory events like cycling groups, gardening and primary school open air educational activities. Another descriptor that illustrated the interiorisation of the benefits in the participants is the diffusion of an instrument, similar to one adopted over the time of the meetings, designed to explore the citizens' viewpoints about other urban issues. This indicator reveals the beginning of a fundamental step in the process of participatory action research, that is the transition from citizens as objects of research to the same citizens participating as co-researchers, asking themselves about their community and widening their perspectives.

On the political level, the citizens' ideas were reported in the Local Action Plan, currently under approval by municipal administration.

The participatory process described here represents a "pilot study" which has been established in local territory for the first time and is innovative on a national level. The methodologies developed obtained active engagement which was far from formal as is usually seen in many processes that call themselves participatory. As far as the research objective, namely to explore the problems and proposals of the citizens regarding potential green areas, and the possible co-management of the parks are concerned, the project achieved its objective and also revealed interesting, controversial and creative ideas provided by the engaged citizens. These are reported briefly in this volume.

The limit of this research was that it did not involve a large number of citizens and above all those living near the parks.

As far as the research objective and an intervention is concerned, namely the idea of promoting empowering participation, the project mostly achieved individual and group empowerment, and had little impact on the level of community empowerment (Labonte and Laverack, 2008). Significant limits were also reported if we classify empowerment in reference to the criteria mentioned above, namely formal, psychological, instrumental and substantial empowerment. The latter two forms are still lacking and as far as this is concerned participation is still at a consultation stage: the uncertainty of political conditions of support has particularly affected the unclear definition of a timeframe for planning and co-management.

In the future the data collected and the guidelines drafted by the citizens will prove useful in guiding administrators and experts in the creation of specific projects. The group that participated in the meetings could, in this sense, acts as gatekeepers for an involvement of more than just the stakeholders.

The promotion of the project would therefore overcome time limits dedicated to the promotion on a local level, this being perhaps one of the factors which did not allow us to reach a larger number of participants.

Another important limit to overcome is that regarding conflict management. In a culture oriented towards mediation and cooperation, divergences are neither avoided nor escalated; they lead to constructive debate and generate new possibilities for new interpretations and solutions to problems. It is essential for future planning to think about experiential development, destined for the competent leadership of institutional, organisational and informal groups, that knows how to value lateral and divergent thinking and that is educated in conflict resolution management, non-violent communication strategies and skilled in sustainability-oriented decisions. Actually, often irreconcilable positions, when one works on communication and the clarification of each party's needs and interests, underneath these positions interests emerge that can be compatible and the solutions reached may be win-win-win ones, meaning both sides win and so do nature and future generations.

This project contributed, albeit minimally, in showing that it is possible to find an alternative to consolidated decisional models, vertical hierarchy, self-reference, institutions and groups, and the prevalence of technique-based planning. Listening to citizens is not only a possible but effective instrument for results to be achieved, as long as it is regulated by a method and by specific skills of facilitation and action research, which can be provided by community psychologists.

When participation works, not only does it produce useful data for decision makers, but it also establishes a wholeness in communication by working on different levels (cognitive, emotional and body) through a playful and pleasant setting. It activates networks of relations that form so-called social capital, the driving force for well-being and happiness.

Citizens become active organisers of knowledge, carrying forward the logic of the research, themselves learning and formulating open and stimulating questions for a wider and more complex consideration of problems, benefiting for the diversity of voices, viewpoints, diverging and minority ideas, far from a distorted logic of dichotomy and in most cases, polarised extreme positions.

Transnational Meeting of Sub>urban. Reinventing the fringe network in Casoria. Workshop in the Museum of Contemporary Art, Casoria. (Alessandro Capozzoli)

The highest ambition of the author is to know that even when the expert has gone away the community can find within itself the resources to change by activating democratic steps, integrating cooperative and problem-solving skills; that it can definitively perceive itself as cohesive in its common interests, with fewer uncertainties and more questions, towards the Liberation of all that constitutes Oppression (Nelson, Prillenltesky, 2010).

2.4.5

Dossiers

Asse Mediano Stories. Living in an infrastructured wasteland

Fabrizia Ippolito

A selection of studies on the metropolitan area of Naples carried out in recent years is the starting point for a reflection on the 'infrastructured' wasteland of the plains of the Campania region. This investigates the ways of living in this territory and its many stories[1]. The field of investigation is the plain located between Naples and Caserta, between inland and the sea. This area is home to many infrastructural elements and waste deposits; where, above all, the condition of dumping waste seems to have affected the entire urban landscape, spoilt and wasting away[2]. starting from infrastructure. The hypothesis is that to understand a landscape like this, elusive to any consolidated interpretation, gathering stories and attempting to find ways in which to tell them may be of help.

If the infrastructural elements are the main origin of urbanisation of this landscape and the main residue of its neglect, then roads could be the main viewpoint from which to view it and collect its stories; and if the waste is concentrated particularly along these, then waste could become the key for interpretation of this whole landscape, which has been removed from urban conscience and that the stories can help to reveal.

An introduction must first be made to the naming of the landscape when referring to this lost urban territory. It refers to a concept, now shared[3], of a lived in, anthropised and predominantly urban landscape: not a painting, nor a green field, but the result of the relation between the features of the territory and its populations' ways of living. An ordinary landscape, like that depicted in photo-

---

1. The research referred to in this text is found in the volume by F. Ippolito (2012), *Tattiche, Genova: Il melangolo.*

2. The term is used in reference to the title *"Wasting Away"* by Kevin Lynch. (Lynch, 1990).

3. For signs of sharing described in the European Landscape Convention, 2000.

graphic campaigns of the last decades that around here[4] reveal temporary structures that become permanent; signs, buildings and commercial spaces that change owners and use; permanent or non-permanent residential enclaves that house foreigners, from the U.S. soldiers to Africa immigrants; abandoned factories, uncompleted or requisitioned buildings that remain unused. It is an anti-city, like that described in recent urban studies[5]. Here it is mostly made up of homes built in the countryside, by the sea, near the roads, under the overpass, as long as nature and orography allow it: they are constructions available for any use, strongholds of criminal powers, shelter for seasonal or refugee inhabitants. The road – the overpass – is, in turn, a shelter for populations and shacks, and other shelters are the natural caves and quarries, in a context where nature and urbanisation get confused, or else, like the silhouette of the Vesuvius identifies this generic city as a particular place, so emerges this place[6].

The second premise involves the definition of discarded infrastructured landscape[7] and the logical thought processes, evident or concealed, that preside over this condition. The Regional and Provincial administration regulations supplied this territory, rather than with a vision of a city, with the infrastructural elements to make a city work, while, what Legambiente describes as a criminal urban plan, supplied the territory with urban waste. Here we can find major works– like highways, freeways and main roads connecting provinces - and major projects - like the U.S. bases, a port and an airport - that can be listed like in a catalogue, reporting size and cost: from The NATO Base in Lago Patria covering 333,000 sq. m. to the Gricignano Base (250,000 sq. m.); from the port of Village Coppola which cost €16,000,000 to the €1.1 billion for the Grazzanise airport.

This is where one can see all the visible elements of the waste cycle – like rubbish dumps, incinerators and storage facilities. One can also trace the dynamics of clandestine waste disposal like in an investigation: common places in urban landscapes become significant in the story of illegal waste disposal. One such place is the La Lanterna restaurant on the "Strada degli Americani", where, in 1989, there was a meeting between politicians, entrepreneurs and criminals in which the scheme was put into place.

Another is the Asse Mediano, that since opening in the eighties, has been the main transport route, with its Selex bridge, and which was the location for serious fires at an intersection of Via Domitiana in the Lago Patria area, and where in 1991 a spillage incident revealed illegal trafficking. These aspects of the landscape confirm the investigation, from quarries to artificial lakes used as dumping grounds, to open air tips, to widespread fires[8].

Telling these stories may be a way to bring to light a city which otherwise would be invisible, by overcoming central observation to view it laterally, from inside, discovering elements, materials and dynamics in its everyday transformation. The hypothesis is that the city, particularly in a complex place like this, changes day by day in an adaptive and tactical process which can be useful to learn about in order to intercept reality by practising tactical urban planning and adopting a tactical approach to the project. The tactics are not ascribable to a system or to fixed rules, but they can

4. This refers to photographic campaigns of the mid-nineties, with Datar's photographic mission and *Viaggio in Italia* led by Luigi Ghirri, shooting European urban landscapes.

For a more recent contribution and for the images in question, see the study by Francesco Jodice, (Jodice, 2004).
5. Boeri, 2011.

6. For the relationship between general nature and local identity see Ippolito, 2002.
7. Ippolito, 2014.
8. Ippolito, 2012b.

be studied through examples, more than through models and interpretative protocols, building a collection of samples in which the approach to the study varies depending on the sample.

A study of the infrastructured wasteland in the metropolitan area of Naples can start from these premises to take samples from the variations that the tactically built city assumes around this area. Here the tactical city is generic, individualistic, obscure, discarded or dissolving; it can be traced along the "Strada degli Americani", from inland to the coast, or in the residential areas of Varcaturo, to the highway exit towards the sea, or in the anti-city between Naples and Caserta, all traversed by these roads, or along the Asse Mediano with its concentration of rubbish, or on the *domitio* coastal road along Via Domitiana: it can be told by composing catalogues, playing a game, carrying out an investigation, digging archaeological sites and collecting the artefacts.

A brief mention of individual studies may be useful to illustrate the collection of samples, bringing to light the relation that, case by case, is established between the object and the ways of telling the story.

One can describe the city of tactics as a generic city along the *Strada degli Americani* which offers a succession of landscapes: related to beach going, commerce, production, dwellings and immigration, by composing catalogues of its materials and matching photographs and travel notes. These catalogues, which refer to other catalogues of ugly ordinary architecture, starting from those of Las Vegas in the 70s, and through the shared eye of the photographer and the viewer, remind us of other shared travels in banal landscapes, from America to Italy. The generic city displays features and aberrations that reveal its identity and suggest a more obscure side[9].

One can describe the city of tactics as an individualistic city in Varcaturo, at the exit of the highway towards the sea, where day after day a city of houses has grown. One can present this growth as a game, with its players (inhabitants, private entrepreneurs and administrators), its own rules (zoning plans and laws) and its moves (fence off, merge, elevate, close off, cover) and its results (variations of generic buildings in the shape of a house). From this game, which goes back to the theories of daily invention and the significance of tactics compared to strategies, this landscape displays an adaptive tendency in which rules are bypassed by exceptions and are subject to the interests of the private citizens[10].

One can describe the city of tactics as an obscure and illegal city in the anti-city between Naples and Caserta, a *terrain vague* between well-known cities. It can be tested for samples, collected as clues in an investigation: the abandoned complex of Villaggio Coppola Pinetamare, the hidden strongholds in Casal di Principe, the buildings functioning as hotels along the *Strada degli Americani*, the built-up rural area along the Asse Mediano. With this clue-based approach that borrows its paradigm from other fields, one can trace, starting from their visible signs, the invisible dynamics that regulate the transformation and construction of this landscape through the phenomena of abandonment, control, adaptation, appropriation, mostly dominated by illegal powers and interests[11].

9. Ippolito 2002, photography by F. Jodice. For reference to Las Vegas, see Venturi et al., 1972.. For Combined trips to ordinary landscapes see Agee, Evans, 1941; Celati, 1989.
10. See also F. Ippolito, *Tattiche*, independent research, 2003; graphics by F. Lancio, photography P. Maisto. For theories of the invention of everyday life and tactics, de Certeau, 1990.
11. This paragraph refers to F. Ippolito, Antinapoli. *La città oscura*, in C. Gambardella, F. Ippolito, F. Jodice, L. Molinari, V. Trione (ed.), Antinapoli, workshop - Seconda Università di Napoli – and exhibition– Galleria Alfonso Artiaco, Napoli, 2005- 2006. For the roots of an evidential paradigm, Ginzburg 1986.

One can describe the city of tactics as a discarded city, a side effect of the dumping of debris from urban development along the Asse Mediano, where rubbish accumulates with particular intensity. There is waste material, residential spaces, objects and people who go beyond their needs and live outside the established uses and order. One can try to collect them, catalogue and exhibit them as evidence, recognising their value. This operation, which adopts an archaeological approach and draws on urban literature about dissipation, can teach one to recognise waste as material for new visions for projects and the discarded cities and societies as elements of the urban condition, accepting the deterioration as part of life[12].

One can conclude by describing the city of tactics as a dissolving city in the urban settlement of Varcaturo, revisited some years after its growth. Here the city of houses displays its limits and the gap between the demand for construction, dictated by the economic cycle of cement, and the demand for housing, linked to actual needs: depreciated, uncompleted, unused, these houses are the remains of a lost city that did not fulfil the expectations of development or that revealed its fallacy. One can organise these houses in a collection of images organised by theme – uncompleted, temporary, public, requisitioned or confiscated, for sale, for foreigners (rich and poor) – and open to further additions. This collection, calling to mind the insignificant construction seen in many photographs of the late twentieth century, could be a source for material for a remediation project[13].

Going back to the starting point, the *litorale Domitio*, representing an emblematic glance of this discarded landscape, from its many stories and its many ways they can be told, rather than being a no man's land, seems to be every mans' land, offering everyone a second chance[14].

12. See also F. Ippolito (ed.), Scarti, in G. Montesano, V. Trione (ed.), *Napoli Assediata*, exhibition, Istituto Cervantes, Napoli 2007 (Pironti catalogue, Naples 2007); curated and graphics by F. Lancio, photography by P. Maisto, research team C. Alvino, L. Bismuto, A. Cassese, A. Colaps, F. Dell'Aversano, A. Gallo, A. Natalizio, V. Santangelo, C. Senatore, S. Vano, F. Vatieri, C. Vigilante. For an archeological approach, see Calvino, 1980; for urban literature on waste, Lynch, 1990 and Berger, 2006.

13. See also *Dissolvenze. A forma di casa*, architectural planning lab, Faculty of Architecture, Seconda Università di Napoli, 2010-2012, F. Ippolito, V. Santangelo; *Collezione di case*, photography P. Maisto. Among the photographic archives of elements of ordinary buildings see works by Edward Rusha e Berndt e Hilla Becher.

14. This phrase is taken from the documentary *Terre in disordine*. by M. Braucci, S. Laf (ed.), *Terre in disordine. Racconti e immagini della Campania da di oggi*, Minimum Fax, Rome 2009.

Uncompleted/interrupted housing
All along the coastline there are uncompleted houses at different stages of completion, so many that they represent a characteristic of the territory, partially covered shells, building that are completed but lacking finishings. The interruption is usually ascribable to them having been seized, but reasons may be varied. Many shells are covered in plants, bearing witness to the time that has passed since construction work was halted.

1. Shell of the building
2. Shell
3. Partially closed up
4. Partially closed up
5. with outer walls
6. with outer walls

(above) Pages 28, 29 and 30 from "Città generica. Paesaggi ordinari" (Research Fabrizia Ippolito, photography Francesco Jodice).
(below) Pages 79 and 81 by Fabrizia Ippolito, "Antinapoli. Città oscura", in Various Authors, (2006), "Antinapoli" (photography Peppe Maisto)

(above) Pages 43 and 44 from "Città di case" (Research Fabrizia Ippolito, photographs Peppe Maisto).

(below) Pages 123, 125 and 127 Fabrizia Ippolito, "Dissolvenze. A forma di casa" (Research Fabrizia Ippolito; Collezione di case – photography Peppe Maisto)

Confiscated properties
Many buildings have been confiscated – due to illegal construction or in connection to organised crime – while awaiting legal proceedings. In the Giugliano area there are over 900 non-sanctionable buildings, equalling approx. 30,000 rooms, pending demolition. Giugliano and Castelvolturno are the Campania municipalities with the highest number of properties seized from the local organised crime network, respectively 128 (of which 72 without any declared purpose) and 102 (of which 56 without any declared purpose).

1. Villaggio Obelisco, Via Ripuana, Varcaturo
2. Green Domitia Village, Lago Patria, Castelvolturno
3. Parco Allocca, Via Cosenza, località Martinenza, Castelvolturno
4. Detached house, Via Mantova, Castelvolturno
5. Two-Family house, Via Verona, Castelvolturno
6. Detached house, Via Verona, Castelvolturno

Collezione di case
photographs Peppe Maisto
6 series of 6 photos of houses that are temporary/ uncompleted/confiscated/public/ for sale/for foreigners

Houses for foreigners/colonisation
On the two ends of the real estate spectrum are houses rented to Americans from the Lago Patria Base and homes rented to Africans in Castelvolturno. For many years American NATO employees, stationed at Bagnoli, have rented homes in this area. The construction of the new base in the Lago Patria area is bringing new inhabitants. The immigrants come mainly from Nigeria, The Ukraine, and Poland and are mostly concentrated in Castelvolturno. They rent houses, seeing that on the coastal road there are 60,000 empty homes. Rent is about €300/400 a month and this is shared among several inhabitants. School enrolment changes yearly and indicates mobility on the part of the families. Empty homes outnumber inhabited ones, foreigners outnumber Italians: A land without citizens, where the inhabitants increase every year.

1. American Base, Lago Patria
2. Americans' house, Lago Patria
3. Alice's home, Baia Verde, outside
4. Alice's home, Baia Verde, outside
5. Alice's home, Baia Verde, inside

CASORIA, ITALY

2.4.6
The Metropolitan Dimension

Dossiers

Michelangelo Russo

The metropolitan dimension plays a key role in the interpretation of contemporary territory, and it certainly cannot be discovered by the activation of the form of inter-Province government, which, for that matter, only arrived thirty years too late and because of an executive order purely inspired by the rationalisation of expenses.

Five key words will help us reflect on the points, places and strategies, in the prospect of constructing a new metropolitan spatiality, fertile from an innovative vision of contemporaneity. The starting point is that the government of metropolitan-scale urban areas constitutes a privileged perspective with which to interpret the phenomena of today's social and territorial change, the place where the metropolitan scale is the emblematic place in which to unfold a project for the territory seen as a vision of the future, a vision projected in the long term, intrinsically political as well as urbanistic.

1. BOUNDARIES

The issue of boundaries was one of the central themes of the debate at the time of Law. 142 of 1990: the relocation of the perimeter of areas was conceived by political powers as a means of redesigning administrative geography with power and jurisdiction over the territory. Purging the theme of boundaries from this meaning of management of power widens the cultural and planning value that boundaries acquire in metropolitan-scale projects: the definition of new boundaries allows for an interpretation of the territory, its socio-economic and physical-spatial morphology, that is not artificially drawn up on the basis of administrative terms. Drawing a boundary means recognising the development model, but also the relevance of phenomena of settlement (historical and current), the type of landscape and the potentiality of its transformation.

Boundaries, in this conception, have a variable substance and geography; their topography cannot be imposed by a law. They are part of a project which must recognise the identity, values, critical elements and their distribution, their dysfunctions and their potentiality, their networks of visible, and especially hidden relations of the territory. The definition of boundaries cannot be a pre-established fact that is stable and fixed in time: it defines the form of a process centred around the meeting of collective subjects of diverse nature, on the recognition of the coherence and the convergences between interests and demand for change, on the interpretation of the regulator processes, and on the opportunities for development and growth of resources.

It is a mobile process, which by definition is discontinuous and variable, and which must be managed by the project. A boundary – challenging the dogmas of modernity –cannot be identified as the perimeter in zoning, but it must focus on the variability of its geometry on the basis of the construction of one or more visions, viewed as strategies in which to place liveability of the territory and innovation of the process. There are multiple visions made up of stable and variable elements, hard and soft parts, coalitions and projects.

2. THE MULTI-SCALE APPROACH – From Place to System

The multi-scale approach is the interpretative model of the metropolitan territory itself. The variation of focal points with which to describe the urban territory, the iteration on different scales of the same settlement and morphological principles, the need to view places in the identity and systems like networks beyond the local boundaries, all lead to the tightening of the dimensions in which it is possible to recognise the phenomena that pass through and give shape to the territory.

The approach overlays wide-scale visions with material exploration, without hierarchy between the two. It is the dialectic between the scale of the project and the event that a spatial metamorphosis is produced and that, over time, a general vision progressively becomes more defined, losing its adaptive and partly indefinite character that characterises a vision.

This methodology allows us to break down the complexity of the contemporary metropolis, deconstructing it into systems, the jumble and tangles of relations that lie between places societies and natural elements.

In regards to emerging themes in the contemporary metropolis priority is given to reflections on environment sustainability and accessibility: systems related to these themes give rise to a field of noteworthy connections insofar as the two themes present close interrelations and mutual interferences. Ecological networks, fragments of landscape ecology, environmental mosaics: a continual process of assembly of heterogeneous materials, guarantees the future conservation and survival of the ecosystem as structure of the territory, and sheds light on the close integration that is needed to be established in local action and interventions on micro-areas of the territory.

On a different level but following the same logic, we find the system for mobility and infrastructure: infrastructure networks shorten distances, allowing for the redesign of the metropolitan topology, and have a crucial impact on the design of spaces and the centrality of new urban living.

3. CONTEMPORANEITY - The Coexistence of Phenomena of Change

The metropolitan dimension traditionally refers to the city rather than the territory: it works on the principles of contiguity, density, concentration, interconnection, centrality, but it is brought up to today's extensive, fragmented, discontinuous conurbation. The metabolism of the city is often "pathological", it destroys non-renewable resources and it contrasts with the idea of an exchange of flows between the ecological and the urban system that, governed by adaptive strategies of mitigation and virtuous interaction (water cycle, waste disposal cycle, energy production, forms of soft mobility etc.) represents extraordinary potential for the metropolitan territory (Gandy, 2004).

The metabolism of peri-urban areas in particular assumes a metastatic and destructive form. Waste is due to settlement and social phenomena: from the overflow of settlement dispersion in the juxtaposition of agriculture and industrial production, to rampant illegal land consumption, to the settlement models of Regional logistics systems or the illegal or hidden dumping grounds of toxic waste.

The regeneration of these "remains" – ever more ethically urgent as far as environmental sustainability and saving the territory are concerned (Ciorra, Marini, 2011) –and their reintroduction into new life cycles can only occur within the context of a multiscale system that is rooted in the specificity of the context. The dimension which is most pertinent to this planning logic is the metropolitan area: waste and wasteland becomes new public spaces, new land, new resettlement opportunities, new landscapes. A project in this unprecedented space will rationalise the use of resources, utilising its assets and lengthening or inverting the life cycles of territorial materials, this becoming the strategic alternative of contemporaneity.

4 RISKS AND MOBILITY - Providing Infrastructure to the Territory

Risk management and mobility management represent some classic interpretative models of the sector for the knowledge and management of the territory, but they can represent areas of interest for intervention that can have extraordinary effects on shaping the metropolitan city.

Danger becomes a collective issue when associated with density: the risk in urban areas multiplies the extent of factors of danger and exposed value, as is well known. But risk management is more viable in the metropolitan area: namely in a territory that is interpreted as a city, like a metropolitan community (Martinotti, 1999). In Campania, for instance – after years during which this theme has sometimes been misused in terms of the media – the issue of the Vesuvius Risk has been completely removed (Russo, 2004). The metropolitan dimension is the only one that deals with risk in its preventive phase and in the prospect of mitigating its effects.

Similarly, the hydrogeological risk, in terms of water systems, is another subject of equal importance in the urban mechanisms on the metropolitan scale (Pötz, Bleuzé, 2012). Believing to solve this delicate issue, placing bans and regulating any possible action in detail, (even the most minute operations performed by the local Water Authority) is, to say the least, an impracticable operation. Making things worse is the "irreparable" interference of entire legal or illegal agglomerations on the areas that are the most hydro-geologically and seismically vulnerable, that determines risk conditions that require rigorous indications over time to reduce and relocate, on their localisation and possible intervention strategies.

5 NEW GOVERNANCE - Administrating and Governing the Territory.

What is the character of a structural choice? How can a structural choice activate a strategic dimension if it is contextualised within strict territorial boundaries defined by the administrative perimeter of the municipalities?

The selection of an active structure plan in a small municipality is, for example, a paradox. The attribution of competences to various Authorities is uncertain and the principle of subsidiarity is often proven untrue in the actual facts, still deeply rooted in a waterfall planning logic based on interdiction and "negotiation" on the points of balance rather than on efficient co-planning between authorities. Structural choices involve the scale of the networks (of value, of ecological components, of the distribution of functions, of invariants and areas of transformability). The dimension and the context of a structure plan define a territory with homogenous characteristics, in terms of relevant interconnection, as well as of identity: the structure form of the plan makes sense in the metropolitan territory (not just the Provincial), in the agreement between intersectoral institutional actors on the basis of long term value.

The primary task of new metropolitan cities should indeed be that of launching overarching structural instruments capable of providing a convincing vision, to be defined and put into place over time, with patience and foresight. In order for this to occur we need a spatial project and the skills to make it, through a real co-planning process, a shared legacy, the founding "statute" of the developing metropolitan city.

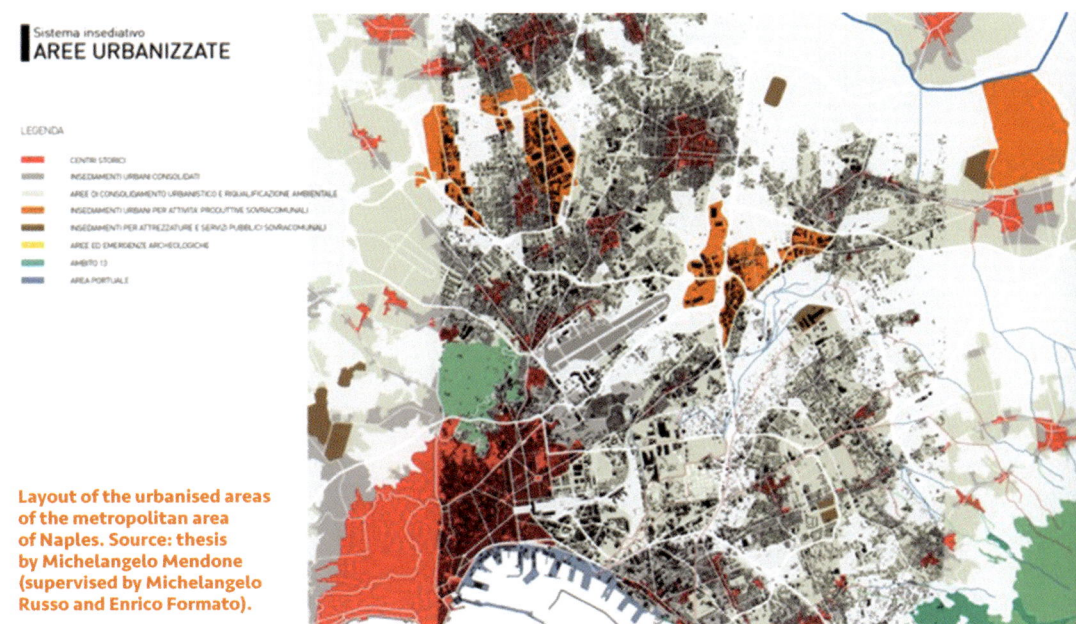

Layout of the urbanised areas of the metropolitan area of Naples. Source: thesis by Michelangelo Mendone (supervised by Michelangelo Russo and Enrico Formato).

2.4.7 Dossiers

SbS_Lab after URBACT. Starting points for innovation in facing the new challenges of the fringe

Francesca Avitabile, Ermelinda Clarino, Pietro Salomone, Bianca Senese, Pasquale Volpe[1]

1. European Cohesion Policies and Place-Based Approach

The main objective of European Cohesion Policies, as established in Art. 174 of the Lisbon Treaty[2] consists in the reduction of the gap between levels of development in the various regions of the Old World, in order to strengthen economic, social and territorial cohesion. In its most recent budget for 2014/2020, the Union allocated a good third of its resources to strengthening territorial cohesion: approximately €350 billion, structured into different operative programmes (PON, POR, etc.) and complementary ones, such as the URBACT project, financed with ERDF funds.

Despite this, in recent years the gap between the more advanced regions and the more backward ones has grown substantially. This is described in the "OECD: Regions and city 2018" report[3], in which the fact that Italy is one of the European countries in which the regional gap is among the most evident is highlighted.

The cohesion strategies have not, therefore, produced the desired effects. Among the causes of this partial failure, as seen elsewhere, is the "blindness" of several EU policies regarding the contexts in question: it was long believed that the policies could be applied independently of territorial differences; this transformed cohesion into a compensatory logic and the objective of overcoming the gaps into a mere distribution of financial resources.

---

1. This chapter was conceived collectively, through discussion that also involved the director Salvatore Napolitano. However, the single paragraphs were written, in order by: Pasquale Volpe, Francesca Avitabile, Ermelinda Clarino, Bianca Senese and Pietro Salomone.
2. *Treaty of Lisbon that amends the Treaty on European Union and the Treaty on the Functioning of the European Union* signed 13 December 2007, which modified the EU Treaty. This entered into force in 2009.
3. See OECD: Regions and city 2018, report assessing disparities within nations and their evolution.

For these reasons, in 2008 the EU Commission pressed for a redrafting of its Cohesion Policy, and it was put into action with the 2013 regulations. From the report on Italy[4] it emerged that it was important to focus on a place-based approach, as *"[...] a long-term strategy aimed at tackling persistent underutilisation of potential and reducing persistent social exclusion in specific places through external interventions and multilevel governance. It promotes the supply of integrated goods and services tailored to contexts, and it triggers institutional changes. In a place-based policy, public interventions rely on local knowledge [...]"* (Barca, 2009).

Local knowledge, multilevel governance, integration of strategies, social inclusion and planning long-term interventions – these are the key elements in an innovative approach, as described by Fabrizio Barca[5], which require, on a European level, the integration of programmes for the investment in the expert human resources.

The City of Casoria, during the three years of participation in *Sub>urban. Reinventing the Fringe*, worked following these principles, transferring them onto the local context: The *SbS_Lab*, which, as is described in detail elsewhere, was actually founded to define renewal strategies, attempting to start from target areas, used to "trigger" future incremental transformations. Attention was paid to how to manage and overcome, on a municipal level, the existing gap between the activation of EU policies, the usual planning procedures (3-year plans, urban plans, economic management plans, welfare plans etc.) and in general the interventions promoted on a local level by governing public authorities. In examining the recent past, this gap produced a lack of cohesion in effects on the territory, especially in metropolitan areas made up of many different municipalities, such as the Naples metropolitan area.

In the light of this, what emerged was the need for a permanent planning lab within the public administration, composed of human resources that, thanks also to the strong roots within the context and the knowledge of the current state of affairs, could deal with long-term planning, in order to provide management that would be organic and integrated with public policies on different levels. The lab intended to assume the role of liaison between public administration and stakeholders, with local associations and active citizens, with a view of pursuing the objectives of participation and social inclusion, in a way that is consistent with a place-based approach.

2. Planning in the Public Administration: research and organisation

The current conditions of the City of Casoria are particularly critical. The difficulties are the reflection of national and regional issues as well as specifically local ones: some indeed depend on the functioning of the Public Administration itself (Tuzi, 2016).

Generally, in Italy the reduction of financial resources available to local administrations, as well as the need to apply methods of distribution of substantial funds and the ability to assess the spending power of the allocated funds, are determining the conditions for a radical transformation in the way the local authorities are working. In the field of planning, especially urban planning, the need to adopt experimental, innovative and diversified approaches based on the context is guiding the change towards ways of programming/ planning /management that need to be both unprecedented and concrete.

4. An Agenda for a Reformed Cohesion Policy, Barca Report 2009.

5. *Cohesion Policy: Three Strategies* report by Fabrizio Barca in EU's Multiannual Financial Framework 2021-2027" (2018)

The URBACT experience in Casoria can thus be positioned in the scope of wider research in modernisation and adaptation to the standards of more advanced European countries as far as organisation and public governance is concerned.

In the case under examination, given the organisational gap and the insufficient human and economic resources available in the administration of Casoria, the gap between the efficiency of other network cities and Casoria was reduced by work that was similar, in many aspects, to that carried out in research workshops in postgraduate studies.

Despite the positive results of the *Sub>urban* experience, one must also recognise the method through which the work was carried out. This was based on the growing intensification of activities within a limited time frame, not fully achieving optimal conditions to put into practice the constant workload, projected over the long term, that territorial transformations of the fringe require.

On the basis of what was learnt in observing the partner cities' ways of working, what needs to be pursued is an attempt to structure the administrative machine in a way that, without bridling the attention on individuals and the passion for research, can be capable of ensuring a consistency in the territorial management process. This is a paradoxical situation: personnel are being reduced in public offices, yet, to be successful in this endeavour, additional highly competent staff should be added.

One final aspect pertains to the relations between the office for public planning and the territory: this relationship cannot be viewed, as is amply supported elsewhere in this volume, as a mere administration of irrelevant formulas by a small group of experts, approved by decision-makers and many representatives. On the contrary, in order to achieve successful urban renewal, it is necessary to actively involve stakeholders and promote and stimulate their interest to encourage them to act, compose and guide the conflicts towards the interests that are compatible with the structural strategic visions.

In this sense, the planning lab must be transformed into a living lab, open to non-experts, capable of fostering the interaction between public and private parties and citizens (Leminen, Westerlund, Nyström, 2012; Russo et al., 2018). In this model, the users' communities are not only seen as object of study or analysis, but rather as promoters for change that, therefore, are "living" in a creative space, in which social planning and concrete solutions for the future are brought to life (Russo et al., 2017).

In this sense the action project for Via Michelangelo Park – the pilot in the Local Action Plan – was carried forward in the knowledge that it represented a tangible manifestation of a replicable, exportable and adaptive methodology of integrated and participatory planning.

In two years, starting from November 2016, utilising financial resources as they became available, the ideas formulated in the co-creation labs were put into action by both impromptu actions of social gardening, and regular procedures like bids for tenders for safety measures and installation of services. The living lab participated in bids for public tenders for the planting of new trees; it found private sponsors for the construction of equipment, it promoted temporary events with associations and educational campaigns in local schools.

The fundamental characteristic of an approach like this lies in asking questions and reviewing one's role and action prospects, taking into consideration all the factors in play, without preconceptions, in the attempt to face the complexities of extensive transformations and to guarantee the conservation and continuous regeneration of the peri-urban environment.

3. Working in stages, integrating different sources of financing

It is becoming ever clearer that the multiple challenges that urban areas must face – economic, environmental, climactic, social and demographic – are closely intertwined. For this reason, efficient urban development can only be achieved through an integrated approach. It is necessary, therefore to marry the measures for physical improvement of the urban environment with measures designed for promotion, education, economic development, social inclusion and environmental protection. The formation of intense collaboration between citizens, civil society, local economy and different levels of administration constitutes the key element in allowing the process to unfold. The ability to put together skills and local know-how is fundamental in identifying shared solutions and in pursuing sustainable results that can fulfil expectations. An approach like this is of the utmost importance in this moment of history, considering the challenges that our cities are called upon to face today – ranging from specific demographic changes to the consequences of economic stagnation in terms of employment opportunities and service provision. The identification of efficient answers to these challenges is decisive for the realisation of the intelligent, sustainable and inclusive society envisioned in the Europe 2020 Strategy.

The URBACT programme, in which the City of Casoria participated, represented an instrument with which the administration put into action strategies and methods for integrated action, both material and immaterial, to achieve a concrete objective: the redevelopment of Michelangelo Park. Immaterial actions as a whole represented the catalyser of social capital, and material actions as a whole constituted all the technical and operational strategies that brought about small but concrete changes.

The main effort that the Public Works department of the public administration had to face was probably finding the funds needed for the regeneration work in the park area. The strategy was to work simultaneously on several fronts: on one hand, using public financing as it became available, proceeding in small but functional interventions; on the other hand, finding private funding through manifestations of interest and affiliations.

The first real action, carried out thanks to resources from the authority's budget (approx. €60,000) allowed us, through bidding for a tender, to install safety measure in the central building in the target area destined as a public park, clear green areas and plant new trees. One manifestation of interest in which private businesses and operators of the sector participated supplied the park with a series of outdoor wooden furnishings like tables and benches, designed by the same municipal technical office. A second call for bids provided the area with hygienic services, new tree plantings and a well for the water supply needed for irrigation. Further works were carried out thanks to an agreement signed by administration and a wholesale supply company to build, on behalf of the public administration, a walking path inside the park, new fencing and more tree planting. Last but not less important was funding obtained through the participation in a tender from Città Metropolitana di Napoli for the planting of a considerable number of trees and their irrigation.

These tangible actions, as a whole, which gave rise to a real process of transformation of the park aimed at its opening, doubtlessly contributed to building up faith in the URBACT programme on the part of the citizens, associations and civil society, who, as the occasion required, were called upon to participate. During the regeneration actions the park was used several times for public and local events with citizens and school children.

4. The Search for Social Capital: A Mosaic of Actions

Participating in URBACT was the lifeblood that gave the *SbS_Lab* the surge and energy needed to take on what can be defined as a true challenge within a challenge. Within a context like that of Casoria, a municipality which covers in general all the northern area of Naples, characterised by strong social disintegration and distrust of the institutions, research and the attempt to regenerate social capital can prove to be the condition necessary to identify strategies and planning directed at efficient transformation and sustainable urban regeneration.

The objective of the Local Action Plan was not only a transformation of places, but the rethinking of instruments for activating mechanisms of participation. The incentivisation of the use of the participatory model and a public-private integrated approach proved, indeed, to be of fundamental importance within an urban regeneration vision that hopes to become not only a physical and functional transformation of the place, but also an element for social and economic revitalisation. The latter can then not only contribute to the activation of the process, but also be a trigger for future planning.

Right from the start, in order to familiarise the Casoria community with the participatory practices that were intended, it was decided to appeal to the curiosity believed to be generable from an event of an international nature. It was significant to coincide the launch of participatory events with the visit of the delegation from Antwerp (Lead Partner) to Casoria, in December 2015, to verify the advancement of the local programme, the organisation of the structure and to visit the spaces of the city that were the most significant for the urban regeneration actions under development.

The strategy chosen proved to be a winner in attracting the preliminary interest of a large number of participants. The participatory planning labs that were organised over the following three years were held with the concrete objective of having the citizens and all the stakeholders actively participate within a programming and planning process designed not only *for* the people but *with* the people, so this could generate a sense of identity and belonging, which would then be the engine for the regeneration hoped for.

Following this, to strengthen and consolidate the sense of connection, practical participation was utilised in the regeneration of the area selected as a pilot scheme, the park in Via Michelangelo; in what we could call "shovel in hand" participation, in a literal sense, like on the occasion of the social gardening event organised during the Transnational Meeting, held in Casoria in November, 2016 (Georgieff, 2018). The local action group was formed and consolidated as a community of persons interested in actively participating in the renewal process, and wanting to feel like they were taking an active role in it.

Another relevant aspect was the discussion launched on the future possibility of co-management and organisation of temporary uses that were experimented. The use of sums from the municipal budget for the realisation of tangible actions, aimed at effective transformation and the opening of the park, definitely proved to be fundamental in increasing trust in public institutions and providing proof of the start of progress.

Among the strategies put into practice with URBACT was the involvement of several local schools. In March 2017 an educational programme for children and teens was launched: *Conosci URBACT e partecipa anche tu!* (Get to Know URBACT and Be a Part of It!). The initiative was aimed at increasing awareness in the younger stakeholders who were active on the local scene, so their contribution could be focused and informed. The youngsters were excited and provided an undeniable contribution of enthusiasm, vitality and freshness to the process of achieving the expected result.

The massive use of multimedia communication served as fuel in keeping attention and interest alive. Social media and multi-platform Instant Messaging represented alternative modes of communication to those traditionally used in public administrations for information and news distribution (websites and public notices), allowing all those interested, who increased exponentially in number, to continuously interact with *SbS_Lab* members, and to participate constantly in all the initiatives that were being held within the programme.

The activities that were launched by the participation in URBACT still continue today and will be put into full practice with the permanent opening of Via Michelangelo Park to the public. Experimenting, therefore, worked as a catalyser of attention and energy, aimed at the expected re-activation of social capital.

5. The Active Search for Financing

Despite not expecting direct funding for public works, the URBACT programme offered a good opportunity for modifying the way in which municipal technical departments are used to planning and implementing their works. Full awareness of the processual nature of urban renewal has effects on the way of planning and realising public works: without giving up on the hopes for more complex transformations, it is possible to deconstruct the works on an open timeline, in order to work more pragmatically over time, using resources as they become available. For those who are appointed to invest public funds this is an important lesson that, ever since the URBACT experience, has changed the way *SbS_Lab* now plans and thinks about interventions outlined in municipal urban plans and drafted in local action plans.

Here is a brief review of the sources of financing utilised and utilisable in the near future:

Municipal Budget Funds and urbanisation costs

During the URBACT programme several financial resources were identified.

The 2017 and 2018 Municipal budgets for the renewal of the Via Michelangelo Park target area, destined for the permanent usability of the ex-military base. Over two years sums totalling €140,000 were allocated, used for the clearing and setting up of green spaces and the reconversion of a service block in the pre-existing entrance post on Via Michelangelo, as well as the construction if an artesian well to provide a sustainable irrigation system, and the planting of an additional number of trees.

The scarceness of resources and the desire to involve private parties triggered a process to obtain further financing. In 2017, the Globo company acquired the ex- Euromercato facility along the Circumvallazione Esterna and started a reconversion process on the site, not far from Michelangelo Park.

Public administration saw the opportunity to be able to use the resources destined for primary urbanisation and compensatory works in the Park area, so, thanks to a specific urbanistic agreement, works at a reduced cost, like the redevelopment of the avenues and the regeneration of the southern edge of the park regeneration, were identified.

Region Administration funds

During its participation in the URBACT programme, Casoria was identified as one of the cities destined to host the sporting events of the 2019 Universiade World University Games. During the various meetings with international sports delegations and with the Regional Agency for the Universiade, three sports facilities - the San Mauro stadium, the sports hall and the public swimming pool -all located in areas bordering on the target area of Via Michelangelo Park, were identified for this purpose.

The financing allocated for the redevelopment of the sport structures totalled €3.5 million, assigned from European and national funds. Apart from the opportunity to redevelop the sports facilities, all the actions financed by the Agency for the Universiade were inserted into a strategy that was being defined by the Local Action Plan. For example, upgrading and improvement in public spaces connecting the sport facilities, the historical centre and Michelangelo Park were planned. These redevelopment projects of public spaces obtained, in a competitive call for bids organised by the Campania Regional Administration, further financing of €5 million. Over the next few months cycling paths, permeable green belts, wide convenient footpaths, diverse and abundant trees will change the face of the city spaces that connect the centre with the outskirts of Casoria. Over the course of 2018, lastly, *SbS_Lab* participated in a call for bids by the Citta Metropolitana di Napoli to provide plans for upgrading the urban green spaces and obtained approximately €400,000 for the realisation of an additional "green infrastructure" within the more compact urban fabric and along the *Strada Sannitica,* one of the main historical routes passing through Casoria and which nowadays is one of the most heavily congested.

SbS_Lab, in collaboration with the Department of Architecture of the University of Naples, participated in the 2016 and 2017 calls organised by the Urban Innovative Actions programme.[6] Although the proposals presented did not obtain the financing requested, the ideas and innovative solutions outlined in those proposals will be able to be put into practice collectively over the next three months, in search, again, of public and private partners interested in investing in the project to make Casoria a better, greener, more sustainable and inclusive city.

---

6. For more information see: http://pianifcazionecasoria.blogspot.com/p/progetto-urbaninnovative-actions.html

Transnational Meeting of Sub>urban Reinventing the fringe (Casoria). Social Gardening in Via Michelangelo Park.
On the right, the Sbs_Lab members (Alessandro Capozzoli).

2.5.1
Interviews
From here to diversity

Interview with Pablo and Miguel Georgieff
by Danilo Capasso

"The real "War on Nature" that intensifies day by day before our very eyes needs an armed response. And this begins, like any military operation, with a reconnaissance mission, defined by the manuals as the process of locating present forces, their position and arrangement, and the nature of the terrain. If we don't have adequate means of information available, any strategy is in vain and we can give up. This conflict is unprecedented in history, because war on the environment from which we are absolutely inseparable and without which we cannot live: is a war against ourselves. It is our conscience, the origin of phenomenal power of creation and destruction that we, the human species, have acquired, it is our only hope for reconciliation. Abetted by our conveniences, laziness, greed and the art of looking away, the conservation of our inviolable standard of living seems to have become our only objective" P. Georgieff

Atelier COLOCO is a studio of French landscape designers founded in 1999. They have always been associated with the "third landscape" theorist Gilles Clèment, with whom they frequently collaborate.

Atelier COLOCO are partisans of nature as a force for renewal and against incipient planetary entropy. They define themselves as "explorers of human diversity" and they don't identify with disciplinary corporate logic, but they operate as a symbiotic structure that invites new skills according to the objectives of the project (www.coloco.org).

Both *practitioners* of public spaces and landscape designers, COLOCO are carriers of eclectic and multi-scale sensitivity that views the ecological challenge with a new spirit, that measures the health of a city based on the biological and cultural diversity it contains.

This is summed with a project dimension that expresses itself through art and performance as a liminal element and the sublimation of contents towards an open air urban project. For these young French landscape designers, the project, therefore, is the evolution of experiences on different dimensional levels: it is constructed in a relational and processual manner, though the collective construction of gardens, shared leisure spaces and rituals of transformation in the residual space, put into practice in a pragmatic way, inscribed into everyday life. We met Pablo and Miguel Georgieffin Palermo during Manifesta 12, while engaged in a project in the Zen Quarter.

Pablo and Miguel, what do you think of the ecological networks in the structure of the urban plan?

PABLO: In my opinion the role of ecological networks is more closely connected to the development of life than to an urban plan that today seems to be a fairly inefficient instrument, so I think it is a question of defence. These days the urban plan is no longer the relevant instrument to promote collective intelligence to make a city. We are, instead, facing a much more urgent problem: the ability to conserve the fertility of the planet, the metropolis, the city-countryside system, and it is in this sense that ecological networks become fundamental, because if we don't conserve a system of habitats for biodiversity, we are endangering the food chain, agriculture and all that is needed for the phenomenon of life itself to continue to be sustainable.

Se we're talking about cities but the problem is on a larger scale...

PABLO: I believe the difference between city and non-city is another theme to defend ourselves against. Today we are in a complex system made up of networks of industrial and housing settlements, governed by infrastructure and industrial production. What remains between these structures is the famous *third landscape*, a space for biological and cultural diversities, a space where the dynamics of nature go on and we take for granted that they will function forever.

Another recurrent theme is that of "crisis of the blueprint" and the relationship between design and action. It seems to me that in COLOCO operations this is an important topic

MIGUEL: Depending on the context, there is always a big difference between the plan designed, imagined or even dreamt of, and its ability to transform itself into reality: it is as if the project wanted to model the space to its convenience. However, in the concept of invitation to work together, it is the interaction between people and spaces that succeeds in allowing visions and projects to emerge. Ours is not only a dynamic vision, but a process of collaboration between the idea the planner has before stepping foot on the terrain, and the experience of interacting directly with it and with the people who live there. The path towards action is, for us, part of the project, actually it is what gives it birth, like a magic surprise born from meeting the inhabitants and inviting them to collaborate.

The *crisis of the blueprint* perhaps depends on how the public administration has made the planning process into an infinite sequence of bureaucratic steps, rather than a direct action on the bodies of spaces. This is clearly visible during operations meeting with public administrators, when generally things end up with a division of roles and skills that complete specific tasks, instead of activating a chain of relations between local actors who could be useful in transforming a determined space. For these reasons, we do all that is possible to invite administrators onto the sites of the project, we have them tread on the ground, we engage them on a human level. The project emerges from this rapport, not before, and not without.

But is any of your work less relations-based, where, despite this vision, there is still the need for a "traditional" method of working?

MIGUEL: It is important to understand that it is not a conflict between one vision and another, but a collaboration of two simultaneous movements: the understanding of reality and the long term vision. This is, perhaps the sense of the blueprint. Or maybe, rather than blueprints being in crisis, it is a crisis of methodologies to adapt to different projects. In any case, we have never put into conflict a classical project against a participatory intervention, for us it is another opportunity for operation. While some conflicts in planning turned out to be easy to solve through negotiation and impromptu creation, there are others that don't necessarily require participation.

PABLO: This crisis is a crisis of field work, it is a crisis on two levels: the level of Public Administration that functions through bureaucratic routes, sequential procedures, closing one thing before passing onto the next. And then there is the teaching level, the professors of architecture, landscape design, urban planning, among those who are the knowledgeable, the experts, unfortunately there are many who have never had direct experience with these practices, but they have to teach them anyway, because students are starting to request it in order to do a job like ours. The problem is they don't know exactly what they're talking about and how can you teach certain practices? We always invite them to participate, to accompany the projects, to come to the site to understand how they work. The issue is to give shape to this experience, but trying to understand these processes starting from literature or documents, without experiencing them, doesn't lead to a sensitive, physical understanding of what is happening, and so one finds oneself theorising about the theory, far from reality. Sensitivity cannot be delegated, and for this reason we prepare different types of documents like the map of public well-being and we construct mobile instruments to explore urban reality.

It is true that we can't expect a politician to spend three weeks in a place to understand how it works, they can surely come for a day and experience the perception of the place, the relationships, the smells, the social dynamics, the movement of the people, the tone of communication between the inhabitants. These are things that are not normally described in project reports. So, it is crucial for not only the citizens to participate, but also the people who make the decisions, who have important roles in public administration and in the development of these projects, to experience this through our mediation.

In your experience, how does the interaction with citizens come about in the definition of structural elements of a project for a public space?

PABLO: These days we are seeing a multiplication of models of interaction with citizens for the realization of small and mid-scale urban projects, and we can definitely say that the participatory model does not completely replace other urban or landscape planning dynamics. With COLOCO, in 2005 we began experimenting with an experimental participatory model. We were in search of freedom of action, but above all we followed our instinct, because we like to make gardens in this way, being physically involved in the construction, in following this path we created ways of doing things. Just like us, now there's an interesting constellation of experiences that are more or less similar, especially on a European scale. Today, after 10-15 years, there is an attempt to make what is actually empirical experience into a method. I think this dynamic is important, in order for these experiments to transform into territorial government policy, for them to enter onto the public operations circuit,

Fig. 1 – *Incontri Del Terzo Luogo* workshop with Gilles Clement, *Asfalto Mon Amour.* Transforming a parking lot into a garden. Knos manufacturers. Photography Danilo Capasso, Lecce 2013

Fig 2 Greening Ciompi Square, workshop with DIDA LAB, University of Florence. Photography Danilo Capasso, Florence 2016

with their own financing and regulations. At the same time, for us it is a challenge to not lose our freedom of action by entering into contact with these systems.

Wouldn't it, on the other hand, be a shame if these experiments, once formalised and regulated within a method, lost their value or their efficacy?

PABLO: This is one of the battles for autonomy, but at the same time there's a need for the power of the public administration to succeed in launching 200 projects on a European scale, perhaps with a good line of financing, with programmes and all the rest, without which everything stays patchy and not coherent. You have to find a line of conduct that elevates these practices to an economically manageable scale and timeline. For this reason, we tend to defend our different positions, for example when I participate in think tanks for the development of the Grand Paris project, I often find myself saying: be careful not to transform all this energy into projects that just have to fill in forms, because you are killing a whole lot of energy that shouldn't be so bridled. At the same time, when you go to places where there is no relationship with the administration, no organisational know how of relations with public institutions, you try, instead, to create this rapport, this connection.

Fig 3 *Incontri Del Terzo Luogo* **workshop with Gilles Clement,** *Asfalto Mon Amour***. Transforming a parking lot into a garden, depaving action. Knos manufacturers. Photography Danilo Capasso, Lecce 2013**

Reference
https://colocoplaces.wixsite.com/italile
https://coloco.org
https://www.paris.fr/vosplaces
http://www.manifattureknos.org
http://m12.manifesta.org/becoming-garen-2018/?lang=

Fig. 4/5 - URBACT III Reinventing the Fringe, URBACT Local Group, Via Michelangelo Park. Photography Danilo Capasso, Casoria 2016.

Fig. 6/7 -Incontri Del Terzo Luogo, Workshop with Gilles Clement, Asfalto Mon Amour. Transformation of a parking lot into a Garden, Manifatture Knos. Photography Danilo Capasso, Lecce 2013.

Fig. 8 – "Jardination", "Vos Places": renovation of seven squares in Paris, Place de La Nation, "Demolition Party". Photography Ana Bloom, Paris 2017.

Fig. 9/10 - "Ital'île" !, "Vos Places": renovation of seven squares in Paris, new uses and construction experiments. Photography Danilo Capasso, Paris 2017.

Fig. 11/12 - Jardin Demain, 24 hour garden construction, Croix d'Argent, Citè Lemasson. Photography Danilo Capasso, Montpellier 2010.

Fig. 13/14 - Incontri Del Terzo Luogo workshop with Gilles Clement, Asfalto Mon Amour. Transformation of a parking lot into a garden, Manifatture Knos, Photograpy Danilo Capasso, Lecce 2014.

Fig. 15/16 - Incontri Del Terzo Luogo workshop with Gilles Clement, Asfalto Mon Amour. Transformation of a parking lot into a garden, Manifatture Knos, Photography Danilo Capasso, Lecce 2015.

CASORIA, ITALY

Fig. 17 - "Jardination", "Vos Places": renovation of seven squares in Paris, Place de La Nation, "Gardening". Photography Ana Bloom, Paris 2017.

Fig. 18/19/20 - Diventare Giardino, Manifesta 12, with the Terzo Luogo School and the Laboratorio ZEN. Photography Lucia Pergolizzi, Palermo 2018.

CASORIA, ITALY

2.5.2
Interview
Eco-Regional perspective

Interview with Michael Neuman
Libera Amenta, Anna Attademo, Enrico Formato, Federica Vingelli

The Metropolitan area of Naples consists of about 100 municipalities, with about 3.5 million inhabitants, in a relatively small territory. The density is very high. In 2015 the former Province of Naples was transformed into the Metropolitan City, without changing its boundaries. However, its functional area (or large urban zone) extends itself beyond this old nineteenth-century border, including part of the Provinces of Caserta and Salerno. Moreover, the subdivision of the municipalities is absolutely inadequate, as today the urbanizations clustered into much wider poles, with no clear separation between the boundaries of the different towns. Each municipality govern its own territory; in addition, the provincial urban plan has never been approved. In recent decades, the introduction of metropolitan and regional infrastructures (highways) and new railways, as well as national and European level ones (High Speed Train and airport reinforcement) have actually changed the scale and complexity of territorial and environmental issues. In order to adequately address current problems, it is our opinion that the level of municipalities and of the current Città Metropolitana is inadequate, because of its lack of multi-scales richness and features.
Based on your experience, how do you think this current condition can be solved?

I think that the existing metropolitan city could use this new form of territorial government as an opportunity to do a legal, institutional, and meaningful new metropolitan plan. Then, it would be possible to implement the plan considering both the new reality, such as the new train station located in the municipality of Afragola, and the continuing realities of the fragmented landscape and wastescapes of the peri-urban area.
This is a big opportunity even if it could lead to an incomplete structure of the territory for the time being. Even while considering that the scale of the metropolitan city could be insufficient, a new plan can be seen as a starting point.

Which could be the way to promote 'clustering' of neighboring municipalities, for example in cases like the municipalities of Acerra and Afragola, that share the high speed railway, in order to solve the planning fragmentation?

Is there an institutional framework of the new Metropolitan City to enable clustering?

No, there isn't.

In this case, the reply should be multisectorial: the Metropolitan City could work through sub-regions or areas, composed by different municipalities, with a neutral mediator entity, like the University. The University has a technological background and its knowledge is generally perceived as neutral, compared to other actors of the private sector with its profit interests, or of the governmental sector with its political interests.
It doesn't matter who starts the process as long as it happens. The University could be a key player in this multisectorial perspective, but the real question is with which municipalities? For example Acerra and Afragola are connected but is this enough? Or do they need more municipalities? Who decides the dimensions of the clusters? What are the criteria? The criteria have to be not too complicated; basic, clear, direct, maybe several but not too many. It also depends on the realities of the territories, including the political reality. For example two municipalities that have agreed to work together with the metropolitan city government and with a university/private consultant: that could be a good nucleus to start and then, if It works, it could be extended to other neighbor municipalities. Clustering has to focus on real municipalities problems, It's not just a planning exercise made up by someone.

From the environmental point of view, Naples is characterised by a peri-urban territory in which the anthropic and natural-rural components are strongly interwoven.
How do you think these features can be enhanced and improved?

The starting point has to be a common understanding based on the analysis of historical trajectories and of future possibilities. This calls for a process.
Typically environmental planning processes focus on environmental goals such as agriculture, ecosystem, and so on. Yett the problems in this periurban area are really specific, complex and deep-rooted. I think that everything that has ecological value has also an economical value, and everything that has an economical value has ecological value. Therefore, the way to 'shake loose' the situation could be to get something to happen, choosing an issue that has immediate economic value, and maybe provide economic incentives to get specific actions. A strategic environmental action could involve something that has a specific economic value, for example in relation to waste. Maybe this is not an innovative idea but typically policies, regulations and laws are used to achieve environmental goals; that is good but not enough. Maybe they could be more effective and immediate if they focus on economical benefit.

Given that many of these areas are abandoned or underused, how could their reuse be promoted?

This is connected to the first question because the Metropolitan City, through the new metropolitan plan, can qualify the land in a way that get a productive use but also a social and ecological use value.

It is related to the discussion on drosscape, flows, reconnections; but it is also a huge challenge for planning and for the new metropolitan plan.

There is a strong architectural and landscape gap between large upper level equipment such as the High Speed Train station of Afragola and the surrounding urban fabric.
How do you see this asymmetry? Do you think that it constitutes an element of weakness or a possibility to be enhanced? How (in both cases)?

Clearly national and regional governments, for whatever reason, made a big investment in the long term future in this part of the metropolitan area and, like any investment, it has risks.
The intention of the investments is raising the value of the surrounding area and to develop it in a urban way. Perhaps it could become urban in 50 or 100 years, a kind of second center of the metropolitan area, but this would call for a good planning and obviously for a connection between infrastructures and public transport networks.
The new metropolitan plan has to provide a future vision of the 'new city' in this general empty area around the station, to take advantage of it. For example Cerda, with his plan, had a vision about five times the size of the old Barcelona and it is still working today. New York City as well had the famous grid plan in 1811. The future vision for the area has not to be strictly a grid, but it could be based on a multimodal transport network to create connections within the area but also to the regional and national networks.
Another important idea is to change the mental image everyone has about the area: it is not just a drosscape, not just a train station, not just peri-urban; peri-urban has a negative sense in my opinion, and it sounds like inferior. On the contrary it may be the nucleus of the second city of the metropolitan area.

The investment is like a bet that could return a lot of money, if there is a plan: the beginning of a plan is the analysis, including an analysis of multimodal transports networks that are well-interconnected. Even if this could seem the most obvious thing to a planner, it is fundamental in order to design efficient cities.
It's not too late for planning this. And better late than never.

Regenerating these territories means to bring innovation in institutional and governance approaches, and giving back a sense of belonging to community and stakeholders.
How do you think that political, financial and institutional structures should be re-designed over time?

I think the question contains the answer, which is the recognition that institutions need to be re-designed. Part of this recognition was made by the national government through the creation of Metropolitan cities, and it is a start, even if Province is probably not adequate for the true new metropolitan reality, and I faced this problem also during a peri-urban planning project that I co-led in Florence last year with Professor Camilla Perrone.
Moreover, in a democracy the different stakeholders have to participate in the long term. It is an ongoing process, and designing this kind of process and managing it takes leadership, authority and resources. A government or an agency can do it, maybe the Region or the Metropolitan City.
It is an opportunity to create a new plan and to continue to re-design the institutions, maybe not the structures right now but the processes of planning, of financing, of land development. Different processes have to change to keep up with the new reality and to be resilient. Designing a resilient process is very hard.

CASORIA, ITALY

When you have problems like criminality, unemployment, low incomes, involving people in planning or environmental topics is not so simple. How to promote the participation of people in collaborative processes?

Everyone has ideas about where they live, but governments spends lots of money for consultants while they could, with the guidance of professionals, design a participative process with the unemployed, poor people, immigrants, representative of different ages, sectors, places; people could become "part-time planners" and even get paid to participate.
In this way the role of private consultants would change and they would become designers and managers of the process.

Are there other projects like this, with people paid to participate?

Why not be the first? It could be an interesting experiment.
I would ask people why they'd participate or not participate, because when we planners don't have all the answers, people could have the answers, in the form of local knowledge and what they need.
People usually participate if there is something really meaningful to them and if they have the time to afford voluntary participation. Without meaning, some people do not have the time or they believe participating is not meaningful.

If the municipality has a lot of publicly owned places, they could also 'exchange' participation with the use of public spaces, to make up economical and socio economic activities.

It could be an idea.
When I don't have answers, I always ask the people.

CASORIA, ITALY

References

- Adams D., Hardman M. (2013) Observing guerrillas in the wild: reinterpreting practices of urban guerrilla gardening. *Urban Studies*, 51 (6), pp. 1–17.
- Agee J., Evans W. (1941) *Let us now praise famous men*. Boston: Houghton Mifflin.
- Amenta L. (2015) *Reverse Land. Wasted Landscapes as a resource to re-cycle contemporary cities*. University of Naples Federico II.
- Amenta L., Attademo A. (2016) Circular Wastescapes. Waste as a resource for periurban landscapes planning. *CRIOS, Critica Degli Ordinamenti Spaziali*, 12, pp. 79–88.
- Arena G. (2006) *Cittadini attivi*. Bari: Laterza.
- Attademo A. (2017) Infrastrutture e rischio idraulico. In: Curci F., Formato E. e Zanfi F. *Territori dell'Abusivismo. Un progetto per uscire dall'Italia dei condoni*. Roma: Donzelli.
- Becattini G. (2015) *La coscienza dei luoghi. Il territorio come soggetto corale*. Roma: Donzelli.
- Belli A. (2013) *Spazio, differenza, ospitalità, La città oltre Henri Lefebvre*, Roma: Donzelli.
- Belli A., Formato E. (2015) Ammaliare e sopire. Spunti sull'influenza dell'urbanistica americana nell'Italia del secondo dopoguerra. *Territorio*, 75, pp. 7-29.
- Basco L., Formato E., Lieto L. (2012) *Americans. Città e territorio ai tempi dell'Impero*. Napoli: Cronopio.
- Beauregard R.A. (2006) *When America became Sub>urban*. Minneapolis, MN: University of Minnesota Press.
- Berger A. (2006) *Drosscape: Wasting Land in Urban America*. New York: Princeton Architectural Press.
- Berger A. (2009) *Systemic Design Can Change the World*. The Netherlands: SUN Publishers.
- Bergevoet T., van Tuijl M. (2016) *The Flexible City Sustainable Solutions for a Europe in Transition*. Rotterdam: nai010.
- Bianchetti C. (2003) *Abitare la città contemporanea*. Milano: FrancoAngeli.
- Bianchetti C. (2014), *Territori della condivisione. Una nuova città*. Macerata: Quodlibet.
- Boal A. (2005). *Il Teatro degli Oppressi*. Molfetta (BA): La Meridiana.
- Boeri S., Lanzani A., Marini E. (1993) *Il territorio che cambia. Ambienti, paesaggi e immagini della regione milanese*. Milano: Abitare Segesta.
- Boeri S. (2011) *L'anticittà*. Roma-Bari: Laterza.
- Calvino I. (1980) *Una pietra sopra. Discorsi di letteratura e società*. Torino: Einaudi.
- Celati G. (1989) *Verso la foce*. Milano: Feltrinelli.
- Chiodelli F. (2009) La cittadinanza secondo Henri Lefebvre: urbana, attiva, a matrice spaziale. *Territorio*, 51, pp. 103-109.
- Ciorra P., Marini S. (2011) *Re-Cycle / Strategie per l'architettura, la città e il pianeta*. Milano: Electa.
- Clèment G. (2004) *Manifeste pour le Tiers paysage*. Paris: Éditions Sujet/Objet.
- Clementi A. (2013) *Paesaggi interrotti*. Roma: Donzelli.
- Corner J. (2006) Terra fluxus. In Waldheim C. *The Landscape Urbanism Reader*, New York: Princeton Architectural Press.
- Cotta M. (1979) Il concetto di partecipazione politica: linee di un inquadramento teorico. *Rivista italiana di scienza politica*. 9 (2), pp. 193-227.
- Cremaschi M. (2008) *Tracce di Quartieri: Il Legame Sociale nella Città che Cambia*. Milano: FrancoAngeli.
- Dardot P., Laval C. (2015) *Del Comune o della rivoluzione nel XXI secolo*. Roma: DeriveApprodi.
- De Certeau M. (1990) *L'invention du quotidien*. Parigi: Gallimard.
- Dehaene, M. e Kristiaan B. (2015) Towards a renewal of urban renewal. In Grafe C. Verhaert I. , *LAB XX : opting for the twentieth-century belt*. Antwerp: City of Antwerp, p. 133.
- De Piccoli, N. (2005). Sulla partecipazione. *Psicologia di Comunità*. 2, pp. 27-36.
- Desvigne M. (2012) The Landscape as Precondition. Lotus International, 150, pp. 20-26.
- Discepolo B. (2012) *Downsizing Napoli. Il declino della città partenopea, cinquant'anni dopo e quarant'anni prima*. Napoli: Edizioni Graffiti.
- Donadieu P. (1998) *Campagnes urbaines*, Arles-Versailles: Actes Sud / E.N.S.P.
- EC (2013) *Social economy and social entrepreneurship*. Social Europe guide, 4.
- EC (2012) *Eco-innovation the key to Europe's future competitiveness*. European Commission, Environment.
- EC (2014) *Towards a circular economy: A zero waste programme for Europe*. European Commission.
- EC (2016) Grant Agreement n. 688920, "REPAiR: REsource Management in Peri-urban AReas: Going Beyond Urban Metabolism".
- EEA (2016) *Circular economy in Europe. Developing the knowledge base*. European Environment Agency.
- Ellen MacArthur Foundation (2013) *Towards the Circular Economy. Economic and business rationale for an accelerated transition*.
- Ellen MacArthur Foundation (2015) *Growth within: a circular economy vision for a competitive europe*.

- Ferguson F. (2014) *Make _ Shift city: renegotiating the urban commons*. Berlin: Jovis.

- Fini G., Pezzoni N. (2011), Il Piano Strutturale di Anversa. Un nuovo linguaggio urbanistico per la città del XXI secolo. Urbanistica, 14, pp.90-98.

- Forman R.T. (1995) *Land Mosaics. The ecology of landscapes and regions*. Cambridge/New York: Cambridge University Press.

- Forman R.T.T. (2008) *Urban Regions. Ecology and Planning Beyond the City*, Cambridge/New York: Cambridge University Press.

- Formato E. (2010) Paesaggi dell'abiezione urbana, in AA.VV., *Abitare il futuro... dopo Copenaghen*. Napoli: Clean.

- Formato E. (2012) *Terre comuni. Il progetto dello spazio aperto nella città contemporanea*. Napoli: Clean.

- Formato E. (2013) Tempo, natura, città. Casoria, Italia. Progettare nuovi metabolismi ibridi. *ECOWEB TOWN*. 8, pp. 1-23.

- Formato E. (2015) Recombinant' hybrid ecologies and landscapes. In Lieto L., Beauregard R., *Planning for a material world*. London - New York: Routledge.

- Formato E. (2016) Differenza. In: Marini S., Corbellini G., *Recycled Theory: Dizionario illustrato*. Macerata: Quodlibet.

- Formato E., Amenta L., Attademo A. (2017) Wastescape e flussi di rifiuti: materiali innovativi del progetto urbanistico. *Urbanistica Informazioni*. 272, pp. 986-993.

- Formato E., Attademo A. (2017) No. Wall: S. Un progetto di rigenerazione, per l'ospitalità e la condivisione. *Territorio*. 82, pp. 129-139.

- Formato E., Napolitano S., Sacco P. (2017) Il piano e il parco. Nuovi metabolismi eco-urbani nella prima corona di Napoli. In Lucchini C. *Pratiche, politiche e progetti per la città dismessa*, pp. 366-398, Politecnico di Torino.

- Gallent N., Bianconi M., Andersson J. (2006) Planning on the edge: England's rural – urban fringe and the spatial-planning agenda. *Environment and Planning B: Planning and Design*. 33 (3), pp. 457–476.

- Geldermans B. et al. (2017) REPAiR D3.1 Introduction to methodology for integrated spatial, material flow and social analyses.

- Geldermans B. et al. (2018) D3.3 Process model for the two pilot cases: Amsterdam, the Netherlands & Naples, Italy, REPAiR.

- Georgieff P. (2018) *Poetica della zappa*, Roma: DeriveApprodi.

- Gandy M. (2002) *Concrete and Clay: Reworking Nature in New York City*. Cambridge: The Mit Press.

- Gandy M. (2004) Rethinking urban metabolism: Water, space and the modern city. *City*, 8 (3), pp. 363-379

- Gasparrini C. (2012) Città da riconoscere e reti eco-paesaggistiche. *Piano progetto città*.

- Gasparrini C. (2015) The Waste Side of Change. Drosscape and Reverse City. *CRIOS*, 8, pp. 63-72.

- Ginzburg C. (1986) *Miti, emblemi e spie*. Torino: Einaudi.

- Girardet H. (2010) *Regenerative Cities*. World Future Council and HafenCity University Hamburg (HCU) Commission on Cities and Climate Change.

- Gustafson P. (2001) Meanings of place: everyday experience and theoretical conceptualizations. *Journal of Environmental Psychology*. 21 (1), pp. 5-16.

- Hall T. (2006) *Urban geography*. Londra-New York: Routledge.

- Harvey D. (2012) *Rebel cities*, trad.it: (2013) *Città ribelli*, Milano: Il Saggiatore.

- Houk M., Koutsomarkou J., Moulin E., Scatamburlo M., Tosics I. (2015) *Sustainable regeneration in urban areas*. Saint Denis: URBACT Press.

- Jackson T. (2011) *Prosperità senza crescita. Economia per il pianeta reale*. Milano: Edizioni Ambiente.

- F. Jodice (2004) *What we want. Landscape as a Projection of People's Desire*. Milano: Skira.

- Keil R. (2003) Urban political ecology, *Urban geography*, 24.

- Kennedy C., Cuddihy J., Engel-Yan J. (2007). The Changing Metabolism of Cities. *Journal Of Industrial Ecology*, 11, pp. 43-59.

- Knox P. (1987) *Urban social geography, An introduction*. Harlow (UK): Longman.

- Innovation Alcotra (2013) *La creazione di Living Lab transfrontalieri*.

- Inti I. (2011) «Che cos'è il riuso temporaneo?». *Territorio*, 56, pp. 18–43.

- Ippolito F. (2002) *Il paesaggio ordinario contemporaneo tra genericità e identità locale*, Università di Napoli Federico II.

- Ippolito F. (2012a) *Tattiche*. Genova: Il melangolo.

- Ippolito F. (2012b) Forme di scarto e abbandono lungo il litorale campano. In A. Lanzani, C. Merlini and F. Zanfi *Urbanistica dopo la crescita. Esplorazioni geografiche e prospettive progettuali*, convegno, Politecnico di Milano.

- Ippolito F. (2014) Dissolvenze. Paesaggi scartati infrastrutturati. In A. Ferlenga, I. Valente *L'architettura del mondo. Infrastrutture, mobilità, nuovi paesaggi*, convegno, Triennale di Milano 2013. Published in C. Cozza, I. Valente (2014) *La freccia del tempo, Ricerche*

· *e progetti di architettura delle infrastrutture*. Milano: Pearson Mondadori.

· Labonte R., Laverack G. (2008) *Health Promotion in Action: from local to global empowerment*. London: Palgrave McMillan.

· Lanzani A., Pasqui G. (2011) *L'Italia al futuro. Città e paesaggi, economie e società*. Milano: FrancoAngeli.

· Latour B. (2018) *Tracciare la rotta. Come orientarsi in politica*, Milano: Raffaello Cortina Editore.

· Leminen S., Westerlund M. & Nyström A.G. (2012) Living Labs as Open-Innovation Networks. Technology Innovation Management Review, 2(9), pp. 6-11.

· Lynch K. (1990) *Wasting Away. An Exploration of Waste: What It Is, How It Happens, Why We Fear It, How To Do It Well*. San Francisco: Sierra Club Books.

· Maddalena P. (2014) *Il territorio bene comune degli italiani. Proprietà collettiva, proprietà privata e interesse pubblico*. Roma: Donzelli.

· Magnaghi A. (2012) *Il territorio come bene comune*. Firenze: University Press.

· Mannarini T. (2004). *Comunità e partecipazione*. Milano: FrancoAngeli.

· Martinotti G. (1999) La dimensione metropolitana. Sviluppo e governo della nuova città. *Il nuovo governo locale*, 3. Milano: FrancoAngeli.

· Mattei U. (2012) *Beni comuni. Un manifesto*. Roma-Bari: Laterza.

· McHarg I. (1969) *Design with nature*. Garden City, N.Y.: Natural History Press.

· Micciarelli G. (2017) *Introduzione all'uso civico e collettivo urbano. La gestione diretta dei beni comuni urbani*. Munus, 1, pp. 135-161.

· Nelson G. Prilleltensky I. (2010) *Community Psychology in pursuit of Liberation and Well-being*. London: Palgrave MacMillan.

· Ostrom E. (2006) *Governare i beni collettivi*. Venezia: Marsilio.

· Ostrom E. (2009) *La conoscenza come bene comune. Dalla teoria alla pratica*. Milano: Bruno Mondadori.

· Oswalt P., Rieniets T., Schirmel H., 1Kilo and Bundes. K. des. (2006) *Atlas of shrinking cities. Atlas Der Schrumpfenden Städte*. Berlin: Hatje Cantz.

· Oswalt P., Overmeyer K., Misselwitz P. (2013) *Urban catalyst: the power of temporary use*. Berlin: Dom Pub.

· Paba G. (1998) *Luoghi comuni. La città come laboratorio di progetti collettivi*. Milano: FrancoAngeli.

· Peirson L.J. et al. (2011) An ecological Process Model of Systems Change. American Journal of Community Psychology, 47, pp. 307–321.

· Pellizzoni, L. (2008) Politiche pubbliche e nuove forme di partecipazione. *Partecipazione e conflitto*, 0, pp. 93-116.

· Pötz H., Bleuzé P. (2012) *Urban Green-Blue Grids For Sustainable And Dynamic Cities*. Delft, The Netherlands: Coop for life.

· Repishti F. (2012) Dalla prassi alla teoria nel landscape urbanism. *Lotus International*, 150, pp. 36-45.

· Ricci M. (2013) *Nuovi paradigmi*. Trento: ListLab.

· Rigillo M. et al. (2018) Eco-Innovative Solutions for Wasted Landscapes, *RI-VISTA*, 01, pp. 146-159.

· Rodotà S. (2018) *Verso i beni comuni*. In Preterossi G. e Capone N., *Stefano Rodotà. I beni comuni. L'inaspettata rinascita degli usi collettivi*, Napoli: La Scuola di Pitagora Editrice, pp. 31-89.

· Roesems V., Public value through co-creation. *Are you working on your fringe?*, *Volume*, 52, p. 33-34.

· Russo M. (2004) Napoli metropoli a rischio. In Savino M. *Pratiche di pianificazione alla prova*. Milano: FrancoAngeli.

· Russo M. (2012) Terre di mezzo: l'interconnessione come strategia. In Lucci R., Russo M. *Napol verso oriente*. Napoli: Clean Edizioni.

· Russo M. (2014) *Urbanistica per una diversa crescita*. Roma: Donzelli

· Russo M. et al. (2017) D5.1 PULLs Handbook. REPAiR

· Russo M. et al. (2018a) D5.4 Handbook: how to run a PULL. REPAiR

· Russo M. et al. (2018b) D5.3 Eco-Innovative Solutions for Naples. REPAiR

· Sassen S. (2013), Forgotten spaces, definizione data nel convegno internazionale "Technologies, Global Cities and Law", tenutosi a Milano il 18 giugno 2013.

· Scafuto F., La Barbera F. (2016). Protest Against Waste Contamination in the 'Land of Fires': Psychological Antecedents for Activists and Non activists. *Journal of Community & Applied Social Psychology*, 26 (6), pp. 481-495.

· Scafuto F. et al. (2011) Costruire percorsi di partecipazione civica. L'esperienza in un Comune di Napoli (Promoting a path of civic participation. A study in a province of Naples). Psicologia di Comunità, 2, pp. 57-67.

· Scafuto F. et al. (2018) What drives recycling behavior? The role of social trust, perceived risk and self-efficacy. *Quality - Access to Success*, 19 (s1), pp. 463-469.

· Secchi B. (a cura di Bianchetti C.) (1994) *Tre piani. La Spezia, Ascoli, Bergamo*. Milano: FrancoAngeli.

· Secchi B. (2006) Progetto di suolo 2. In Aymonino A., Mosco V.P. *Spazi pubblici contemporanei. Architettura a volume zero*, Milano: Skira.

· Secchi B., Viganò P. (2009) *Antwerp: territory of a new modernity*. Antwerp: Sun architecture.

· Secchi B. (2011) La nuova questione urbana, *CRIOS*, 1, pp. 83-92.

· Secchi B. (2005) *La città del ventesimo secolo*. Roma-Bari: Laterza.

· Secchi B. (2013) *La città dei ricchi e la città dei poveri*. Roma-Bari: Laterza.

· Shane D.G. (2004) On Landscape. The emergence of Landscape Urbanism. *Harvard Design Magazine*, 1 9, pp. 1-8.

· Soja E. (2000) *Postmetropolis: Critical Studies of Cities and Regions*. Oxford: Basil Blackwell.

· Steen K. and Bueren E. van (2017) *Urban Living Labs. A living lab way of working*. Amsterdam Institute for Advanced Metropolitan Solutions - Delft University of Technology.

· Tuzi F. (2016) *Amministrazione pubblica: all'egoismo alla competizione. Manuale per una sopravvivenza operosa*, Catanzaro: Rubettino ed.

· Van Tuijl, Verhaert, 2018, "The city of the future is already here", in "Are you working on your fringe?", supplement to Volume n. 52/2018, initiated by the 'Sub>urban. Reinventing the fringe' network and supported by the EU program URBACT III, p. 6-7.

· Verhaert I. (2018) Lab XX – creating a living lab. *Are you working on your fringe?, Volume*, 52, p. 12-13.

· Venturi R., Scott Brown D., Izenour S. (1972) Learning from Las Vegas. Cambridge: MIT Press.

· Viganò P. (2012) I territori dell'urbanistica. *Lotus International*, 150, pp. 107-113.

· Viganò P. (2014) Metamorfosi dell'ordinario: per una nuova urbanistica. In Russo M. *Urbanistica per una diversa crescita*. Roma: Donzelli.

· Wandl A., Nadin V., Zonneveld W.A.M. & Rooij R.M. (2014) Beyond urban & rural classifications: Character- izing and mapping territories-in-between across Europe. *Landscape and Urban Planning*, 130, pp. 50-63.

· Waldheim C. (2006) *The Landscape Urbanism Reader*. New York: Princeton Architectural Press.

· Wolman A. (1965) The Metabolism of Cities. *Scientific American*, 213, pp. 179-190.

· Zanfi F. (2010) Dopo la crescita: per una diversa agenda di ricerca. *Territorio*, 53, p. 110-116.

web sites
- http://ec.europa.eu/
- http://pianificazionecasoria.blogspot.it/
- http://urbact.eu/sub.urban
- http://h2020repair.eu/
- https://urbanmetabolism.weblog.tudelft.nl/repair/
- http://recycleitaly.net/
- http://www.postmetropoli.it/
- http://www.callinghome.it
- http://www.uia-initiative.eu/en
- http://www.coloco.org/
- http://www.luoghisingolari.net/

FRINGE SHIFTS
Transforming planning for new sub>urban habitats

Author
Anna Attademo and Enrico Formato

Published by
LISt Lab
info@listlab.eu
listlab.eu

Art Director & Production
Blacklist Creative, BCN
blacklist-creative.com

Editorial Director of LIStLab
Alessandro Martinelli

ISBN 9788899854300

Printed and bound in the European Union
2019

All rights reserved
© of the edition LISt Lab
© of the text the authors
© of the images the authors, all the images of the cities are taken from URBACT Local Action Plans.

serie BABEL INTERNATIONAT

Prohibited total or partial reproduction
of this book by any means, without permission of the author and publisher.

Sales, Marketing & Distribution
distribution@listlab.eu
listlab.eu/en/distribuzione/

Scientific Committee of the List editions
Eve Blau – Harvard GSD (U.S.A.), Maurizio Carta – Università di Palermo (IT), Alfredo Ramirez – Architectural Association London (UK), Alberto Cecchetto – Università di Venezia (IT), Stefano De Martino – Università di Innsbruck (AU), Corrado Diamantini – Università di Trento (IT), Antonio De Rossi – Università di Torino (IT), Franco Farinelli – Università di Bologna (IT), Carlo Gasparrini – Università di Napoli (IT), Manuel Gausa – Università di Genova (IT), Giovanni Maciocco – Università di Sassari/Alghero (IT), Mosè Ricci – Università di Trento (IT), Roger Riewe – Università di Graz (AU), Pino Scaglione – Università di Trento (IT)

LIStLab is an editorial workshop, based in Europe, that works on contemporary issues. LISt Lab not only publishes, but also researches, proposes, promotes, produces, creates networks.

LIStLab is a green company committed to respect the environment. Paper, ink, glues and all processings come from short supply chains and aim at limiting pollution. The print run of books and magazines is based on consumption patterns, thus preventing waste of paper and surpluses. LISt Lab aims at the responsibility of the authors and markets, towards the knowledge of a new publishing culture based on resource management.